THE FOUNDATIONS OF EXPECTED UTILITY

THEORY AND DECISION LIBRARY

AN INTERNATIONAL SERIES
IN THE PHILOSOPHY AND METHODOLOGY OF THE
SOCIAL AND BEHAVIORAL SCIENCES

Editors

GERALD EBERLEIN, *University of Technology, Munich*
WERNER LEINFELLNER, *University of Nebraska*

Editorial Advisory Board:

VOLUME 31

PETER C. FISHBURN

Bell Telephone Laboratories, Inc., Murray Hill, New Jersey

THE FOUNDATIONS OF EXPECTED UTILITY

D. REIDEL PUBLISHING COMPANY

DORDRECHT: HOLLAND/BOSTON: U.S.A.

LONDON: ENGLAND

Library of Congress Cataloging in Publication Data

CIP

Fishburn, Peter C.
    The foundations of expected utility.

    (Theory and decision library; v. 31)
    Bibliography: p.
    Includes indexes.
    1.   Utility theory.   I.   Title.   II.   Series.
    HB201.F54   1982   330.15′7   82-9138
    ISBN 90-277-1420-7   AACR2

Published by D. Reidel Publishing Company,
P.O. Box 17, 3300 AA Dordrecht, Holland.

Sold and distributed in the U.S.A. and Canada
by Kluwer Boston Inc.,
190 Old Derby Street, Hingham, MA 02043, U.S.A.

In all other countries, sold and distributed
by Kluwer Academic Publishers Group,
P.O. Box 322, 3300 AH Dordrecht, Holland.

D. Reidel Publishing Company is a member of the Kluwer Group.

To Jan

TABLE OF CONTENTS

PREFACE

This book offers a unified treatment of my research in the foundations of expected utility theory from around 1965 to 1980. While parts are new, the presentation draws heavily on published articles and a few chapters in my 1970 monograph on utility theory. The diverse notations and styles of the sources have of course been reconciled here, and their topics arranged in a logical sequence.

The two parts of the book take their respective cues from the von Neumann–Morgenstern axiomatization of preferences between risky options and from Savage's foundational treatment of decision making under uncertainty. Both parts are studies in the axiomatics of preferences for decision situations and in numerical representations for preferences. Proofs of the representation and uniqueness theorems appear at the ends of the chapters so as not to impede the flow of the discussion.

A few warnings on notation are in order. The numbers for theorems cited within a chapter have no prefix if they appear in that chapter, but otherwise carry a chapter prefix (Theorem 3.2 is Theorem 2 in Chapter 3). All lower case Greek letters refer to numbers in the closed interval from 0 to 1. The same symbol in different chapters has essentially the same meaning with one major exception: $x, y, \ldots$ mean quite different things in different chapters.

I am indebted to many people for their help and encouragement. Werner Leinfellner's generous invitation to contribute to the series in which this book appears was essential and is deeply appreciated. Fred Roberts and Peter Farquhar shared ideas that led to jointly-authored papers I have relied on in Chapter 2, 6, and 7. Ed Zajac provided the moral and organizational support on behalf of Bell Laboratories' management that enabled the book to be written, and Janice Ivanitz did a truly superb job of typing the manuscript. My greatest debt is to Jimmie Savage, whose influence is beyond reckoning.

For the record, I would like to acknowledge the works I had a part in that served as source material for the book. Complete references are given here only for papers not cited later: F(xy) signifies Fishburn (19xy) in the References. Chapter 2 is based in part on F(70, Chapter 8) and Fishburn and Roberts (1978). Chapter 3 is based on F(67), F(70, Chapter 10), F(75a), and my 'Unbounded Utility Functions in Expected Utility Theory', *Quarterly Journal of Economic* **90** (1976), 163–168. Chapter 4 grew out of F(71a): its proofs have not appeared previously. Chapter 5 is based on F(71b); 'Alternative Axiomatizations of One-Way Expected Utility', *Annals of Mathematical Statistics* **43** (1972), 1648–1651; 'Bounded One-Way Expected Utility', *Econometrica* **43** (1975), 867–875; and 'A Note on Linear Utility', *Journal of Economic Theory* (1982). Chapter 6 relies on Fishburn and Farquhar (1979); 'Independence in Utility Theory with Whole Product Sets', *Operations Research* **13** (1965), 28–45; and 'Additive Representations of Real-Valued Functions on Subsets of Product Sets', *Journal of Mathematical Psychology* **8** (1971), 382–388. Chapters 7 and 8 devolved from F(76), Fishburn and Roberts (1978), and F(80).

In Part II, Chapter 9 is based on F(70, Chapter 13); 'Preference-Based Definitions of Subjective Probability', *Annals of Mathematical Statistics* **38** (1967), 1605–1617; and 'Additivity in Utility Theory with Denumerable Product Sets', *Econometrica* **34** (1966), 500–503. Chapter 10 is also based on F(70, Chapter 13) as well as 'A General Theory of Subjective Probabilities and Expected Utilities', *Annals of Mathematical Statistics* **40** (1969), 1419–1429, and 'Subjective Expected Utility with Mixture Sets and Boolean Algebras', *Annals of Mathematical Statistics* **43** (1972), 917–927. Material in the first part of Chapter 11 was adapted from F(75b), and Chapter 12 was developed from F(73) and F(74).

Murray Hill, New Jersey   PETER C. FISHBURN
July 1981

CHAPTER 1

INTRODUCTION

Early in the Eighteenth Century, the mathematicians Daniel Bernoulli and Gabriel Cramer (Bernoulli, 1738) argued that the maximization of expected profit or wealth could not adequately describe the choices of reasonable individuals among risky monetary options. Consider, for example, an individual who can invest a sum of money in one of two options, A and B. Option A is riskless and guarantees $1000 profit, whereas B is a risky venture that yields either a $2000 loss or a $4200 profit, each with probability $\frac{1}{2}$. Despite the fact that B has a larger expected profit, a prudent individual may well prefer A to B. Based on related examples, Bernoulli and Cramer proposed that risky monetary options be evaluated not by their expected returns but rather by the expectations of the utilities of their returns. Although utility of money could be expected to increase in the amount, there is no compelling reason why it should be linear in the amount. In particular, if an individual's utility of wealth increases at a decreasing rate, then he will prefer some options to others that have higher expected returns but are also perceived to involve more risk.

Despite its early beginning, expected utility lay in relative obscurity until John von Neumann and Oskar Morgenstern axiomatized it for their theory of games more than two hundred years after Bernoulli's paper was published (von Neumann and Morgenstern, 1944). Several years earlier, Frank P. Ramsey outlined a theory of subjective probability and expected utility (Ramsey, 1931), but this went virtually unnoticed until the appearance of Leonard J. Savage's classic on the foundations of statistics (Savage, 1954). Drawing on Ramsey as well as von Neumann and Morgenstern for expected utility and de Finetti (1937) for subjective probability, Savage presented the first complete axiomatization of subjective expected utility, in which the notion of personal or subjective probability is integrated with expected utility.

Part I of the present work is devoted to the von Neumann–Morgenstern theory and to generalizations and extensions of their basic idea. Part II then considers subjective expected utility, showing how aspects of the theory in Part I can be used to derive representations of preferences that

1

involve subjective probability. Further introductory comments and pre-
views of the two parts of the book are provided in the remainder of this
chapter.

1.1. PART I: EXPECTED UTILITY

The importance of the von Neumann–Morgenstern contribution lies
in its derivation of a linear utility representation for preferences from
simple, appealing axioms for a qualitative preference relation on a set
of objects that is closed under an operation that resembles convex combinations. Although their formulation seems far removed from the des-
cription given above for Bernoulli and Cramer, I shall note shortly how
the expected-utility form arises from the linear utility representation
derived by von Neumann and Morgenstern.

Their axioms, which are presented in a slightly different form in Chapter
2, apply a binary relation $\succ$ ('is preferred to') to a set $\mathcal{M}$ that is closed under
an operation on triples $(\lambda, x, y) \in [0, 1] \times \mathcal{M} \times \mathcal{M}$. We denote the element
in $\mathcal{M}$ that results from the operation on (λ, x, y) by $\lambda x \oplus (1 - \lambda)y$. Appropriate assumptions about $\oplus$, along with the preference axioms for $\succ$ on
$\mathcal{M}$, imply the existence of a real-valued function u on $\mathcal{M}$ that preserves
$\succ$ and is linear:

$$x \succ y \quad \text{iff} \quad u(x) > u(y),$$

$$u(\lambda x \oplus (1 - \lambda)y) = \lambda u(x) + (1 - \lambda)u(y),$$

for all $x, y \in \mathcal{M}$ and all $\lambda \in [0, 1]$. The latter property, which says that u
is linear in $\oplus$, should not be confused with the notion of a utility function
on a real variable (such as money) that is a linear function of the variable.
Although the abstract theory can be applied to cases in which $\mathcal{M}$ is a
real variable and $\lambda x \oplus (1 - \lambda)y$ is the convex combination $\lambda x + (1 - \lambda)y$,
interesting applications endow $\mathcal{M}$ with considerably more structure.

A case in point arises by taking $\mathcal{M}$ as the set $\mathcal{P}_0(\mathcal{C})$ of all simple probability measures on a set $\mathcal{C}$ of consequences or outcomes. By definition,
$p \in \mathcal{P}_0(\mathcal{C})$ iff p maps $\mathcal{C}$ into $[0, 1]$ such that $p(c) = 0$ for all but a finite
number of $c \in \mathcal{C}$, and $\Sigma p(c) = 1$. Let $\lambda p \oplus (1 - \lambda)q$ be the convex combination $\lambda p + (1 - \lambda)q$ of measures $p, q \in \mathcal{P}_0(\mathcal{C})$, so that this combination is
the simple measure that assigns probability $\lambda p(c) + (1 - \lambda)q(c)$ to each
$c \in \mathcal{C}$. Given the foregoing linear utility representation for $\succ$ on $\mathcal{P}_0(\mathcal{C})$,
extend u from $\mathcal{P}_0(\mathcal{C})$ to $\mathcal{C}$ by defining the utility of consequence c to be

the utility of the measure that assigns probability 1 to c:

$$u(c) = u(p) \quad \text{when} \quad p(c) = 1.$$

Then the linearity property $u(\lambda p + (1 - \lambda)q) = \lambda u(p) + (1 - \lambda)u(q)$ leads, by a simple inductive argument, to the expected-utility form

$$u(p) = \sum_{\mathscr{C}} p(c)u(c)$$

for all $p \in \mathscr{P}_0(\mathscr{C})$. Thus, this application of the basic theory yields a utility function on $\mathscr{C}$ such that p is preferred to q iff the expected utility of p exceeds the expected utility of q.

Although consequences in $\mathscr{C}$ are profits or wealths in the Bernoulli–Cramer context, elements in $\mathscr{C}$ could be anything. They might be real vectors, qualitative descriptions of the future, pure strategies or n-tuples of pure strategies in a game context, Savage acts, and so forth. Many of our later developments will be based on specialized $\mathscr{C}$ sets.

Preview

The first chapter in Part I presents two sets of axioms for the linear utility representation of von Neumann and Morgenstern. Both assume that $\mathscr{M}$ is a mixture set as defined by Herstein and Milnor (1953), but use somewhat different axioms for $\succ$ on $\mathscr{M}$. It is then shown how the basic theory can be generalized by replacing the equality relation in the mixture-set axioms by the symmetric complement $\sim$ of $\succ$, where $x \sim y$ means that neither $x \succ y$ nor $y \succ x$. The relation $\sim$ is often referred to as an indifference relation.

Chapter 3 extends the expected-utility form for simple probability measures to more general probability measures, with

$$u(p) = \int_{\mathscr{C}} u(c)\, dp(c)$$

for all p in a set $\mathscr{P}$ of measures that includes $\mathscr{P}_0(\mathscr{C})$. New axioms, involving closure properties for $\mathscr{P}$ and dominance axioms for $\succ$ on $\mathscr{P}$, are used in the extension. Both finitely additive and countably additive measures are considered. The question of whether u on $\mathscr{C}$ must be bounded is also examined.

The axioms in Chapter 2 are ordering, independence and continuity conditions. Independence is primarily responsible for linearity, whereas the continuity or Archimedeam axiom ensures that utilities will be real numbers. Chapter 4 investigates the structure of preferences on $\mathcal{M}$ when the Archimedean axiom is omitted. A special condition on preference hierarchies leads to a quasilinear utility representation in which real-valued utilities $u(x)$ are replaced by utility vectors $(u_1(x), \ldots, u_n(x))$ whose lexicographic ordering preserves preference:

$$x \succ y \quad \text{iff} \quad u_1(x) > u_1(y) \quad \text{or} \quad [u_1(x) = u_1(y), u_2(x) > u_2(y)]$$

$$\text{or} \ldots \text{or} \quad [u_1(x) = u_1(y), \ldots, u_{n-1}(x) = u_{n-1}(y),$$

$$u_n(x) > u_n(y)].$$

Unlike the other chapters in Part I, Chapter 5 does not assume that the indifference relation $\sim$ is transitive, but it does presume that $\succ$ or its transitive closure is a partial order. Suitable independence and Archimedean axioms yield a 'one-way' linear utility representation in which $u(x) > u(y)$ whenever $x \succ y$, but not conversely. A lexicographic one-way representation arises when the Archimedean axiom is omitted.

The final three chapters of Part I involve specializations with Cartesian product sets. Chapter 6 begins with a linear u on $\mathcal{P}_0(\mathcal{C})$ and shows first that a simple marginal indfference condition is necessary and sufficient for the additive representation

$$u(c_1, c_2, \ldots, c_n) = \sum_{i=1}^{n} u_i(c_i)$$

for all $(c_1, \ldots, c_n) \in \mathcal{C}$ whenever $\mathcal{C}$ is a subset of a product set $\mathcal{C}_1 \times \mathcal{C}_2 \times \cdots \times \mathcal{C}_n$. We then consider $\mathcal{C} = \mathcal{D} \times \mathcal{E}$ and identify a necessary and sufficient condition for the multiadditive form

$$u(d, e) = \sum_{j=1}^{n} f_j(d) g_j(e) + h(d),$$

where the f_j and h are real-valued functions on $\mathcal{D}$, and the g_j are real-valued functions on $\mathcal{E}$.

Chapters 7 and 8 are concerned with a preference relation $\succ$ defined on a product of mixture sets $\mathcal{M}_1 \times \mathcal{M}_2 \times \cdots \times \mathcal{M}_n$ rather than on a single mixture set. This formulation applies directly to n-person games when $\mathcal{M}_i$ is the set of mixed strategies for player i and $\succ$ is the preference relation of a designated player. Chapter 7 shows how the axioms of Chapter 2 can be generalized to yield a multilinear utility function u on

$\mathscr{M}_1 \times \cdots \times \mathscr{M}_n$ that preserves $\succ$, where u is multilinear if

$$u(x_1, \ldots, x_{i-1}, \lambda x_i \oplus (1 - \lambda)y_i, x_{i+1}, \ldots, x_n)$$
$$= \lambda u(x_1, \ldots, x_i, \ldots, x_n) + (1 - \lambda)u(x_1, \ldots, y_i, \ldots, x_n)$$

whenever $i \in \{1, \ldots, n\}$, $x_j \in \mathscr{M}_j$ for all $j \neq i$, and $x_i, y_i \in \mathscr{M}_i$. Chapter 8 discusses the extension of this form to the multilinear expected-utility representation

$$u(p_1, \ldots, p_n) = \int_{\mathscr{C}} u(c_1, \ldots, c_n) \, dp_n(c_n) \ldots dp_1(c_1)$$

when $\mathscr{M}_i$ is a set $\mathscr{P}_i$ of probability measures on $\mathscr{C}_i$, $p_i \in \mathscr{P}_i$ for $i = 1, \ldots, n$, and $\mathscr{C} = \mathscr{C}_1 \times \cdots \times \mathscr{C}_n$.

Uniqueness properties for the utility functions involved in the various representations given above will be established when we encounter these representations later. Readers who may wish to scan ensuing chapters should also be advised that the sometimes cumbersome notation $\lambda x \oplus \oplus (1 - \lambda)y$ will be written as $x \lambda y$, and that $\lambda p + (1 - \lambda)q$ will always denote the literal convex combination of real-valued functions p and q.

1.2. PART II: SUBJECTIVE EXPECTED UTILITY

We have already noted that Savage (1954) presented the first complete axiomatization of subjective expected utility. A thorough account of Savage's theory is given in Chapter 14 of Fishburn (1970), and I shall therefore provide only a brief sketch of his ideas here.

Savage's basic primitives are a set $\mathscr{C}$ of consequences, a set S of states of the world, and a preference relation $\succ$ on the set $\mathscr{C}^S$ of all functions $f, g, \ldots$ from S into $\mathscr{C}$. The functions in $\mathscr{C}^S$ are Savage's acts: if the individual does f and state $s \in S$ obtains – or is the true state – then he will experience consequence $f(s)$ in $\mathscr{C}$. The individual is presumed to be uncertain about the state that obtains, or will obtain. In Savage's representation, this uncertainty is reflected by a finitely additive probability measure P on the set $\mathscr{S}$ of all subsets of S. An element $A \in \mathscr{S}$ is called an event, and $P(A)$ is a quantitative measure of the individual's degree of belief that event A obtains, i.e. that some state $s \in A$ obtains. Hence $P(A)$ is the individual's personal or subjective probability for event A.

Savage uses seven axioms for $\succ$ on $\mathscr{C}^S$. These include a typical ordering axiom, several independence conditions, a continuity axiom, and a dominance postulate. His axioms imply that there exists a bounded real-valued function u on $\mathscr{C}$ and a finitely additive probability measure P on $\mathscr{S}$ such that expected utilities preserve $\succ$:

$$f \succ g \quad \text{iff} \quad \int_S u(f(s)) \, dP(s) > \int_S u(g(s)) \, dP(s).$$

In addition, P is uniquely determined, and u is unique up to a positive affine transformation, i.e. v on $\mathscr{C}$ satisfies the representation in place of u if and only if there are real numbers a and b with $a > 0$ such that $v(c) = au(c) + b$ for all $c \in \mathscr{C}$. His axioms also imply that events in $\mathscr{S}$ are continuously divisible in the sense that, for any $A \in \mathscr{S}$ and any $\lambda \in [0, 1]$, there is a $B \subseteq A$ such that

$$P(B) = \lambda P(A).$$

Although this forces S to be uncountably infinite, $\mathscr{C}$ can have as few as two members.

The influence of de Finetti (1937) and von Neumann and Morgenstern (1944) on Savage is evident in the proof of his representation theorem. Let $\succ^*$ be a binary relation on $\mathscr{S}$, with $A \succ^* B$ interpreted as "A is more probable than B". Formally, $A \succ^* B$ holds if and only if $f \succ g$ whenever c and d are consequences such that c is preferred to d, $f(s) = c$ for all $s \in A$, $f(s) = d$ for all $s \in S \backslash A$, $g(s) = c$ for all $s \in B$, and $g(s) = d$ for all $s \in S \backslash B$. In other words, $A \succ^* B$ if the individual would rather take his chances on A than B to obtain a preferred consequence.

Following de Finetti's lead, Savage proves that his axioms imply that there is a unique finitely additive probability measure P on $\mathscr{S}$ for which

$$A \succ^* B \quad \text{iff} \quad P(A) > P(B),$$

for all $A, B \in \mathscr{S}$. He then uses P to construct simple probability measures on $\mathscr{C}$ from specialized acts, and shows that his axioms imply those of von Neumann and Morgenstern for preferences on the simple measures. This yields the expected-utility representation for 'simple acts', and the representation for more general acts then follows from Savage's dominance postulate.

A number of other writers, including Suppes (1956), Anscombe and Aumann (1963), Pratt et al. (1964, 1965), Pfanzagl (1968), Bolker (1967), and Luce and Krantz (1971), have devised other axiomatizations for representations of subjective expected utility. These were motivated in part by a desire to generalize certain aspects of Savage's system, including his continuously divisible events and the very rich structure of his act set. A detailed review of these and related theories is given in Fishburn (1981).

Preview

My own work in subjective expected utility, which is closely allied with the approach taken by Anscombe and Aumann (1963) and Pratt *et al.* (1964, 1965), was also motivated by a desire to weaken some of the strong structural presumptions in Savage's theory. At the same time, it employs other structures that are not used by Savage. In part, these additional structures make direct use of concepts developed in Part I, so that Part II of the book can be viewed as a natural sequel to Part I.

The initial chapter of Part II considers $\succ$ on the product $\mathcal{M}_1 \times \cdots \times \mathcal{M}_n$ of a finite number of mixture sets, as in Chapter 7. However, instead of using the axioms in Chapter 7, it applies axioms like those in Chapter 2 to $\succ$ on $\mathcal{M}_1 \times \cdots \times \mathcal{M}_n$ and shows that these lead to additive linear utilities of the form

$$U(x_1, \ldots, x_n) = \sum_{i=1}^{n} u_i(x_i),$$

where u_i on $\mathcal{M}_i$ is linear for each i. In the context of decision making under uncertainty, we can suppose that i indexes a finite set of states and that $\mathcal{M}_i$ applies to state i. If $\mathcal{M}_i = \mathcal{P}_0(\mathcal{C}_i)$, where $\mathcal{C}_i$ is the set of relevant consequences for state i, then the probabilities used in the simple measures in $\mathcal{P}_0(\mathcal{C}_i)$ can be viewed as 'extraneous scaling probabilities' that are generated by random mechanisms not directly associated with the states in S.

When minimal structural overlap among the $\mathcal{M}_i$ is presumed along with an interstate monotonicity axiom, it is shown that the u_i in the preceding expression can be aligned on a common scale so that U can be written as

$$U(x_1, \ldots, x_n) = \sum_{i=1}^{n} \rho_i u(x_i),$$

where u is linear on each $\mathcal{M}_i$ and the ρ_i are nonnegative numbers that sum to unity. In the states context, ρ_i is interpreted as the individual's subjective probability for state i. When $\mathcal{M}_i = \mathcal{P}_0(\mathcal{C}_i)$ for each i, the preceding form gives $\rho_1 u(c_1) + \cdots + \rho_n u(c_n)$ as the subjective expected utility of the act that assigns consequence c_i to state i for $i = 1, \ldots, n$.

This finite-states approach is then generalized to accommodate arbitrary state sets in Chapter 10. Rather than using a different mixture set for each state, Chapter 10 adopts the same mixture set $\mathcal{M}$ for all states, and views acts as mappings from S into $\mathcal{M}$. It also views the set of events as an arbitrary Boolean algebra $\mathcal{S}$ of subsets of S. Suitable axioms are then used to imply the existence of a finitely additive probability measure P on $\mathcal{S}$ and a linear function u on $\mathcal{M}$ such that

$$f \succ g \quad \text{iff} \quad \int_S u(f(s)) \, dP(s) > \int_S u(g(s)) \, dP(s),$$

for 'most' functions f and g from S into $\mathcal{M}$. Special considerations that arise from the generality of the formulation used in Chapter 10 are noted.

Chapter 11 examines a one-way version of the subjective expected utility model in which the indifference relation $\sim$ is not assumed to be transitive. It is based on the formulation of Chapter 10 in much the same way that Chapter 5 relates to Chapter 2.

The final chapter of the book considers a formulation for subjective expected utility based on conditional preference comparisons. It applies $\succ$ to $\mathcal{M} \times \mathcal{S}'$, where $\mathcal{M}$ is a mixture set (e.g., the set of simple probability measures defined over a set of Savage-type acts) and $\mathcal{S}'$ is a Boolean algebra of subsets of S with the empty event $\emptyset$ removed. The ordered pair $xA \in \mathcal{M} \times \mathcal{S}'$ is to be thought of as 'act' x under the supposition that event A obtains. The axioms of Chapter 12 lead to a quasi-conditional utility representation of the form

$$u(xA) = \sum_{i=1}^{n} P_A(A_i) u(xA_i)$$

when $\{A_1, \ldots, A_n\}$ is a partition of A. Here P_A is a (conditional) probability measure on $\{A \cap B : B \in \mathcal{S}\}$. These measures satisfy the chain rule

$$P_C(A) = P_C(B) P_B(A) \quad \text{when} \quad A \subseteq B \subseteq C.$$

Chapter 12 also considers the extension of the preceding representation to the general integral form

$$u(xA) = \int_A u(xs) \, dP_A(s).$$

PART I

EXPECTED UTILITY

CHAPTER 2

LINEAR UTILITY ON MIXTURE SETS

We begin with the definitions of a mixture set and a linear function on a mixture set. Each of two sets of axioms for a binary relation $\succ$ on a mixture set $\mathcal{M}$ is then shown to imply the existence of a linear function on $\mathcal{M}$ that preserves $\succ$ and is unique up to a positive affine transformation. The mixture-set axioms are replaced later by weaker assumptions that use the symmetric complement $\sim$ of $\succ$.

Here, and later, lower case Greek letters will always denote numbers in $[0, 1]$, *and all sets identified by capital script Latin letters will be presumed to be nonempty except when noted otherwise.*

2.1. MIXTURE SETS AND LINEAR FUNCTIONS

A set $\mathcal{M}$ is a *mixture set* (Herstein and Milnor, 1953) if for any λ and any ordered pair $(x, y) \in \mathcal{M} \times \mathcal{M}$ there is a unique element $\lambda x \oplus (1 - \lambda)y$ in $\mathcal{M}$ such that

    M1. $1x \oplus 0y = x,$
    M2. $\lambda x \oplus (1 - \lambda)y = (1 - \lambda)y \oplus \lambda x,$
    M3. $\lambda[\mu x \oplus (1 - \mu)y] \oplus (1 - \lambda)y = (\lambda\mu)x \oplus (1 - \lambda\mu)y,$

for all $x, y \in \mathcal{M}$ and all λ and μ. If $\mathcal{P}$ is a set of probability measures defined on an algebra $\mathcal{A}$, and if $\mathcal{P}^+$ is the set of finite convex combinations of measures in $\mathcal{P}$ (the convex hull of $\mathcal{P}$), then $\mathcal{P}^+$ is a mixture set when $\lambda p \oplus (1 - \lambda)q = \lambda p + (1 - \lambda)q$.

Although $\lambda x \oplus (1 - \lambda)y$ is useful in suggesting similarities to convex combinations, I shall henceforth write it as $x \lambda y$, except when $\lambda p + (1 - \lambda)q$ is used to denote a convex combination of real-valued functions. The mixture-set axioms appear in the new notation as

    M1. $x 1 y = x,$
    M2. $x \lambda y = y(1 - \lambda)x,$
    M3. $(x \mu y)\lambda y = x(\lambda\mu)y.$

In the later proofs, we show that M1 through M3 imply

    M4. $x \lambda x = x,$
    M5. $(x \beta y)\alpha(x \gamma y) = x(\alpha\beta + (1 - \alpha)\gamma)y.$

We shall say that u is a *linear function* on a mixture set $\mathcal{M}$ if it is a real-valued function for which

$$u(x \lambda y) = \lambda u(x) + (1 - \lambda)u(y)$$

for all λ and $x, y \in \mathcal{M}$. Two linear functions u and v are related by a *positive affine transformation* if there are real number $a > 0$ and b such that

$$v(x) = au(x) + b \quad \text{for all} \quad x \in \mathcal{M}.$$

When u on $\mathcal{M}$ satisfies specified properties, such as linearity and order preservation, we shall say that it is *unique up to a positive affine transformation* if all functions v related to u by positive affine transformations, but no others, satisfy the same properties.

2.2. AXIOMS FOR LINEAR UTILITY

Here, and later, $\succ$ will always signify an *asymmetric* $(x \succ y \Rightarrow \text{not } [y \succ x])$ binary relation on a designated set, which we denote for the time being as X. We define $\sim$ and $\succsim$ on X from $\succ$ by

$$x \sim y \quad \text{iff not} \quad (x \succ y) \text{ and not } (y \succ x),$$
$$x \succsim y \quad \text{iff} \quad x \succ y \quad \text{or} \quad x \sim y.$$

When $\succ$ is a preference relation, $\sim$ is its induced indifference relation, and $\succsim$ is a preference-or-indifference relation. Since $\succ$ is asymmetric, $\sim$ is reflexive $(x \sim x)$ and symmetric $(x \sim y \Rightarrow y \sim x)$.

The relation $\succ$ is *negatively transitive* if $x \succ z \Rightarrow (x \succ y \text{ or } y \succ z)$, or, equivalently, if $[\text{not } (x \succ y) \text{ and not } (y \succ z)] \Rightarrow \text{not } (x \succ z)$, for all $x, y, z \in X$. We shall say that $\succ$ is an *asymmetric weak order* if it is negatively transitive. It is easily verified that $\succ$ is an asymmetric weak order if, and only if, both $\succ$ and $\sim$ are *transitive* $(x \succ y$ and $y \succ z \Rightarrow x \succ z; x \sim y$ and $y \sim z \Rightarrow x \sim z)$. Note also that if $\succ$ is an asymmetric weak order then $\sim$ is an *equivalence relation* (reflexive, symmetric, transitive).

The Axioms

Our first set of three axioms for $\succ$ on a mixture set $\mathcal{M}$ is due to Jensen (1967):

A1. $\succ$ *on $\mathcal{M}$ is an asymmetric weak order,*
A2.   *For all $x, y, z \in \mathcal{M}$ and $0 < \lambda < 1$, if $x \succ y$ then $x \lambda z \succ y \lambda z$,*
A3.   *For all $x, y, z \in \mathcal{M}$, if $x \succ y$ and $y \succ z$ then there are $\alpha, \beta \in (0, 1)$ such that $x \alpha z \succ y$ and $y \succ x \beta z$.*

Axiom A1 is a typical ordering assumption, A2 is an independence or cancellation condition, and A3 is an Archimedean axiom. In the context of preferences between probability distributions, A2 is usually defended by appealing to a two-stage process. Since $\lambda p + (1 - \lambda)r$ can be realized by first selecting p or r with probabilities λ and $1 - \lambda$, respectively, and then choosing a consequence according to the probabilities in the one of p and r selected at the first stage, it stands to reason that if p is preferred to q then $\lambda p + (1 - \lambda)r$ will be preferred to $\lambda q + (1 - \lambda)r$. Although some people are compelled by this argument to accept A2, at least as a normative principle, others suggest that the two-stage interpretation for holistic probability distributions is misleading. Allais's (1953) famous example against the reasonableness of A2 in a monetary setting has led other writers, including Savage (1954, pp. 101–103), MacCrimmon (1968), and Slovic and Tversky (1974), to comment at length on that axiom.

In the probability setting, A3 is usually defended by the argument that if $p \succ q \succ r$, then some convex combinations $\alpha p + (1 - \alpha)r$ with α near to 1 should be preferred to q, and q should be preferred to $\beta p + (1 - \beta)r$ for some β near to 0. In Chapter 4, we shall drop A3 and investigate in more detail the 'pure' implications of A1 and A2. The Archimedean axiom is then reinstated in Chapter 5, where A1 is weakened by not assuming that $\sim$ is transitive.

Our second combination of order, independence and Archimedean axioms for $\succ$ on $\mathcal{M}$ is due to Herstein and Milnor (1953):

B1. $\succ$ *on $\mathcal{M}$ is an asymmetric weak order,*

B2.   *For all $x, y, z \in \mathcal{M}$, if $x \sim y$ then $x\frac{1}{2}z \sim y\frac{1}{2}z$,*

B3.   *For all $x, y, z \in \mathcal{M}$, $\{\alpha: x\alpha z \succsim y\}$ and $\{\beta: y \succsim x\beta z\}$ are closed subsets of the unit interval.*

In B3, the indicated sets are closed with respect to the relative usual topology on $[0, 1]$. Although A1 and B1 are identical, neither of A2 and B2 implies the other, and B3 implies A3 (but not conversely) as will be noted later.

Axioms B2 and B3 emphasize different aspects of linear utilities than do A2 and A3. Axiom B2 highlights indifference preservation under simple 50–50 mixtures, while B3 is a continuity condition. It says, for example, that if $x\alpha_i z \succsim y$ for all i and $\alpha_i \to \alpha$, then $x\alpha z \succsim y$. Despite differences between the axiom sets, we shall observe that $\{A1, A2, A3\}$ and $\{B1, B2, B3\}$ are formally equivalent.

The Representation-Uniqueness Theorem

The essential features of the von Neumann–Morgenstern linear utility theory are given in the following theorem. The proof is presented is Section 4. Since the axioms are clearly necessary for the utility representation, our proof will focus on sufficiency.

THEOREM 1. *Suppose $\mathcal{M}$ is a mixture set. Then the following three statements are mutually equivalent:*
(a) A1, A2 *and* A3 *hold;*
(b) B1, B2 *and* B3 *hold;*
(c) *There is a linear function u on $\mathcal{M}$ that preserves $\succ$: for all x, $y \in \mathcal{M}$, $x \succ y$ iff $u(x) > u(y)$.*

In addition, a linear order-preserving u on $\mathcal{M}$ is unique up to a positive affine transformation.

As noted in the introduction, a linear u leads to the expected-utility form for simple probability measures when $\mathcal{M}$ includes such measures in a suitable formulation. Expected utility for more general measures is discussed in the next chapter.

It should be noted that nonlinear order-preserving utility functions exist in abundance when the axioms in part (a) or (b) of Theorem 1 hold. For, if u satisfies (c), then every monotonic transformation of u also preserves $\succ$. We note also that the theorem says nothing about boundedness for u. If $\mathcal{M}$ is finitely generated (all elements in $\mathcal{M}$ can be obtained from a finite subset using the mixture operation), then u is trivially bounded, but otherwise it could be either bounded or unbounded, above or below. Boundedness in the context of nonsimple probability measures is considered in Chapter 3.

2.3. GENERALIZED MIXTURE AXIOMS

Several writers, including Fishburn (1964, p. 8), Chipman (1971), and Fishburn and Roberts (1978), have presented utility axiomatizations in which the mixture-set axioms have been replaced by axioms that employ the indifference relation $\sim$ in place of equality, such as with

M1($\sim$). $x1y \sim x$,

M2($\sim$). $x\lambda y \sim y(1-\lambda)x$,

M3($\sim$). $(x\mu y)\lambda y \sim x(\lambda\mu)y$.

Such a replacement is feasible when $\sim$ is an equivalence relation, as when A1 holds, but would appear to encounter serious difficulties otherwise.

The following theorem, due to Fishburn and Roberts (1978), constitutes a generalization of Theorem 1 since its axioms are obviously implied by the axioms of Theorem 1.

THEOREM 2. *Suppose $\mathcal{M}$ is a set that contains $x\lambda y$ for any λ and any $(x, y)\in\mathcal{M}\times\mathcal{M}$, and that $\succ$ is a binary relation on $\mathcal{M}$ that satisfies* M2($\sim$), M3($\sim$), A1, A2, *and* A3. *Then there exists a linear, order-preserving function u on $\mathcal{M}$, and such a u is unique up to a positive affine transformation.*

Axiom M1($\sim$) is omitted from the theorem since it is implied by the other axioms. A proof of Theorem 2 appears in Section 5.

2.4. PROOF OF THEOREM 1

In this section we shall first establish M4 and M5, then show that B3 $\Rightarrow$ A3, and that the Herstein–Milnor axioms yield a number of intermediate results which are used to verify that A2 is implied by B1, B2, and B3. Hence $\{B1, B2, B3\}\Rightarrow\{A1, A2, A3\}$. Jensen's axioms are then used to derive a series of lemmas that we shall make use of in constructing a linear, order-preserving utility function on $\mathcal{M}$. The section concludes with a proof of uniqueness.

M4 and M5

To verify

    M4. $x\lambda x = x,$

we observe that M1, M2, M3, M2, and M1, applied in order, give $x\lambda x =$
$= (x1x)\lambda x = (x0x)\lambda x = x0x = x1x = x.$

It is easily seen that

    M5. $(x\beta y)\alpha(x\gamma y) = x(\alpha\beta + (1-\alpha)\gamma)y$

follows from M1–M3 if $\{\beta, \gamma\}\cap\{0, 1\}\neq\emptyset$. Assume then that $0 < \beta \leq \gamma < 1$: the proof for $\gamma \leq \beta$ is similar. Following Luce and Suppes (1965, p. 288) and using M3, M2, M3, M2, and M3 in that order for the first through the fifth equalities, we get

$$(x\beta y)\alpha(x\gamma y) = \left[(x\gamma y)(\beta/\gamma)y\right]\alpha(x\gamma y)$$
$$= \left[y(1-\beta/\gamma)(x\gamma y)\right]\alpha(x\gamma y)$$

$$= y(\alpha - \alpha\beta/\gamma)(x\gamma y)$$
$$= (x\gamma y)(1 - \alpha + \alpha\beta/\gamma)y$$
$$= x(\alpha\beta + \gamma(1 - \alpha))y.$$

B3 Implies A3

Given B3 and $x \succ y \succ z$, we are to show that $x\alpha z \succ y$ and $y \succ x\beta z$ for some $\alpha, \beta \in (0, 1)$. If $x\alpha z \succ y$ for no $\alpha \in (0, 1)$, then $(0, 1) \subseteq \{\beta : y \succsim x\beta z\}$ and in fact $\{\beta : y \succsim x\beta z\} = [0, 1]$ by B3. But then $\beta = 1$ and M1 give $y \succsim x$, which contradicts $x \succ y$ and asymmetry. A similar contradiction obtains when $y \succ x\beta z$ for no $\beta \in (0, 1)$.

Herstein-Milnor Results

This subsection proves the following implications of B1, B2, and B3, using proofs that are like those in Herstein and Milnor (1953):

H1. $x \succsim y \succsim z \Rightarrow y \sim x\lambda z$ for some λ,

H2. $\{\alpha : x\alpha y \sim z\}$ is closed,

H3. $x \succ y \Rightarrow x \succ x\frac{1}{2}y \succ y$,

H4. $(x \succ y, 0 < \lambda < 1) \Rightarrow x \succ x\lambda y \succ y$,

H5. $x \sim y \Rightarrow x \sim x\lambda y$,

H6. $x \sim y \Rightarrow x\lambda z \sim y\lambda z$,

H7. $x \succ y \Rightarrow (x\lambda y \succ x\mu y \text{ iff } \lambda > \mu)$.

H1. By B3, $\{\alpha : x\alpha z \succsim y\}$ is closed, and by $x \succsim y$ and M1 it contains $\alpha = 1$. Similarly, $\{\beta : y \succsim x\beta z\}$ is closed and contains $\beta = 0$. By the definition of $\succsim$, the union of $\{\alpha : x\alpha z \succsim y\}$ and $\{\beta : y \succsim x\beta z\}$ is $[0, 1]$ and, since both sets are nonempty and closed, they must have a nonempty intersection. If λ is in their intersection, then $y \sim x\lambda z$.

H2. This follows from B3 and the fact that the intersection of two closed sets is closed.

H3. Contrary to H3, suppose $x\frac{1}{2}y \succsim x \succ y$. By H1 and M3, $x \sim (x\frac{1}{2}y)\lambda y = x(\lambda/2)y$ for some λ. Let $T = \{\lambda : x \sim x(\lambda/2)y\}$, which is closed by H2 and therefore has a smallest element λ_0, which is positive since M1, M2 and $x \sim x0y$ imply $x \sim y$, contradicting $x \succ y$. According to B2 and M3, $x\frac{1}{2}y \sim [x(\lambda_0/2)y]\frac{1}{2}y = x(\lambda_0/4)y \succsim x \succ y$, so that, by H1 and M3, $x \sim [x(\lambda_0/4)y]\mu y = x(\lambda_0\mu/4)y$ for some μ. But then $\lambda_0\mu/4 < \lambda_0/2$, contradicting the choice of λ_0. Therefore $x \succ y \Rightarrow x \succ x\frac{1}{2}y$. Similarly, $x \succ y \Rightarrow x\frac{1}{2}y \succ y$.

REMARK. In the next three proofs, ρ generically represents a rational number of the form $\rho = \sum_{i=1}^{n(\rho)} \alpha_i/2^i, \alpha_i \in \{0, 1\}$ for each i.

H4. Given $x \succ y$, successive applications of H3 along with the mixture-set axioms imply that, if $\rho_2 > \rho_1$, then $x \succ x\rho_2 y \succ x\rho_1 y \succ y$. For $0 < \lambda <$ < 1, choose ρ_1 and ρ_2 so that $0 < \rho_1 < \lambda < \rho_2 < 1$. Let $x' = x\rho_2 y$ and $y' = x\rho_1 y$. Then, for any $\rho_i \in (\rho_1, \rho_2), x' \succsim x\rho_i y \succsim y'$. By a suitable choice of such ρ_i, $\lim \rho_i = \lambda$, and, by B3, we then get $x \succ x' \succsim x\lambda y \succsim y' \succ y$. Hence $x \succ x\lambda y \succ y$ from B1.

H5. Successive applications of B2 imply that $x\rho_i y \sim x$ when $x \sim y$. Choose ρ_i so that $\lim \rho_i = \lambda$. Then H2 implies $x \sim x\lambda y$.

H6. Given $x \sim y$, suppose first that $z \sim x$. Then $x\lambda z \sim y\lambda z$ by H5 and the transitivity of $\sim$. Suppose next that $x \succ z$. It then follows from B2 and the mixture-set axioms that $x\rho z \sim y\rho z$ for any ρ. Given λ, let $T = \{\mu : x\mu z \succsim y\lambda z\}$, and choose $\rho_i \to \lambda$ with $\rho_i \geq \lambda$ for all i. Then $x\rho_i z \sim$ $\sim y\rho_i z \succsim y\lambda z$ follows easily from H4. Therefore all ρ_i are in T and, by B3, $\lambda \in T$, so that $x\lambda z \succsim y\lambda z$. By symmetry, $y\lambda z \succsim x\lambda z$, so that $x\lambda z \sim y\lambda z$. A similar proof gives this result if $z \succ x$.

H7. Suppose $x \succ y$ and $\lambda > \mu > 0$. Then $x\lambda y \succ y$ by H4 or $x \succ y$ and M1 (if $\lambda = 1$). Since $0 < \mu/\lambda < 1$, H4 and M3 imply that $x\lambda y \succ (x\lambda y) \times$ $\times (\mu/\lambda)y = x\mu y$. Similarly, if $x \succ y$ and $x\lambda y \succ x\mu y$, then $\lambda > \mu$. The case for $\mu = 0$ is obvious.

The B Axioms Imply A2

We now prove that the Herstein–Milnor axioms imply A2: $(x \succ y,$ $0 < \lambda < 1) \Rightarrow x\lambda z \succ y\lambda z$. Given $x \succ y$ and $0 < \lambda < 1$, suppose first that $z \succ x \succ y$. Then $x \sim z\alpha y$ for some $\alpha < 1$ by H1, and $x\lambda z \sim (z\alpha y)\lambda z =$ $= [y(1 - \alpha)z]\lambda z = y(\lambda(1 - \alpha))z \succ y\lambda z$ by H6, M2, M3, and H7, so that $x\lambda z \succ y\lambda z$ by B1. Suppose next that $z \sim x \succ y$. Then $x\lambda z \sim z \succ y\lambda z$ by H5 and H7 with M2 and M4. The desired conclusion is reached in similar fashion for the other ways that z can relate to x and y.

Implications of Jensen's Axioms

This subsection proves the following implications of A1, A2, and A3, using proofs like those in Fishburn (1970, p. 112):

J1. $(x \succ y, \lambda > \mu) \Rightarrow x\lambda y \succ x\mu y$,

J2. $(x \succsim y \succsim z, x \succ z) \Rightarrow y \sim x\lambda z$ for a unique λ,

J3. $(x \succ y, z \succ w) \Rightarrow x \lambda z \succ y \lambda w,$

J4. $x \sim y \Rightarrow x \sim x \lambda y,$

J5. $x \sim y \Rightarrow x \lambda z \sim y \lambda z.$

It may be noted that J1 is part of H7, J2 is closely related to H1, J4 = H5 and J5 = H6. Moreover, B2 is the special case J5 with $\lambda = \frac{1}{2}$.

J1. Assume that $x \succ y$ and $\lambda > \mu$. Then $x \succ x\mu y$, by M1 and M2 if $\mu = 0$, and by A2 and M4 if $\mu > 0$. Hence, $x\lambda y \succ x\mu y$, by M1 if $\lambda = 1$, and by M2, M3, M4, and A2 as follows if $\lambda < 1$: $x\lambda y = y(1 - \lambda)x = [y(1 - \mu)x]$ $((1 - \lambda)/(1 - \mu))x = (x\mu y)((1 - \lambda)/(1 - \mu))x = x((\lambda - \mu)/(1 - \mu))(x\mu y) \succ$ $\succ (x\mu y)((\lambda - \mu)/(1 - \mu))(x\mu y) = x\mu y.$

J2. Given $x \succsim y \succsim z$ and $x \succ z$, suppose first that $x \sim y$, so $y \sim x \succ z$. Then $y \sim x 1 z = x$ by M1, and $x 1 z \succ x\mu z$ for any $\mu < 1$ by J1, so that $y \sim x\lambda z$ for a unique λ. A similar proof applies when $y \sim z$. Finally, suppose that $x \succ y \succ z$. It then follows from A1, A3, and J1 that there is a unique $\lambda \in (0, 1)$ such that

$$x\alpha z \succ y \succ x\beta z \quad \text{for all} \quad \alpha > \lambda > \beta.$$

We claim that $y \sim x\lambda z$. For, if $x\lambda z \succ y$ then $x\lambda z \succ y \succ z$, and, by M3 and A3, $x(\lambda\mu)z = (x\lambda z)\mu z \succ y$ for some $0 < \mu < 1$, contradicting $y \succ x(\lambda\mu)z$ since $\lambda > \lambda\mu$. A similar contradiction obtains if we suppose that $y \succ x\lambda z$.

J3. If $0 < \lambda < 1$ and $\{x \succ y, z \succ w\}$, then A2 gives $x\lambda z \succ y\lambda z =$ $= z(1 - \lambda)y \succ w(1 - \lambda)y = y\lambda w.$

J4. Suppose $x \sim y \succ x\lambda y$. Then J3 and M4 imply $x\lambda y \succ (x\lambda y)\lambda(x\lambda y) =$ $= x\lambda y$, contrary to asymmetry. Hence $x \sim y \Rightarrow x\lambda y \succsim x$. Similarly, $x \sim y \Rightarrow x \succsim x\lambda y.$

J5. We are to show that $x \sim y \Rightarrow x\lambda z \sim y\lambda z$. Since this is obvious if $\lambda \in \{0, 1\}$, assume henceforth that $x \sim y$ and $0 < \lambda < 1$. If $z \succ x$, then J4 gives the desired result, so henceforth take $x \succ z$. (The proof with $z \succ x$ is similar.) Then $x\lambda z \succ z$ by A2 and M4. Suppose also that $y\lambda z \succ x\lambda z$. Then J2 and M3 give $x\lambda z \sim (y\lambda z)\alpha z = y(\lambda\alpha)z$ for a unique $\alpha \in (0, 1)$; and, since $y \succ z$, two applications of A2 with M4 and then M3 give $y \succ y\alpha z$, hence $x \succ y\alpha z$, and therefore $x\lambda z \succ (y\alpha z)\lambda z = y(\lambda\alpha)z$, which contradicts $x\lambda z \sim y(\lambda\alpha)z$. Hence, $y\lambda z \succ x\lambda z$ is false. Similarly, $x\lambda z \succ y\lambda z$ is false. Therefore $x\lambda z \sim y\lambda z.$

Construction of Linear Utilities

We now show that A1–A3 and the results just proved imply the existence of a linear, order-preserving u on $\mathcal{M}$. Since there is nothing to prove if $\succ$ is empty, assume that $x \succ y$ for some $x, y \in \mathcal{M}$ and for the time being let such x and y be fixed with

$$[xy] = \{z : x \gtrsim z \gtrsim y\}.$$

By J2 there is a unique $f(z) \in [0, 1]$ for each $z \in [xy]$ such that

$$z \sim xf(z)y, \quad \text{with} \quad f(x) = 1 \quad \text{and} \quad f(y) = 0.$$

Suppose $z, w \in [xy]$ and $f(w) > f(z)$. Then, by J1, $xf(w)y \succ xf(z)y$. Transitivity then gives $w \succ z$. If $f(w) = f(z)$ then $z \sim xf(z)y \sim w$, hence $z \sim w$. Therefore

$$w \succ z \quad \text{iff} \quad f(w) > f(z), \quad \text{for all} \quad z, w \in [xy].$$

Therefore f preserves $\succ$ on $[xy]$.

To establish linearity, we first note that $[xy]$ is closed under the mixture operation, i.e. that $z, w \in [xy] \Rightarrow z\lambda w \in [xy]$. If $\lambda \in \{0, 1\}$, this follows from M1 and M2. If $0 < \lambda < 1$ then $x = x\lambda x \gtrsim x\lambda w = w(1 - \lambda)x \gtrsim w(1 - \lambda)z = z\lambda w \gtrsim z\lambda y = y(1 - \lambda)z \gtrsim y(1 - \lambda)y = y$, using M2, M4, A2, and J5 as needed.

Therefore, if $z, w \in [xy]$ then the definition of f gives

$$z\lambda w \sim xf(z\lambda w)y.$$

In addition, two applications of J5 and M2 give $z\lambda w \sim [xf(z)y]\lambda[xf(w)y]$ so that, by M5,

$$z\lambda w \sim x(\lambda f(z) + (1 - \lambda)f(w))y.$$

Therefore $xf(z\lambda w)y \sim x(\lambda f(z) + (1 - \lambda)f(w))y$ by the transitivity of $\sim$, so that, by J1,

$$f(z\lambda w) = \lambda f(z) + (1 - \lambda)f(w),$$

which shows that f is linear on $[xy]$.

Hence, whenever $x \succ y$, there is a linear, order-preserving f on $[xy]$. To show that one such function covers all of $\mathcal{M}$, fix $x \succ y$ as before and let $[x_1 y_1]$ and $[x_2 y_2]$ be any two sets like $[xy]$ for which $x_i \gtrsim x$ and $y \gtrsim y_i$. Let f_i be a linear, order-preserving function on $[x_i y_i]$ scaled so that $f_i(x) = 1$ and $f_i(y) = 0$ for $i = 1, 2$. We show that $f_1(z) = f_2(z)$ for any $z \in [x_1 y_1] \cap [x_2 y_2]$. If $z \sim x$ or $z \sim y$ then $f_1(z) = f_2(z)$ by the definitions. The other possibilities for z are as follows, shown with the unique number for indifference according to J2:

$$x \succ y \succ z : \quad y \sim x\alpha z,$$

$$x \succ z \succ y : \quad z \sim x\beta y,$$

$$z \succ x \succ y : \quad x \sim z\gamma y.$$

Under linearity and $\sim$ preservation for the f_i, these give

$$0 = \alpha + (1 - \alpha)f_i(z) \qquad (\alpha \neq 1)$$

$$f_i(z) = \beta$$

$$1 = \gamma f_i(z) \qquad\qquad\qquad (\gamma \neq 0)$$

respectively for $i = 1, 2$. Therefore $f_1(z) = f_2(z)$ in each case.

Finally, let $u(z)$ be the common value of $f_i(z)$ for every $[x_i y_i]$ that contains x, y, and z. Since every pair $z, w \in \mathcal{M}$ is in at least one $[x_i y_i]$, it follows that u is defined on $\mathcal{M}$ and is linear and order-preserving.

Uniqueness

Let u be order-preserving and linear on $\mathcal{M}$. Then if $v(x) = au(x) + b$, $a > 0$, v shares the same properties. Conversely, suppose that v too is order-preserving and linear. If u is constant then so is v, and $v(x) = u(x) + b$ for all x and some b. If u is not constant, fix $x \succ y$ and let

$$f_1(z) = \frac{u(z) - u(y)}{u(x) - u(y)}, \qquad f_2(z) = \frac{v(z) - v(y)}{v(x) - v(y)}$$

for all $z \in \mathcal{M}$. Since these are positive affine transformations of u and v, they too are order-preserving and linear. In addition, $f_1(x) = f_2(x) = 1$, $f_1(y) = f_2(y) = 0$, and an indifference analysis like that given above shows that $f_1 \equiv f_2$. Then, by the definitions of the f_i,

$$v(z) = au(z) + b,$$

where $a = [v(x) - v(y)]/[u(x) - u(y)] > 0$ and $b = v(y) - u(y)a$.

2.5. PROOF OF THEOREM 2

The proof of Theorem 2 is similar to the proof given above for the construction of linear, order-preserving utilities on the basis of M1–M3 and J1–J5. Our main concern in modifying the preceding proof is to make sure that the uses of $=$ from M1–M3 can be replaced by $\sim$ on the basis of the axioms in Theorem 2. Since M2 ($\sim$) and M3 ($\sim$) appear as axioms in Theorem 2, this means that we need to establish the $\sim$ versions of M1, M4, and M5, as well as J1–J5, from the new axioms. The construction of the desired u then parallels the construction given above with a few changes from $=$ to $\sim$, and the uniqueness proof is likewise straightforward.

The $\sim$ versions of M1, M4, and M5 are

M1($\sim$). $x1y \sim x$,

M4($\sim$). $x\lambda x \sim x$,

M5($\sim$). $(x\beta y)\alpha(x\gamma y) \sim x(\alpha\beta + (1-\alpha)\gamma)y$.

These are verified along with J1–J5 for Theorem 2 in the following order: M1($\sim$), M4($\sim$), J1, J2, J3, J4, J5, M5($\sim$). (Note that M5 was not used before until the construction section.) An outline of the proofs follows.

M1($\sim$). Contrary to M1($\sim$), suppose $x \succ x1y$. Then A2 implies $x\frac{1}{2}y \succ (x1y)\frac{1}{2}y$, and $(x1y)\frac{1}{2}y \sim x\frac{1}{2}y$ by M3($\sim$), so A1 is contradicted. A symmetric proof shows that $x1y \succ x$ is false. Therefore $x1y \sim x$.

M4($\sim$). This follows from M1($\sim$) if $\lambda = 1$, and from M1($\sim$), M2($\sim$), and A1 if $\lambda = 0$. Assume henceforth that $0 < \lambda < 1$, and let $\mu = 1/(1+\lambda)$. If $x \succ x\lambda x$ then A2, M3($\sim$), $\lambda\mu = 1 - \mu$, and M2($\sim$) give, in that order

$$x\mu x \succ (x\lambda x)\mu x \sim x(\lambda\mu)x = x(1-\mu)x \sim x\mu x,$$

which contradicts A1. Hence $x \succ x\lambda x$ is false. Similarly, $x\lambda x \succ x$ is false. Therefore $x\lambda x \sim x$.

J1 through J5. See the proofs of these given above, making indicated changes from = to $\sim$ where M1–M4 were used.

M5($\sim$). The proof of M5 early in Section 4 applies here with the usual changes from = to $\sim$. These changes are justified by A1, M1($\sim$), M2($\sim$), M3($\sim$), and J5.

CHAPTER 3

EXPECTED UTILITY FOR PROBABILITY MEASURES

One of the first axiomatizations of expected utility for nonsimple probability measures was given by Blackwell and Girshick (1954). They applied $\succ$ to the set of discrete probability measures on a set $\mathscr{C}$ of consequences, using A1, A3 and a denumerable generalization of A2. Although utilities need not be bounded when only simple measures are used, Blackwell–Girshick utilities must be bounded. Fishburn (1967, 1970, 1975a), DeGroot (1970), and Ledyard (1971) later extended the expected-utility form to other sets of probability measures.

This chapter first presents axiomatizations of expected utility that do not presume countable additivity. The initial axiomatization uses a strong structure that forces utilities to be bounded, but under weaker structural assumptions we shall see that boundedness is not inevitable. We then consider simplifications that obtain when all probability measures are countably additive. Several background definitions will be needed before we specify the axiomatizations.

3.1. MEASURES AND EXPECTATIONS

A *Boolean algebra* $\mathscr{A}$ for $\mathscr{C}$ is a set of subsets of $\mathscr{C}$ that contains $\mathscr{C}$, is closed under complementation $(A \in \mathscr{A} \Rightarrow \mathscr{C} \backslash A \in \mathscr{A})$, and is closed under finite unions $(A, B \in \mathscr{A} \Rightarrow A \cup B \in \mathscr{A})$. A *Borel algebra* ($\sigma$-field) $\mathscr{A}$ for $\mathscr{C}$ is Boolean algebra that is closed under countable unions $(A_i \in \mathscr{A}$ for $i = 1, 2, \ldots \Rightarrow \bigcup_i A_i \in \mathscr{A})$.

Throughout this chapter, $\mathscr{A}$ denotes a Boolean algebra for $\mathscr{C}$ that contains the singleton subset $\{c\}$ for each $c \in \mathscr{C}$.

A *probability measure* on $\mathscr{A}$ is a nonnegative real-valued function p on $\mathscr{A}$ with $p(\mathscr{C}) = 1$ and $p(A \cup B) = p(A) + p(B)$ whenever $A, B \in \mathscr{A}$ and $A \cap B = \emptyset$. The latter property says that p is finitely additive: p is *countably additive* if $p(\bigcup_i A_i) = \Sigma_i p(A_i)$ whenever the A_i are pairwise disjoint elements in $\mathscr{A}$ whose union is in $\mathscr{A}$. It is well known that if p is countably additive, and if $\mathscr{B}$ is a countable subset of $\mathscr{A}$ whose elements are linearly or asymmetrically weak ordered by proper inclusion $\subset$, with $\bigcup_{\mathscr{B}} B \in \mathscr{A}$,

23

then $p(\bigcup_{\mathscr{B}} B) = \sup\{p(B): B \in \mathscr{B}\}$. However, this will not be true if p is only finitely additive.

Henceforth in this chapter, $\mathscr{P}$ will denote a set of probability measures on $\mathscr{A}$ that contains every one-point measure: if $c \in \mathscr{C}$ and $p(\{c\}) = 1$ then $p \in \mathscr{P}$. We shall say that $\mathscr{P}$ is *closed under finite convex combinations* if $\lambda p + (1 - \lambda)q \in \mathscr{P}$ whenever $\lambda \in [0, 1]$ and $p, q \in \mathscr{P}$, and that it is *closed under countable convex combinations* if $\Sigma_i \lambda_i p_i \in \mathscr{P}$ whenever $\lambda_1 + \lambda_2 + \cdots = = 1$ and $p_i \in \mathscr{P}$ for all i.

Given a probability measure p on $\mathscr{A}$, and given $A \in \mathscr{A}$ for which $p(A) > 0$, the *conditional measure* of p given A is the probability measure p_A on $\mathscr{A}$ for which $p_A(B) = p(B \cap A)/p(A)$ for all $B \in \mathscr{A}$. We say that $\mathscr{P}$ is *closed under the formation of conditional measures* if $p_A \in \mathscr{P}$ whenever $p \in P$, $A \in \mathscr{A}$ and $p(A) > 0$.

Expected utilities will be computed with the help of measures conditioned on preference intervals. A subset A of X is a *preference interval* if $z \in A$ whenever $x, y \in A$, $x \gtrsim z$ and $z \gtrsim y$, where in general $c \gtrsim d$ means that $p \gtrsim q$ when $p(\{c\}) = q(\{d\}) = 1$. When all preference intervals are in $\mathscr{A}$, $\mathscr{P}$ is *closed under conditional measures on preference intervals* if $p_A \in \mathscr{P}$ whenever $p \in \mathscr{P}$, A is a preference interval, and $p(A) > 0$. Clearly, closure under the formation of conditional measures implies closure under conditional measures on preference intervals when all preference intervals are in $\mathscr{A}$.

Expectations are defined for $\mathscr{A}$-measurable functions in the usual manner, where f is $\mathscr{A}$-*measurable* if it is a real-valued function on $\mathscr{C}$ and $\{c: f(c) \in I\} \in \mathscr{A}$ for every real interval I. Assume henceforth in this section that f is an $\mathscr{A}$-measurable function and that $p \in \mathscr{P}$. Let $E(f, p)$ denote the expected value of f with respect to p.

Suppose first that f is simple, so that there is a partition $\{A_1, \ldots, A_n\}$ of $\mathscr{C}$ and numbers x_i such that $f(c) = x_i$ for all $c \in A_i$ and all i from 1 to n. Then

$$E(f, p) = \sum_{i=1}^{n} x_i p(A_i).$$

Suppose next that f is bounded, so that $\{c: a \le f(c) \le b\} = \mathscr{C}$ for some numbers a and b. Then

$$E(f, p) = \sup\{E(f_n, p): n = 1, 2, \ldots\},$$

where $f_1, f_2, \ldots$ is any sequence of simple $\mathscr{A}$-measurable functions that converges uniformly from below to f, so that, for all $c \in \mathscr{C}, f_1(c) \le f_2(c) \le$

$\leq \cdots, f(c) = \sup\{f_n(c): n = 1, 2, \ldots\}$, and for any $\varepsilon > 0$ there is an n such that $f(c) \leq f_n(c) + \varepsilon$. Such a sequence always exists, and $\sup E(f_n, p)$ is the same for any such sequence (Fishburn, 1970, p. 136) regardless of whether p is countably additive.

Is f is bounded below but not necessarily bounded above, let $f_{[x]}$ be defined by

$$f_{[x]}(c) = \begin{cases} f(c) & \text{when} \quad f(c) \leq x \\ f(x) & \text{when} \quad f(c) > x, \end{cases}$$

and define $E(f, p)$ by

$$E(f, p) = \sup\{E(f_{[x]}, p): x \text{ real}\}$$
$$= \lim_{x \to \infty} E(f_{[x]}, p).$$

Analogously, if f is bounded above, let $E(f, p) = -E(-f, p)$. Finally, for general f, let $f^+(c) = c$ if $f(c) \geq 0$ and $f^+(c) = 0$ otherwise, and let $f^-(c) = c$ if $f(c) < 0$ and $f^-(c) = 0$ otherwise. Then $E(f, p) = E(f^+, p) + E(f^-, p)$ unless $E(f^+, p) = \infty$ and $E(f^-, p) = -\infty$, in which case $E(f, p)$ is not defined.

3.2. AXIOMS WITH FINITE ADDITIVITY

We consider two axiomatizations when measures in $\mathscr{P}$ are not assumed to be countably additive. The different structural presuppositions for these two cases are as follows:

A0.1. $\mathscr{A}$ contains all preference intervals, and $\mathscr{P}$ is closed under count-
        able convex combinations and under the formation of conditional
        measures.

A0.2. $\mathscr{A}$ contains all preference intervals, and $\mathscr{P}$ is closed under finite
        convex combinations and under conditional measures on preference
        intervals.

The second of these two structural axioms is somewhat weaker than the first and therefore requires stronger preference axioms to arrive at the expected-utility representation. Since $\mathscr{P}$ is a mixture set in either case, axioms A1, A2, and A3 of Section 2.2 imply the existence of a linear, order-preserving utility function u on $\mathscr{P}$. When u is defined on $\mathscr{C}$ from u on $\mathscr{P}$ through one-point measures, additional axioms are needed to conclude that $u(p) = E(u, p)$ for each $p \in \mathscr{P}$.

Only one more axiom is required under A0.1. The new axiom is:

A4.   If $p, q \in \mathcal{P}$, $A \in \mathcal{A}$ and $p(A) = 1$, then $p \succsim q$ if $c \succ q$ for all $c \in A$, and $q \succsim p$ if $q \succ c$ for all $c \in A$.

Here $c \succ q$ means that $r \succ q$ when $r(\{c\}) = 1$, and $q \succ c$ has a similar interpretation. The first part of axiom A4 says that if p is certain to yield a consequence in A, and if every consequence in A is strictly preferred to q, then p will be 'weakly preferred' to q. The second part has a dual interpretation. As a normative postulate, this dominance axiom seems uncontroversial. In the following theorem, A1, A2, and A3 apply to $\succ$ on $\mathcal{P}$ with $p \lambda q = \lambda p + (1 - \lambda)q$.

THEOREM 1. *Suppose A0.1, A1, A2, A3, and A4 hold. Then there is a bounded real-valued function u on $\mathcal{C}$ such that, for all $p, q \in \mathcal{P}$,*

$$p \succ q \quad iff \quad E(u, p) > E(u, q),$$

and such a u is unique up to a positive affine transformation.

This is proved in Section 4, where we note that bounded utilities are caused in large part by the assumption in A0.1 that $\mathcal{P}$ is closed under countable convex combinations. When this assumption is weakened, as in A0.2, u can be unbounded. Because of this, it is necessary to introduce another axiom in the context of A0.2 which will ensure that $u(p) = E(u, p)$. To state this axiom, several notational conventions will be adopted.

First, certain preference intervals in $\mathcal{C}$ will be identified as follows:

$$(-\infty, c) = \{d \in \mathcal{C} : c \succ d\}$$
$$(-\infty, c] = \{d \in \mathcal{C} : c \succsim d\}$$
$$(c, \infty) = \{d \in \mathcal{C} : d \succ c\}$$
$$[c, \infty) = \{d \in \mathcal{C} : d \succsim c\}.$$

Second, let

$$\mathcal{P}^+ = \{p \in \mathcal{P} : p([c, \infty)) = 1 \text{ for some } c \in \mathcal{C}, \text{ and}$$
$$p((d, \infty)) > 0 \text{ for all } d \in \mathcal{C}\},$$
$$\mathcal{P}^- = \{p \in \mathcal{P} : p((-\infty, c]) = 1 \text{ for some } c \in \mathcal{C}, \text{ and}$$
$$p((-\infty, d)) > 0 \text{ for all } d \in \mathcal{C}\}.$$

Thus, measures in $\mathcal{P}^+$ are bounded below but have 'upper preference tails', and measures in $\mathcal{P}^-$ are bounded above but have 'lower preference tails'. As before, $\mathscr{P}_0(\mathscr{C})$ is the set of all simple measures in $\mathscr{P}$. Finally, let c^* denote the simple measure in $\mathscr{P}$ that assigns probability 1 to consequence c, i.e. to $\{c\}$.

A5. (a) *If* $p \in \mathscr{P}^+, p_1 \succ p_0$ *with* $p_0, p_1 \in \mathscr{P}_0(\mathscr{C})$, *and* $p((-\infty, c]) > 0$ *for some* $c \in \mathscr{C}$, *then there is a* $d \in \mathscr{C}$ *such that*

$$p((-\infty, d])p_1 + p((d, \infty))d^* \succsim p((-\infty, d])p_0 + p((d, \infty))p_{(d, \infty)};$$

(b) *If* $p \in \mathscr{P}^-, p_1 \succ p_0$ *with* $p_0, p_1 \in \mathscr{P}_0(\mathscr{C})$, *and* $p([c, \infty)) > 0$ *for some* $c \in \mathscr{C}$, *then there is a* $d \in \mathscr{C}$ *such that*

$$p((-\infty, d))p_{(-\infty, d)} + p([d, \infty))p_1 \succsim p((-\infty, d))d^* + p([d, \infty))p_0.$$

To interpret A5(a), suppose u is unbounded above since otherwise this part of the axiom follows from preceding axioms. Then, given $p \in \mathscr{P}^+$, $p((-\infty, c]) > 0$ for some $c \in \mathscr{C}$, and $p_1 \succ p_0$, part (a) says that there is some $d \in \mathscr{C}$ for which Gamble 1 is preferred or indifferent to Gamble 2, where

Gamble 1 yields	p_1	with probability $p((-\infty, d])$,
or	d	with probability $p((d, \infty))$;
Gamble 2 yields	p_0	with probability $p((-\infty, d])$,
or	$p_{(d, \infty)}$	with probability $p((d, \infty))$.

As $u(d)$ gets large, it follows from preceding assumptions (A0.2, A1 through A4) that $p((d, \infty))$ approaches 0. Hence, even though every consequence in (d, ∞) is preferred to d, when $u(d)$ is sufficiently large it does not seem unreasonable that – in view of $p_1 \succ p_0$ – Gamble 1 will be weakly preferred to Gamble 2. The interpretation of A5(b) is similar.

The inelegance of A5 is the price extracted for our use of the weaker structure in A0.2. As shown by the following theorem, A5 is necessary *and* sufficient for the usual expected-utility representation in the presence of the other preference axioms. As in Theorem 1, A1, A2, and A3 apply to $\succ$ on $\mathscr{P}$ with $p \lambda q = \lambda p + (1 - \lambda)q$.

THEOREM 2. *Suppose A0.2 holds. Then there is a real-valued function* u *on* $\mathscr{C}$ *for which* $E(u, p)$ *is well defined and finite for all* $p \in \mathscr{P}$ *and such that, for all* $p, q \in \mathscr{P}$,

$$p \succ q \quad iff \quad E(u, p) > E(u, q),$$

if and only if A1 *through* A5 *hold.*

Since $\mathscr{P}_0(\mathscr{C}) \subseteq \mathscr{P}, u$ in Theorem 2 must of course be unique up to a positive affine transformation. The theorem is proved later in Section 5.

3.3. AXIOMS WITH COUNTABLE ADDITIVITY

When all measures in $\mathscr{P}$ are countably additive, A4 can be replaced by a dominance axiom that uses $d \in \mathscr{C}$ in place of $q \in \mathscr{P}$:

A4*.   *If* $p \in \mathscr{P}$, $A \in \mathscr{A}$, $p(A) = 1$ *and* $d \in \mathscr{C}$, *then* $p \gtrsim d^*$ *if* $c \gtrsim d$ *for all* $c \in A$, *and* $d^* \gtrsim p$ *if* $d \gtrsim c$ *for all* $c \in A$.

THEOREM 3. *The conclusions of Theorem 1 remain true when A4 in its hypotheses is replaced by* A4*, *provided that all measures in* $\mathscr{P}$ *are countably additive.*

An example illustrating the difference between Theorem 1 and 3 is provided by $\mathscr{C} = \{0, 1, 2, \ldots\}$ with $u(c) = c/(1 + c)$ for all $c \in \mathscr{C}$. Let $\mathscr{A}$ be the set of all subsets of $\mathscr{C}$, let $\mathscr{P}$ be the set of all probability measures on $\mathscr{A}$, and define u on $\mathscr{P}$ by

$$u(p) = E(u, p) + \inf\{p(\{c: u(c) \geq 1 - \varepsilon\}): 0 < \varepsilon \leq 1\}.$$

It is not hard to show that u is linear on $\mathscr{P}$: hence, when $\succ$ on $\mathscr{P}$ is defined by $p \succ q$ iff $u(p) > u(q)$, axioms A1, A2, and A3 hold. Moreover, it is easily seen that A4* holds while A4 fails. Since $\mathscr{P}$ contains measures that are not countably additive, we do not get $u(p) = E(u, p)$ for some $p \in \mathscr{P}$. For example, if p is a diffuse measure with $p(\{c\}) = 0$ for every $c \in \mathscr{C}$, then $\inf\{p(u(c) \geq 1 - \varepsilon): 0 < \varepsilon \leq 1\} = 1$, so $E(u, p) = 1$ but $u(p) = 2$.

A more notable advantage of countable additivity arises in the context of A0.2 since here we can replace the cumbersome A5 with the simpler

A5*.   *If* $p \in \mathscr{P}$ *and* $p_0 \in \mathscr{P}_0(\mathscr{C})$, *then* $p_{(-\infty, d]} \gtrsim p_0$ *for some* $d \in \mathscr{C}$ *if* $p \succ p_0$, *and* $p_0 \gtrsim p_{[d, \infty)}$ *for some* $d \in \mathscr{C}$ *if* $p_0 \succ p$.

This says that if $p \succ p_0$ then some 'upper truncation' of p will be weakly preferred to p_0, and if $p_0 \succ p$ then some 'lower truncation' of p will not be strictly preferred to p_0. Although examples show that A5* is not necessary for the usual expected-utility representation in the finitely-additive setting, it is necessary when all measures are countably additive and $\mathscr{A}$ is a Borel algebra.

THEOREM 4. *Suppose* A0.2 *holds,* $\mathscr{A}$ *is a Borel algebra, and all measures* *in $\mathscr{P}$ are countably additive. Then the conclusion of Theorem 2 holds when A4 and A5 are replaced there by A4* and A5*.*

Theorem 3 is proved in Section 4, and Theorem 4 is proved in Section 5.

3.4. PROOFS WITH A0.1

Assume that A0.1, A1, A2, A3 and either A4 or A4* hold. By Theorem 2.1, let u be a linear, order-preserving function on $\mathscr{P}$, and let $u(c) = u(c^*)$ for all $c \in \mathscr{C}$, where $c^* \in \mathscr{P}$ has $c^*(\{c\}) = 1$. Suppose u is unbounded above. By A0.1, construct $p = \Sigma_i 2^{-i} c_i^*$ in $\mathscr{P}$ with $u(c_i) \geq 2^i$ for $i = 1, 2, \ldots$. Also by A0.1, $\Sigma_i 2^{-i} c_{n+i}^* \in \mathscr{P}$ for $n = 1, 2, \ldots$. By the finite extension of linearity,

$$u(p) = \sum_{i=1}^{n} 2^{-i} u(c_i) + 2^{-n} u(\Sigma_i 2^{-i} c_{n+i}^*)$$

$$\geq n + 2^{-n} u(\Sigma_i 2^{-i} c_{n+i}^0).$$

Since $c_i \succ d$ for some $d \in \mathscr{C}$ and all i greater than some m, the first part of A4 or A4* gives $\Sigma_i 2^{-i} c_{n+i}^* \succsim d^*$ for $n > m$, hence $u(\Sigma_i 2^{-i} c_{n+i}^*) \geq u(d)$, and therefore

$$u(p) \geq n + 2^{-n} u(d) \quad \text{for all} \quad n > m,$$

which is impossible. Therefore u is bounded above. The second parts of A4 and A4* show that u is bounded below.

With u bounded in the context of either Theorem 1 or Theorem 3, we note next that if $p(A) = 1$ for $A \in \mathscr{A}$ then $a \leq u(p) \leq b$, where $a = \inf\{u(c): c \in A\}$ and $b = \sup\{u(c): c \in A\}$. We consider A4 first, then look at A4* under countable additivity.

Suppose to the contrary of $u(p) \leq b$ that $u(p) > u(b)$. Then linearity gives $u(\tfrac{1}{2}p + \tfrac{1}{2}d^*) > u(b) \geq u(c)$ for some $d \in \mathscr{C}$ and all $c \in \mathscr{C}$: hence $\tfrac{1}{2}p + \tfrac{1}{2}d^* \succ c$ for all $c \in A$. Then, by A4, $\tfrac{1}{2}p + \tfrac{1}{2}d^* \succsim p$, contrary to $u(p) > u(\tfrac{1}{2}p + \tfrac{1}{2}d^*) = \tfrac{1}{2}u(p) + \tfrac{1}{2}u(d)$. Therefore $u(p) \leq b$. A similar proof gives $a \leq u(p)$.

To show that $a \leq u(p) \leq b$, given A4* and countable additivity, suppose first that $\{u(c): c \in A\} = \{a, b\}$. Then $a \leq u(p) \leq b$ follows from A4* and order preservation. Assume henceforth in this paragraph that $a < u(e) < b$ for fixed $e \in A$, and let

$$A_e = \{c \in A: e \succ c\}, \qquad \mathscr{P}_e = \{q \in \mathscr{P}: q(A_e) = 1\}$$

$$A^e = \{c \in A: c \succsim e\}, \qquad \mathscr{P}^e = \{q \in \mathscr{P}: q(A^e) = 1\}.$$

It follows from A0.1 that A_e, $A^e \in \mathscr{A}$ and that p is a convex combination of a measure in $\mathscr{P}_e$ and a measure in $\mathscr{P}^e$. Hence linearity for u implies that $a \leq u(p) \leq b$ if $a \leq u(q) \leq b$ for every $q \in \mathscr{P}_e \cup \mathscr{P}^e$. We now show that $a \leq u(q) \leq b$ when $q \in \mathscr{P}^e$: the proof for $q \in \mathscr{P}_e$ is similar. Given $q \in \mathscr{P}^e$, $a \leq u(q)$ follows from $a < u(e)$, A4* and order preservation, and an analysis like that used earlier in this section shows that u on $\mathscr{P}^e$ is bounded above. Thus, let M be such that

$$a \leq u(q) \leq M \quad \text{for all} \quad q \in \mathscr{P}^e.$$

If $u(c) = b$ for some $c \in A^e$ then $u(q) \leq b$ for all $q \in \mathscr{P}^e$ by A4* and order preservation, so that $a \leq u(q) \leq b$ for this case. Suppose henceforth in this paragraph that $u(c) < b$ for all $c \in A^e$, and let

$$A(\varepsilon) = \{c \in A^e : u(c) < b - \varepsilon\}$$

$$B(\varepsilon) = \{c \in A^e : b - \varepsilon \leq u(c)\}$$

for $\varepsilon > 0$. Then $A(\varepsilon) \cup B(\varepsilon) = A^e$, and $\{A(\varepsilon): \varepsilon > 0\}$ is asymmetrically weak ordered by $\subset$ with $\bigcup \{A(\varepsilon): \varepsilon > 0\} = A^e$. Then, by countable additivity,

$$\sup \{q(A(\varepsilon)): \varepsilon > 0\} = q(A^e) = 1$$

for every $q \in \mathscr{P}^e$. If $q(A(\varepsilon)) = 1$ for some $\varepsilon > 0$ then $u(q) < b$ by A4* and order preservation. On the other hand, if $q(A(\varepsilon)) < 1$ for all $\varepsilon > 0$ then, with ε small, it follows from linearity that

$$u(q) = q(A(\varepsilon))u(q_{A(\varepsilon)}) + q(B(\varepsilon))u(q_{B(\varepsilon)}).$$

Hence, by $a \leq u(q) \leq M$ and $q_{A(\varepsilon)}(A(\varepsilon)) = 1$,

$$u(q) < q(A(\varepsilon))b + [1 - q(A(\varepsilon))]M$$

for all small $\varepsilon > 0$, and therefore $u(q) \leq b$ since $\sup \{q(A(\varepsilon))\} = 1$.

Thus, for both Theorems 1 and 3, $\inf \{u(c): c \in A\} \leq u(p) \leq \sup \{u(c): c \in A\}$ when $A \in \mathscr{A}$ and $p(A) = 1$. To complete the proofs of these theorems, let $a = \inf \{u(c): c \in \mathscr{C}\}$ and $b = \sup \{u(c): c \in \mathscr{C}\}$. Since preference intervals are in $\mathscr{A}$, u is $\mathscr{A}$-measurable, and the functions $f_1, f_2, \ldots$ defined by

$$f_n(c) = a + (i - 1)(b - a)/2^n \quad \text{for all} \quad c \in A_{i,n} \quad (i = 1, \ldots, 2^n),$$

where

$$A_{1,n} = \{c : a \leq u(c) \leq a + (b - a)/2^n\}$$

and

$$A_{i,n} = \{c : a + (i - 1)(b - a)/2^n < u(c) \leq a + i(b - a)/2^n\}$$

for $i = 2, \ldots, 2^n$, are simple $\mathscr{A}$-measurable functions that converge uniformly from below to u. Therefore, by definition,

$$E(u, p) = \sup\{\Sigma_i[a + (i-1)(b-a)/2^n]p(A_{i,n}): n = 1, 2, \ldots\}.$$

Moreover, by the first sentence of this paragraph along with the finite extension of linearity,

$$\Sigma_i[a + (i-1)(b-a)/2^n]p(A_{i,n}) \leq u(p) \leq \Sigma_i[a + i(b-a)/2^n]p(A_{i,n}).$$

Since the difference between the two sums here is $(b-a)/2^n$, which vanishes as n gets large, $u(p) = E(u, p)$, and therefore $p \succ q$ iff $E(u, p) > E(u, q)$.

3.5. PROOFS WITH A0.2

We assume throughout this section that A0.2, A1, A2, and A3 hold. With u on $\mathscr{P}$ linear and order-preserving (Theorem 2.1) let $u(c) = u(c^*)$ for all $c \in \mathscr{C}$. It is easily seen that there is a real-valued function v on $\mathscr{C}$ for which $E(v, p)$ is well defined and finite for all $p \in \mathscr{P}$ and gives $p \succ q$ iff $E(v, p) > E(v, q)$, if and only if v only $\mathscr{C}$ is a positive affine transformation of u on $\mathscr{C}$. Hence Theorem 2 will be true if and only if A4 and A5 are necessary and sufficient for $u(p) = E(u, p)$ for all $p \in \mathscr{P}$. And, when $\mathscr{A}$ is a Borel algebra and all measures are countably additive, Theorem 4 is true if and only if A4* and A5* are necessary and sufficient for $u(p) = E(u, p)$.

Necessity

Suppose in fact that $E(u, p) = u(p)$ for all $p \in \mathscr{P}$. If $p(A) = 1$ then $E(u, p) = \int_A u(c)\,dp(c)$, and if $c \succ q$ for all $c \in A$ then $E(u, p)$ must be as great as $E(u, q)$ since $u(c) > E(u, q)$ for all $c \in A$. The necessity of the other part of A4 is established in like manner. The proof of the necessity of A4* is similar.

Continuing with $E(u, p) = u(p)$, suppose the hypotheses of A5(a) hold: $p \in \mathscr{P}^+$, $p_1 \succ p_0$, and $p((-\infty, c]) > 0$ for some $c \in \mathscr{C}$. Then the definition of expectation and linearity give

$$\lim_{u(d) \to \sup u(\mathscr{C})} \{p((-\infty, d])E(u, p_{(-\infty, d]}) + p((d, \infty))u(d)\} =$$

$$= E(u, p) = u(p) = p((-\infty, d])E(u, p_{(-\infty, d]}) + p((d, \infty))u(p_{(d, \infty)}),$$

so that $\lim p((d, \infty))[u(d) - u(p_{(d, \infty)})] = 0$. Since $u(p_1) - u(p_0) > 0$ and $p((-\infty, c]) > 0$ for some $c \in \mathscr{C}$, it follows that there is a $d \in \mathscr{C}$ with $p((-\infty, d]) > 0$ such that

$$p((-\infty, d])[u(p_1) - u(p_0)] + p((d, \infty))u(d) > p((d, \infty))u(p_{(d, \infty)}).$$

Transposition of $p((-\infty, d])u(p_0)$, linearity and order preservation then imply the conclusion of A5(a). The necessity of A5(b) follows from a similar proof.

Although it can be shown that A5* is not necessary in the context of Theorem 2, it is necessary for $E(u, p) = u(p)$ under the hypotheses of Theorem 4. Consider the first part of A5*, with hypotheses $p \in \mathscr{P}$ and $p \succ p_0$. Under countable additivity and finite expected utilities, if $p((-\infty, d]) < 1$ for all d then

$$E(u, p) = \lim_{u(d) \to \sup u(\mathscr{C})} E(u, p_{(-\infty, d]}),$$

so that $E(u, p) > E(u, p_0)$ implies $E(u, p_{(-\infty, d]}) \geq E(u, p_0)$ for some d, hence $p_{(-\infty, d]} \succsim p_0$ for some d. And if $p((-\infty, d]) = 1$ for some d, then $p_{(-\infty, d]} \sim p \succ p_0$. The latter part of A5* is shown to be necessary under countable additivity by a similar proof.

Sufficiency

We shall prove next that $E(u, p) = u(p)$ when A4 and A5 hold, given the items noted in the opening paragraph of this section. We begin with a lemma that does not use A5.

LEMMA 1. *Suppose* A4 *holds. Then, for all* $p \in \mathscr{P}$:
   (a) $E(u, p) = u(p)$ *if* $p(A) = 1$ *for some* $A \in \mathscr{A}$ *for which both* $\inf \{u(c): c \in A\}$ *and* $\sup \{u(c): c \in A\}$ *are finite*;
   (b) $u(p) \geq E(u, p)$ *if* $p(A) = 1$ *for some* $A \in \mathscr{A}$ *for which* $\inf \{u(c): c \in A\}$ *is finite*;
   (c) $E(u, p) \geq u(p)$ *if* $p(A) = 1$ *for some* $A \in \mathscr{A}$ *for which* $\sup \{u(c): c \in A\}$ *is finite*;
   (d) $E(u, p)$ *is well defined and finite*.
   Proof. The proof of part (a) is essentially the same as the proof of Theorem 1 in the preceding section, where closure under countable convex combinations was used only to establish boundedness. Part (d) obviously holds in this case, so assume henceforth in this proof that whenever $p(A) = 1$ for $A \in \mathscr{A}$, either $\inf \{u(c): c \in A\} = -\infty$ or $\sup \{u(c): c \in A\} = \infty$ (possibly both).

For part (b) of the lemma, assume that $p(A) = 1$ with $\inf \{u(c): c \in A\}$ finite. Then $p((d, \infty)) > 0$ for all $d \in \mathscr{C}$. Let $E(u, p_{(-\infty, d]})$ be set at 0 when $p_{(-\infty, d]} = 0$. Then

$$E(u, p) = \lim_{u(d) \to \infty} \{p((-\infty, d])E(u, p_{(-\infty, d]}) + p((d, \infty))u(d)\}.$$

For each $d \in \mathscr{C}$, $p = p_{(d, \infty)}$ if $p((d, \infty)) = 1$, and $p = p((-\infty, d]) \, p_{(-\infty, d]} +$ $+ p((d, \infty))p_{(d, \infty)}$ if $p((d, \infty)) < 1$. Therefore, with $u(p_{(-\infty, d]}) = 0$ by convention when $p((-\infty, d]) = 0$, linearity gives

$$u(p) = p((-\infty, d])u(p_{(-\infty, d]}) + p((d, \infty))u(p_{(d, \infty)})$$

for all $d \in \mathscr{C}$. Now when $p((-\infty, d]) > 0$, we have $p_{(-\infty, d]}(A \cap (-\infty, d]) = 1$ and therefore $u(p_{(-\infty, d]}) = E(u, p_{(-\infty, d]})$ by part (a) of the lemma. Moreover, since $c \succ d$ for every $c \in (d, \infty)$, and since $p_{(d, \infty)}((d, \infty)) = 1$, A4 and order preservation yield $u(p_{(d, \infty)}) \geq u(d)$ for all $d \in \mathscr{C}$. The preceding displayed expressions for $E(u, p)$ and $u(p)$ then show that $u(p) \geq E(u, p)$.

The proof of part (c) is like the proof of (b).

To verify (d) for cases not covered under (a), let $p \in \mathscr{P}$ and let $c \in \mathscr{C}$. If $p((-\infty, c]) = 1$ then $p = p_{(-\infty, c]}$ and $u(p) \leq E(u, p) \leq u(c)$ by part (c); if $p((c, \infty)) = 1$ then $p = p_{(c, \infty)}$ and $u(c) \leq E(u, p) \leq u(p)$ by part (b); otherwise, $p = p((-\infty, c])p_{(-\infty, c]} + p((c, \infty))p_{(c, \infty)}$ and $p((-\infty, c])u(p_{(-\infty, c]}) + p((c, \infty))u(c) \leq E(u, p) \leq p((-\infty, c])u(c) + p((c, \infty))u(p_{(c, \infty)})$. Hence $E(u, p)$ is finite in all cases. ∎

To complete the sufficiency proof for Theorem 2, assume that A4 and A5 hold. Suppose first that $p \in \mathscr{P}^+$ with $p((-\infty, c]) > 0$ for some c. Then, since the difference $u(p_1) - u(p_0)$ with $p_1 \succ p_0$ can be made arbitrarily small by the choice of $p_0, p_1 \in \mathscr{P}_0(\mathscr{C})$, A5(a) along with linearity, order preservation, and $p_{(d, \infty)} \succsim d^*$ implies that $\inf\{p(d, \infty)[u(p_{(d, \infty)}) - u(d)]\} = 0$. Then, since $E(u, p_{(-\infty, d]}) = u(p_{(-\infty, d]})$ by Lemma 1(a), $E(u, p) = u(p)$ follows immediately from the displayed expressions in the proof of Lemma 1. On the other hand, if $p \in \mathscr{P}^+$ and $p((-\infty, c]) = 0$ for all $c \in \mathscr{C}$, i.e. $p((c, \infty)) = 1$ for all c, then Lemma 1(b) and the expression for $E(u, p)$ in its proof require u to be bounded above – in this case, Lemma 1(a) gives $E(u, p) = u(p)$. Hence $E(u, p) = u(p)$ for all $p \in \mathscr{P}^+$.

A similar proof, using A5(b), shows that $E(u, p) = u(p)$ for all $p \in \mathscr{P}^-$. Finally, let $\mathscr{P}^0 = \mathscr{P} \backslash (\mathscr{P}^+ \cup \mathscr{P}^-)$. If $p \in \mathscr{P}$ does not satisfy the condition of Lemma 1(a), then it equals a convex combination of measures in $\mathscr{P}^0$ and $\mathscr{P}^+$, or in $\mathscr{P}^0$ and $\mathscr{P}^-$, or in $\mathscr{P}^-$ and $\mathscr{P}^+$. Then $E(u, p) = u(p)$ follows from linearity of u on $\mathscr{P}$ and of $E(u, \cdot)$, from Lemma 1(a), and the results just noted for $\mathscr{P}^-$ and $\mathscr{P}^+$.

This completes the proof of Theorem 2.

For Theorem 4, assume that all measures in $\mathscr{P}$ are countably additive, that $\mathscr{A}$ is a Borel algebra, and that A4* and A5* hold. Then the conclusions of Lemma 1 hold by a proof that mimics the proof of Theorem 3 for part (a) of the lemma, and the proof of Lemma 1 with A4* in place of A4. To complete the proof that $E(u, p) = u(p)$ in the setting of Theorem 4, it suffices to show that $E(u, p) \geq u(p)$ when $p \in \mathscr{P}^+$ and that $u(p) \geq E(u, p)$ when $p \in \mathscr{P}^-$, for then $E(u, p) = u(p)$ follows from the lemma when $p \in \mathscr{P}^- \cup \cup \mathscr{P}^+$, and $E(u, p) = u(p)$ subsequently follows for all $p \in \mathscr{P}^0$ by the analysis that concludes the proof of Theorem 2. Given $p \in \mathscr{P}^+$,

$$E(u, p) = \lim_{u(d) \to \sup u(\mathscr{C})} E(u, p_{(-\infty, d]}).$$

Contrary to the desired result, suppose $u(p) > E(u, p)$. Then $u(p) > r > > E(u, p_{(-\infty, d]})$ for some number r and all $d \in \mathscr{C}$. Therefore, since $u(c_2) > > r > u(c_1)$ for some $c_1, c_2 \in \mathscr{C}$, there is a $p_0 \in \mathscr{P}_0(\mathscr{C})$ with $E(u, p_0) = r$. But this gives $p \succ p_0$ and $p_0 \succ p_{(-\infty, d]}$ for all $d \in \mathscr{C}$, by order preservation and Lemma 1(a), thus contradicting the first part of A5*. Hence $E(u, p) \geq \geq u(p)$ for $p \in \mathscr{P}^+$. A similar proof shows that $u(p) \geq E(u, p)$ for $p \in \mathscr{P}^-$.

CHAPTER 4

LEXICOGRAPHIC QUASILINEAR UTILITY

The preceding chapter extended the expected-utility model for simple probability measures to more general measures. We now return to an arbitrary mixture set $\mathcal{M}$ and consider axioms that are weaker than the combination of A1, A2, and A3. The initial section drops A3 altogether and investigates the structure of preferences on $\mathcal{M}$ for this case. We then restore part of A3 in a different guise to obtain a lexicographic representation in which $x \succ y$ iff $(u_1(x), \ldots, u_n(x)) >_L (u_1(y), \ldots, u_n(y))$, where $>_L$ is defined on like-dimensional real vectors $a = (a_1, \ldots, a_n)$ and $b = (b_1, \ldots, b_n)$ by

$$a >_L b \quad \text{iff} \quad a \neq b \text{ and } a_i > b_i \text{ for the smallest } i \text{ where } a_i \neq b_i.$$

The lexicographic representation for $\mathcal{M} = \mathcal{P}$ is discussed briefly.

4.1. PREFERENCE INTERVALS AND STRUCTURES

The following axiom will be assumed to hold throughout this section:

A6. $\succ$ *is a nonempty asymmetric weak order on a mixture set $\mathcal{M}$ that satisfies A2 along with*
A2($\sim$). *For all* $x, y, z \in \mathcal{M}$ *and all* $0 < \lambda < 1$, *if* $x \sim y$ *then* $x \lambda z \sim y \lambda z$.

The degenerate case of $\succ = \emptyset$ is forbidden by A6, which requires $x \succ y$ for some $x, y \in \mathcal{M}$. Axiom A2($\sim$) is the obvious indifference counterpart of A2. It is implied (J5, Section 2.4) by A1, A2, and A3, and will be needed for results presented later.

We approach the structure of preferences through closed preference intervals $[xy]$, where

$$[xy] = \{z \in \mathcal{M} : x \succsim z \succsim y\}.$$

Weak order implies that $[xy]$ is empty if $y \succ x$. The set of all nonempty closed preference intervals with nonindifferent end points is denoted by $\mathcal{N}$:

$$\mathcal{N} = \{[xy] : x \succ y\}.$$

When $[xy], [zw] \in \mathcal{N}$, the minimal element in $\mathcal{N}$ that includes both $[xy]$ and $[zw]$ is easily seen to be $[xw] \cup [zy]$.

Two preliminary implications of A6, whose proofs will be omitted since they are similar to the proofs of J1 and J2 in section 2.4, are

J1.   If $[xy] \in \mathcal{N}$ and $\lambda > \mu$ then $x \lambda y \succ x \mu y$,

J2*.   If $[xy] \in \mathcal{N}$ and $z \in [xy]$, then there is a unique λ such that either
(a) $z \sim x \lambda y$, or
(b) $x \mu y \succ z$ for all $\mu \geq \lambda : z \succ x \mu y$ for all $\mu < \lambda$, or
(c) $x \mu y \succ z$ for all $\mu > \lambda$; $z \succ x \mu y$ for all $\mu \leq \lambda$.

Parts (b) and (c) reflect the absence of A3. If A3 holds, then (J2) neither (b) nor (c) can occur. We shall denote the unique λ for $z \in [xy]$ in J2* by $\lambda_{xy}(z)$. That is, when $z \in [xy] \in \mathcal{N}$,

$$x \mu y \succ z \quad \text{for all} \quad \mu > \lambda_{xy}(z),$$
$$z \succ x \mu y \quad \text{for all} \quad \mu < \lambda_{xy}(z).$$

Recall that lower case Greek letters always denote numbers in $[0, 1]$.
Given J2*, we define a binary relation $\geq_0$ on $\mathcal{N}$ by

$$[xy] \geq_0 [zw] \quad \text{iff} \quad [xy] \supseteq [zw] \quad \text{and} \quad \lambda_{xy}(z) > \lambda_{xy}(w).$$

When $[xy] \supseteq [zw]$ and both intervals are in $\mathcal{N}$, the only way that $[xy] \geq_0 [zw]$ can fail is to have $\lambda_{xy}(z) = \lambda_{xy}(w)$, and this can happen only if A3 is false. In a sense, $[xy] \geq_0 [zw]$ indicates that $[zw]$ is commensurable with $[xy]$ since utilities for points in $[zw]$ have the potential of being scaled along with those in $[xy]$ by a single function.

We now define a key binary relation $=_0$ on $\mathcal{N}$ induced by $\geq_0$ as follows:

$$[xy] =_0 [zw] \quad \text{iff} \quad [xw] \cup [zy] \geq_0 [xy]$$
$$\text{and} \quad [xw] \cup [zy] \geq_0 [zw].$$

This says that each of $[xy]$ and $[zw]$ is 'commensurable' with the smallest interval in $\mathcal{N}$ that includes both. Our first theorem notes important properties of $\geq_0$ and $=_0$.

THEOREM 1. $\geq_0$ on $\mathcal{N}$ is reflexive and transitive, and $=_0$ on $\mathcal{N}$ is an equivalence relation.

The proof of Theorem 1 is given along with other proofs in Section 3.
Since $=_0$ on $\mathcal{N}$ is an equivalence relation, we partition $\mathcal{N}$ into equi-

valence classes by $=_0$, letting $\mathcal{N}_0 = \mathcal{N}/=_0$. Thus, $[xy]$ and $[zw]$ are in the same class in $\mathcal{N}_0$ iff $[xy] =_0 [zw]$. $\mathcal{N}_0$ consists of a single class $\mathcal{N}$ if and only if A3 holds.

For each $A \in \mathcal{N}_0$ let $\mathcal{M}(A) = \bigcup_A [xy]$, so that $\mathcal{M}(A)$ is the set of all elements in $\mathcal{M}$ that appear in at least one interval in A. Our next theorem shows how the different $\mathcal{M}(A)$ subsets of $\mathcal{M}$ can be related.

THEOREM 2. *Each $\mathcal{M}(A)$ for $A \in \mathcal{N}_0$ is a mixture set, and for any two distinct $A, B \in \mathcal{N}_0$, either $\mathcal{M}(A)$ and $\mathcal{M}(B)$ are disjoint or one is properly included in the other.*

Hence if $\mathcal{M}(A)$ and $\mathcal{M}(B)$ have a nonempty intersection, either $\mathcal{M}(A) \subset \mathcal{M}(B)$ or $\mathcal{M}(B) \subset \mathcal{M}(A)$. Using the results of Theorem 2, we begin to structure a hierarchy by defining $>$ on $\mathcal{N}_0$ as

$$A > B \quad \text{iff} \quad \mathcal{M}(B) \subset \mathcal{M}(A).$$

Clearly, $>$ is a strict partial order (asymmetric, transitive) on $\mathcal{N}_0$, and, by Theorem 2, if neither $A > B$ nor $B > A$ then every interval in A is disjoint from every interval in B. Adjacent classes in $\mathcal{N}_0$ are identified by $>_1$:

$$A >_1 B \quad \text{iff} \quad A > B \quad \text{and} \quad A > C > B \quad \text{for no} \quad C \in \mathcal{N}_0,$$

and classes separated by $k - 1$ other ordered classes are identified by $>_k$: for $k \geq 2$,

$$A >_k B \quad \text{iff} \quad A >_1 C \quad \text{and} \quad C >_{k-1} B \quad \text{for some} \quad C \in \mathcal{N}_0.$$

We can think of $A >_1 B$ as A 'dominating' B, with A and B in adjacent levels of the $(\mathcal{N}_0, >)$ hierarchy. And $A >_k B$ signifies that $k - 1$ levels separate A and B. When an infinite number of levels separate A and B, we can have $A > B$ and $A >_k B$ for no k. In this case one could use transfinite ordinals to denote separations, but I shall not pursue this here. It is embedded in a somewhat different manner in Hausner's (1954) approach.

Among other things, the following corollary notes that we can never have $A >_k B$ and $A >_j B$ when $j \neq k$.

COROLLARY 1. *If $A >_1 B$, $A >_1 C$ and $B \neq C$ then $\mathcal{M}(B) \cap \mathcal{M}(C) = \emptyset$; for any $B \in \mathcal{N}_0$, $A >_1 B$ for at most one $A \in \mathcal{N}_0$; if $A >_k B$ and $B >_j C$ then $A >_{k+j} C$; if $A > B$ then $A >_k B$ for at most one $k \in \{1, 2, \dots\}$.*

We now show how the levels in a finite $(\mathcal{N}_0, >)$ hierarchy correspond to coordinates in a lexicographic utility representation.

4.2. LEXICOGRAPHIC UTILITY

The following axioms will be used to identify the maximum number of levels in a finite hierarchy for $(\mathcal{N}_0, >)$:

A3(1). $A > B$ for no $A, B \in \mathcal{N}_0$,
A3(n). $n > 1$. $A >_{n-1} B$ for some $A, B \in \mathcal{N}_0$, and for all $A, B \in \mathcal{N}_0$, if $A > B$ then $A >_k B$ for some $1 \leq k \leq n - 1$.

Within the context of A6, axiom A3(1) is easily seen to be equivalent to the Archimedean axiom A3. Axiom A3(n), which says that there are n levels in the hierarchy, is a finite-levels weakening of A3. Suppose A3(n) holds for $n > 1$. It then follows from Corollary 1 that there is a unique class $A \in \mathcal{N}_0$ for which $A > B$ for every $B \in \mathcal{N}_0 \backslash \{A\}$. Let $h(A) = 1$ and $h(B) = k + 1$ when $A >_k B$. Then all B with $h(B) = k$ are in the kth level of the hierarchy. If B and C are in the same level and $B \neq C$ then $\mathcal{M}(B) \cap \mathcal{M}(C) = \emptyset$; if B and C are in different levels and neither $B > C$ nor $C > B$, then again $\mathcal{M}(B) \cap \mathcal{M}(C) = \emptyset$.

We now state a representation theorem in which the dimensionality of the utility vectors equals the number of levels in the hierarchy for $(\mathcal{N}_0, >)$.

THEOREM 3. *Suppose A6 and* A3(n) *hold. Then there are real-valued functions* $u_1, \ldots, u_n$ *on* $\mathcal{M}$ *such that, for all* $x, y \in \mathcal{M}$,

$$x > y \quad \text{iff} \quad (u_1(x), \ldots, u_n(x)) >_L (u_1(y), \ldots, u_n(y)),$$

and, if $u_k(x) \neq u_k(y)$ *and* $u_j(x) = u_j(y)$ *for each* $j < k$, *then for all* λ

$$u_k(x \lambda y) = \lambda u_k(x) + (1 - \lambda) u_k(y).$$

The function u_k will be constructed from linear 'utility' functions on the $\mathcal{M}(B)$ for $B \in \mathcal{N}_0$ that are in the kth level of the hierarchy for $(\mathcal{N}_0, >)$. In particular, if $h(B) = k$ then we define u_k on $\mathcal{M}(B)$ from a linear function u^B on $\mathcal{M}(B)$; and if $x \in \mathcal{M}$ is not in any $\mathcal{M}(B)$ that has $h(B) = k$, then $u_k(x)$ will be set equal to zero.

The last part of Theorem 3 gives a quasilinearity property for u_k. Our proof of the theorem implies that if $B \in \mathcal{N}_0$ with $h(B) = k$, then u_k and u_j for each $j < k$ are linear within $\mathcal{M}(B)$. It should be noted, however, that if $x, y \in \mathcal{M}(B)$ in this case, and $x > y$, we may have $u_j(x) = u_j(y)$ for all $j \leq k$, in which case the strict preference between x and y is accounted for by some u_t for $t > k$, where $u_t(x) > u_t(y)$.

Linear Utilities with Mixture Spaces

The hypotheses of Theorem 3 appear to be insufficient to imply that each u_k can be defined to be linear on all of $\mathcal{M}$. Although it might seem that full linearity for each u_k can be achieved by appropriate alignment under positive affine transformations of the u^B for which $h(B) = k$, an example in Fishburn (1971a) shows that this is not true even when $\mathcal{M}$ has additional structure. For example, to achieve full linearity when $n = 3$, it may be necessary for some B in the *second* level of the hierarchy to have u_1 and u_2 constant on $\mathcal{M}(B)$ and to let u_3 do the full work of characterizing $\succ$ on $\mathcal{M}(B)$. This could happen only if there were no C such that $B > C$, so there is no third-level class in $\mathcal{N}_0$ that is dominated by the second-level class B even though $n = 3$. The cited example has such a structure.

Hausner's (1954) treatment of lexicographic utility contains an assumption that we have not yet needed, but which will be used to prove that every u_k can be defined to be linear on $\mathcal{M}$. We identify this assumption as

M6. $\quad (x\,\mu\,y)\,\lambda\,z = x(\lambda\,\mu)\left(y\dfrac{\lambda(1-\mu)}{1-\lambda\mu}z \right),$

for all $x, y, z \in \mathcal{M}$ and all λ, μ for which $\lambda\mu \neq 1$. Condition M6 is somewhat more complex than M1 through M5 in Section 2.1, and it is not implied by the earlier conditions. The sensibility of M6 can be seen by writing it in convex-combinations form as

$$\lambda(\mu x + (1-\mu)y) + (1-\lambda)z =$$

$$= \lambda\mu x + (1-\lambda\mu)\left[\frac{\lambda(1-\mu)}{1-\lambda\mu}y + \frac{1-\lambda}{1-\lambda\mu}z \right],$$

which is obviously true when $+$ is interpreted in the natural way with $x, y,$ and z real-valued functions on a common domain.

Following Hausner's terminology, we shall call $\mathcal{M}$ a *mixture space* if it is a mixture set that satisfies M6.

THEOREM 4. *Suppose $\mathcal{M}$ is a mixture space that satisfies A6 and A3(n). Then there are linear functions $u_1, \dots, u_n$ on $\mathcal{M}$ such that, for all $x, y \in \mathcal{M}$,*

$$x \succ y \quad \text{iff} \quad (u_1(x), \dots, u_n(x)) >_L (u_1(y), \dots, u_n(y)),$$

and linear functions $v_1, \dots, v_n$ on $\mathcal{M}$ satisfy this representation in place of

$u_1, \ldots, u_n$ respectively, if and only if there are real numbers $a_k > 0$, c_k and b_{kj} ($j = 1, \ldots, k - 1$) for each k such that, for all $x \in \mathcal{M}$,

$$v_k(x) = a_k u_k(x) + \sum_{j=1}^{k-1} b_{kj} u_j(x) + c_k \quad (k = 1, \ldots, n).$$

Since $v_1(x) = a_1 u_1(x) + c_1$, the initial function in the linear lexicographic representation is unique up to a positive affine transformation. Although u_2 is not similarly unique, it is unique up to a positive affine transformation on each subset of $\mathcal{M}$ in which u_1 is constant. Likewise, u_3 is unique up to a positive affine transformation on each subset of $\mathcal{M}$ where both u_1 and u_2 are constant, and so on for succeeding functions.

Sets of Probability Measures

If axioms A6 and A3(n) hold for $\succ$ on the set $\mathscr{P}_0(\mathscr{C})$ of simple probability measures on $\mathscr{C}$, then Theorem 4 and the discussion of $\mathscr{P}_0(\mathscr{C})$ in Section 1.1 imply that there are $u_1, \ldots, u_n$ on $\mathscr{C}$ such that, for all $p, q \in \mathscr{P}_0(\mathscr{C})$,

$$p \succ q \quad \text{iff} \quad (E(u_1, p), \ldots, E(u_n, p)) >_L (E(u_1, q), \ldots, E(u_n, q)).$$

The u_k are unique in the manner specified in Theorem 4. The addition of other axioms, such as A4 and A5 in Chapter 3, leads to the lexicographic expected utility representation for more general sets of probability measures.

A special lexicographic utility representation for the case in which $\succ$ is not assumed to be an asymmetric weak order is discussed in Section 5.2.

4.3. PROOFS

Assume throughout this section that A6 holds, and let λ_{xy} on $[xy] \in \mathcal{N}$ be as defined after J2*. We begin with facts about the λ_{xy} functions.

LEMMA 1. *If* $[xy] \in \mathcal{N}$ *then* λ_{xy} *is linear and, for all* z, $w \in [xy]$, *if* $z \succsim w$ *then* $\lambda_{xy}(z) \geq \lambda_{xy}(w)$.

Proof. The final assertion follows easily from J1 and J2*, which yield $w \succ z$ when $\lambda_{xy}(w) > \lambda_{xy}(z)$. For linearity let z, w be in $[xy]$ with $\beta = \lambda_{xy}(z)$ and $\gamma = \lambda_{xy}(w)$, and fix $\alpha \in (0, 1)$ since linearity in α is obvious when $\alpha \in \{0, 1\}$. Using A2, A2($\sim$), M2 and M5 (Section 2.1), along with J1, J2* and the fact that $t \in [xy] \Rightarrow x \succsim t \succsim y$, we get

$$z \alpha w \succsim (x \beta' y) \alpha w = w(1 - \alpha)(x \beta' y) \succsim (x \gamma' y)(1 - \alpha)(x \beta' y)$$

$$= (x \beta' y) \alpha (x \gamma' y) = x [\alpha \beta' + (1 - \alpha) \gamma'] y$$

and therefore $z \alpha w \succsim x[\alpha \beta' + (1 - \alpha)\gamma']y$ for all $\beta' < \beta$ (or $\beta' \leq \beta$ if $\beta = 0$ or if $\beta > 0$ and (a) or (c) of J2* holds for $\beta = \lambda_{xy}(z)$) and for all $\gamma' < \gamma$ (or $\gamma' \leq \gamma$ if $\gamma = 0 \ldots$). Similarly, $x[\alpha \beta^* + (1 - \alpha)\gamma^*]y \succsim z \alpha w$ for all $\beta^* > \beta$ (or $\beta^* \geq \beta$ if $\beta = 1$ or if $\beta < 1$ and (a) or (b) of J2* holds for β) and for all $\gamma^* > \gamma$ (or $\gamma^* \geq \gamma$ if $\gamma = 1 \ldots$). It then follows from J1 that $z \alpha w \succ x \rho y$ if $\rho < \alpha \beta + (1 - \alpha)\gamma$, and that $x \rho y \succ z \alpha w$ if $\rho > \alpha \beta + (1 - \alpha)\gamma$. Therefore, since $z \alpha w$ is clearly in $[xy]$, we must have $\lambda_{xy}(z \alpha w) = \alpha \beta + (1 - \alpha)\gamma = \alpha \lambda_{xy}(z) + (1 - \alpha)\lambda_{xy}(w)$, and hence λ_{xy} is linear. ∎

LEMMA 2. *If* $[xy] \geq_0 [zw]$ *then, for all* $t \in [zw]$,
$$\lambda_{zw}(t) = \frac{\lambda_{xy}(t) - \lambda_{xy}(w)}{\lambda_{xy}(z) - \lambda_{xy}(w)}.$$

Proof. Given $[xy] \geq_0 [zw]$ let $\alpha = \lambda_{xy}(w)$, $\beta = \lambda_{xy}(t)$ and $\gamma = \lambda_{xy}(z)$, with $\gamma \geq \beta \geq \alpha$ and $\gamma > \alpha$ (by definition of $\geq_0$). Suppose, contrary to the lemma, that $\lambda_{zw}(t) > (\beta - \alpha)/(\gamma - \alpha)$. Then

$$t \succ z\left(\frac{\beta - \alpha}{\gamma - \alpha} + \varepsilon\right)w$$

for small positive ε according to J2*. If $\alpha > 0$, let $\varepsilon' > 0$ be such that $\varepsilon' < \inf\{\alpha, \varepsilon(\gamma - \alpha)\}$. Then $z \succ x(\gamma - \varepsilon')y$ and $w \succ x(\alpha - \varepsilon')y$, and these and the preceding $\succ$ expression for t lead to $t \succ x(\beta + \varepsilon(\gamma - \alpha) - \varepsilon')y$, which contradicts $\lambda_{xy}(t) = \beta$ since $\beta + \varepsilon(\gamma - \alpha) - \varepsilon' > \beta$. On the other hand, if $\alpha = 0$, let $0 < \varepsilon' < \inf\{\varepsilon\gamma^2/(\varepsilon\gamma + \beta), \gamma\}$. Then an analysis like that just given for $\alpha > 0$ implies that $t \succ x(\beta + [\varepsilon\gamma^2 - \varepsilon'(\varepsilon\gamma + \beta)]/\gamma)y$, which again contradicts $\lambda_{xy}(t) = \beta$. Therefore $\lambda_{zw}(t) > (\beta - \alpha)/(\gamma - \alpha)$ is false. A similar proof shows that $\lambda_{zw}(t) < (\beta - \alpha)/(\gamma - \alpha)$ is false. Therefore $\lambda_{zw}(t) = (\beta - \alpha)/(\gamma - \alpha)$. ∎

Another Relation and Theorem 1

The first part of Theorem 1 is

LEMMA 3. $\geq_0$ *on* $\mathcal{N}$ *is reflexive and transitive.*

Proof. Reflexivity is immediate from the definition of $\geq_0$. For transitivity, suppose $[xy] \geq_0 [zw]$ and $[zw] \geq_0 [rs]$. Then $\lambda_{xy}(z) > \lambda_{xy}(w)$ and $\lambda_{zw}(r) > \lambda_{zw}(s)$, and, by Lemma 2,

$$\lambda_{zw}(r) = \frac{\lambda_{xy}(r) - \lambda_{xy}(w)}{\lambda_{xy}(z) - \lambda_{xy}(w)} \quad \text{and} \quad \lambda_{zw}(s) = \frac{\lambda_{xy}(s) - \lambda_{xy}(w)}{\lambda_{xy}(z) - \lambda_{xy}(w)}.$$

Therefore $\lambda_{xy}(r) > \lambda_{xy}(s)$, so that $[xy] \geq_0 [rs]$. ∎

To prepare for the second part of Theorem 1, we introduce the following companion to $\geq_0$ on $\mathcal{N}$:

$$[xy] \gg [zw] \quad \text{iff} \quad [xy], [zw] \in \mathcal{N}, [xy] \supseteq [zw]$$

$$\text{and} \quad \lambda_{xy}(z) = \lambda_{xy}(w).$$

Given $[xy], [zw] \in \mathcal{N}$ and $[xy] \supseteq [zw]$, exactly one of $[xy] \geq_0 [zw]$ and $[xy] \gg [zw]$ must hold. Our next lemma notes other ties between $\geq_0$ and $\gg$.

LEMMA 4. (a) *If* $[xy] \geq_0 [zw]$ *and* $[zw] \gg [rs]$ *then* $[xy] \gg [rs]$; *if* $[xy] \gg [zw]$ *and* $[zw] \geq_0 [rs]$ *then* $[xy] \gg [rs]$;

(b) *If* $[xy] \gg [rs]$, $[zw] \geq_0 [rs]$ *and* $[xy] \supseteq [zw]$, *then* $[xy] \gg [zw]$;

(c) $\gg$ *on* $\mathcal{N}$ *is transitive and irreflexive*;

(d) *If* $[xy] \gg [zw]$, $[xy] \gg [rs]$ *and* $[zw] \cap [rs] \neq \emptyset$, *then* $[xy] \gg [zw] \cup \cup [rs]$;

(e) *If* $[xy] \geq_0 [rs]$ *and* $[zw] \geq_0 [rs]$, *then* $[xy] \cup [zw] \geq_0 [rs]$.

Proofs. (a) If $[xy] \geq_0 [zw]$ and $[zw] \gg [rs]$ then $\lambda_{xy}(z) > \lambda_{xy}(w)$ and $\lambda_{zw}(r) = \lambda_{zw}(s)$. The last part of the proof of Lemma 3 then gives $\lambda_{xy}(r) = = \lambda_{xy}(s)$, so that $[xy] \gg [rs]$. If $[xy] \gg [zw]$ and $[zw] \geq_0 [rs]$ then $\lambda_{xy}(z) \geq \lambda_{xy}(r) \geq \lambda_{xy}(s) \geq \lambda_{xy}(w)$ by Lemma 1, and $\lambda_{xy}(w) = \lambda_{xy}(z)$ by the definition of $\gg$. Therefore $\lambda_{xy}(r) = \lambda_{xy}(s)$, so that $[xy] \gg [rs]$.

(b) If $[xy] \geq_0 [zw]$, contrary to the conclusion, then this and $[zw] \geq_0 [rs]$ imply $[xy] \geq_0 [rs]$ by Lemma 3, which contradicts $[xy] \gg [rs]$.

(c) If $[xy] \gg [zw]$ and $[zw] \gg [rs]$, then $\lambda_{xy}(z) = \lambda_{xy}(w)$, which requires $\lambda_{xy}(r) = \lambda_{xy}(s)$ since $[rs] \subseteq [zw]$.

(d) If $[zw] \cap [rs] \neq \emptyset$, then $[zw] \cup [rs] \in \mathcal{N}$, and therefore $[xy] \gg [zw] \cup \cup [rs]$ when $[xy] \gg [zw]$ and $[xy] \gg [rs]$, since λ_{xy} is constant on $\{z, w, r, s\}$ in view of $[zw] \cap [rs] \neq \emptyset$.

(e) Given $[xy] \geq_0 [rs]$ and $[zw] \geq_0 [rs]$, $[xy] \cup [zw] \in \mathcal{N}$. Suppose $[xy] \cup [zw] \gg [rs]$. Then, by Lemma 4(b), $[xy] \cup [zw] \gg [xy]$ and $[xy] \cup [zw] \gg [zw]$. Hence, by Lemma 4(d), $[xy] \cup [zw] \gg [xy] \cup [zw]$, which is false. Therefore $[xy] \cup [zw] \geq_0 [rs]$. ∎

The proof of Theorem 1 is completed by proving

LEMMA 5. $=_0$ *on* $\mathcal{N}$ *is an equivalence relation.*

Proof. It is obvious that $=_0$ is reflexive (since $\geq_0$ is reflexive) and symmetric. To establish transitivity, we first prove that

$$[xy] \geq_0 [rs] \quad \text{and} \quad [zw] \geq_0 [rs] \Rightarrow [xy] =_0 [zw].$$

Suppose $[xy] \geq_0 [rs]$ and $[zw] \geq_0 [rs]$. Then $[xy] \cup [zw] \geq_0 [rs]$ by Lemma 4(e). If $[xy] \cup [zw] \gg [xy]$ then $[xy] \cup [zw] \gg [rs]$ by Lemma 4(a), a contradiction. Hence $[xy] \cup [zw] \geq_0 [xy]$. Similarly, $[xy] \cup [zw] \geq_0 [zw]$. Therefore $[xy] =_0 [zw]$ by the definition of $=_0$ since $[xy] \cup [zw] = [xw] \cup [zy]$.

For transitivity of $=_0$, assume that $[xy] =_0 [zw]$ and $[zw] =_0 [rs]$. Let I_1, I_2, I_3, and I_4 denote, respectively, the smallest interval in $\mathcal{N}$ that includes $[xy] \cup [zw]$, $[zw] \cup [rs]$, $[xy] \cup [rs]$ and $[xy] \cup [zw] \cup [rs]$. Then $I_1 \geq_0 [xy]$, $I_1 \geq_0 [zw]$, $I_2 \geq_0 [zw]$ and $I_2 \geq_0 [rs]$. By the second and third of these, and the result in the preceding paragraph, $I_1 =_0 I_2$. Therefore, since $I_4 = I_1 \cup I_2$, we have $I_4 \geq_0 I_1$, and $I_4 \geq_0 I_2$. Lemma 3 then gives $I_4 \geq_0 [xy]$ and $I_4 \geq_0 [rs]$. Since $I_4 \supseteq I_3 \supseteq [xy]$ and $I_4 \supseteq I_3 \supseteq [rs]$, Lemma 4(a) implies not $(I_3 \gg [xy])$ and not $(I_3 \gg [rs])$, so that $I_3 \geq_0 [xy]$ and $I_3 \geq_0 [rs]$. Therefore $[xy] = [rs]$. ∎

An Equivalence Class

Throughout this subsection, A is an equivalence class in $\mathcal{N}_0$, with $[xy] =_0 [zw]$ for all $[xy], [zw] \in A$. With $\mathcal{M}(A)$ the union of all $[xy] \in A$, we observe that if $r, s \in \mathcal{M}(A)$ then $r \in [xy]$ and $s \in [zw]$ for some $[xy], [zw] \in A$. Since the smallest interval that includes $[xy] \cup [zw]$ must be in A, and since this interval contains $r \lambda s$ for every λ, $\mathcal{M}(A)$ is closed under the mixture operation. Since the other properties for a mixture set for $\mathcal{M}(A)$ follow from the assumption that $\mathcal{M}$ is a mixture set, we obtain the first part of Theorem 2:

LEMMA 6. *$\mathcal{M}(A)$ is a mixture set.*
The next lemma sets the stage for latter utility representations.

LEMMA 7. *There is a linear function u^A on $\mathcal{M}(A)$ such that, for all $x, y \in \mathcal{M}(A)$, if $[xy] \in A$ then $u^A(x) > u^A(y)$, and if $x \succsim y$ then $u^A(x) \geq u^A(y)$; any such u^A is unique up to a positive affine transformation.*

Proof. Given $\mathcal{M}(A)$, fix $[rs] \in A$ and let $u^A(t) = \lambda_{rs}(t)$ for every $t \in [rs]$. By the definitions and Lemma 1, u^A on $[rs]$ is linear with $u^A(r) = 1$, $u^A(s) = 0$ and $u^A(x) \geq u^A(y)$ when $r \succsim x \succsim y \succsim s$. For any $[zw] \in A$ such that $[rs] \subseteq [zw]$, let u_{zw} be the affine transformation of λ_{zw} obtained by setting $u_{zw}(s) = 0$ and $u_{zw}(r) = 1$:

$$u_{zw}(t) = \frac{\lambda_{zw}(t) - \lambda_{zw}(s)}{\lambda_{zw}(r) - \lambda_{zw}(s)} \quad \text{for all} \quad t \in [zw].$$

Since $[zw] =_0 [rs]$, $\lambda_{zw}(r) - \lambda_{zw}(s) > 0$. Suppose $[xy] \geq_0 [zw] \geq_0 [rs]$

with $[xy]$, $[zw] \in A$. Then, for all $t \in [zw]$,

$$u_{zw}(t) = \frac{\lambda_{zw}(t) - \lambda_{zw}(s)}{\lambda_{zw}(r) - \lambda_{zw}(s)}$$

$$= \frac{\left[\lambda_{xy}(t) - \lambda_{xy}(w)\right] - \left[\lambda_{xy}(s) - \lambda_{xy}(w)\right]}{\left[\lambda_{xy}(r) - \lambda_{xy}(w)\right] - \left[\lambda_{xy}(s) - \lambda_{xy}(w)\right]} \quad \text{(Lemma 2)}$$

$$= \frac{\lambda_{xy}(t) - \lambda_{xy}(s)}{\lambda_{xy}(r) - \lambda_{xy}(s)}$$

$$= u_{xy}(t).$$

Since u_{zw} is a positive affine transformation of λ_{zw}, the properties specified in Lemma 7 hold for u_{zw} on $[zw]$. With A^* a subset of A that is asymmetrically weak ordered by $\subseteq$ such that $\mathcal{M}(A)$ is the union of the $[zw] \in A^*$, it follows that when $u^A(t)$ is defined by

$$u^A(t) = u_{zw}(t) \quad \text{for any} \quad [zw] \text{ with } t \in [zw] \gtrsim_0 [rs],$$

u^A is defined unambiguously on $\mathcal{M}(A)$, and it is linear and satisfies the requirements in the first part of the lemma.

For uniqueness, suppose u_1^A and u_2^A are linear functions on $\mathcal{M}(A)$ which satisfy the ordering conditions in the lemma. Fix $[rs] \in A$ and let $f_i(t) = [u_i^A(t) - u_i^A(s)]/[u_i^A(r) - u_i^A(s)]$ for all $t \in \mathcal{M}(A)$ and $i = 1, 2$. It suffices to show that $f_1 = f_2$ on $\mathcal{M}(A)$. We will prove only that $f_1 = f_2$ on $[rs]$: the proof that $f_1 = f_2$ elsewhere in $\mathcal{M}(A)$ is similar. Given $t \in [rs]$ we consider three cases that correspond to (a), (b), and (c) in J2*, letting λ denote the unique element in each case. We show that $f_i(t) = f_i(r\lambda s)$ for $i = 1, 2$, which implies $f_1(t) = f_2(t)$ since $f_i(r\lambda s) = \lambda$.

(a) $t \sim r\lambda s$. Then, since $u_i^A(t) = u_i^A(r\lambda s)$ by the preservation of $\gtrsim$ in Lemma 7, $f_i(t) = f_i(r\lambda s)$.

(b) $r\lambda s \succ t$. By Lemma 7, $f_i(r\lambda s) \geq f_i(t)$. Suppose $>$ holds here. Then, since $f_i(r\lambda s) = \lambda f_i(r) + (1 - \lambda) f_i(s) = \lambda$, there is a $\mu < \lambda$ such that $f_i(r\mu s) > f_i(t)$. However, this requires $r\mu s \gtrsim t$, a contradiction to J2*(b). Therefore $f_i(r\lambda s) = f_i(t)$.

(c) $t \succ r\lambda s$. This proof is similar to that for (b). ∎

Theorem 2 and Corollary 1

Our proof of the next lemma completes the proof of Theorem 2.

LEMMA 8. *For any distinct* $A, B \in \mathcal{N}_0$, *either* $\mathcal{M}(A) \cap \mathcal{M}(B) = \emptyset$ *or* $\mathcal{M}(A) \subset \mathcal{M}(B)$ *or* $\mathcal{M}(B) \subset \mathcal{M}(A)$.

Proof. Given $A \neq B$ in $\mathcal{N}_0$, assume that $\mathcal{M}(A) \cap \mathcal{M}(B) \neq \emptyset$. We are to show that one of $\mathcal{M}(A)$ and $\mathcal{M}(B)$ is properly included in the other.

Consider $t \in \mathcal{M}(A) \cap \mathcal{M}(B)$ with $t \in [xy] \in A$ and $t \in [zw] \in B$. Since $A \neq B$, not $([xy] =_0 [zw])$. Therefore, either $[xy] \cup [zw] \gg [xy]$ or $[xy] \cup [zw] \gg [zw]$. Suppose for definiteness that $[xy] \cup [zw] \gg [xy]$: then not $([xy] \cup [zw] \gg [zw])$, for otherwise $[xy] \cup [zw] \gg [xy] \cup [zw]$ by Lemma 4(d), contrary to irreflexivity in Lemma 4(c). Therefore $[xy] \cup [zw] \geq_0 [zw]$, so that $[zw] =_0 [xy] \cup [zw]$ and hence $[xy] \cup [zw] \in B$.

Thus, we have $[xy] \cup [zw] \gg [xy]$, $[xy] \in A$ and $[xy] \cup [zw] \in B$. Let r be in $\mathcal{M}(A)$, and let $[x'y']$ be an interval in A that contains r. Also let $[x^*y^*]$ be the smallest interval that includes $[xy] \cup [x'y']$, so that $[x^*y^*] \in A$, $[x^*y^*] \geq_0 [xy]$ and $[x^*y^*] \geq_0 [x'y']$. Since $[xy] \cup [zw] \gg [xy]$, we have $[x^*y^*] \cup [zw] \gg [xy]$, which along with $[x^*y^*] \geq_0 [xy]$ implies $[x^*y^*] \cup [zw] \gg [x^*y^*]$ by Lemma 4(b). Since irreflexivity for $\gg$ would be contradicted if $[x^*y^*] \cup [zw] \gg [zw]$, we have $[x^*y^*] \cup [zw] \geq_0 [zw]$, so that $[x^*y^*] \cup [zw] \in B$. But $r \in [x^*y^*]$, and therefore $r \in \mathcal{M}(B)$. Consequently, $\mathcal{M}(A) \subseteq \mathcal{M}(B)$. (If $[xy] \cup [zw] \gg [zw]$ had been assumed in the preceding paragraph, we would have gotten $\mathcal{M}(B) \subseteq \mathcal{M}(A)$.)

To show that $\mathcal{M}(A) \subset \mathcal{M}(B)$, suppose to the contrary that $\mathcal{M}(A) = \mathcal{M}(B)$, and take $[xy] \in A$. Then there are $[zw]$, $[rs] \in B$ such that $x \in [zw]$, $y \in [rs]$ and $[zw] =_0 [rs]$. Let $[x^*y^*]$ be the smallest interval that includes $[zw] \cup [rs]$. Then $[zw] =_0 [x^*y^*]$ so that $[x^*y^*] \in B$ and $[xy] \subseteq [x^*y^*]$. By a similar proof, beginning with $[x^*y^*] \in B$, there is $[x'y'] \in A$ such that $[x^*y^*] \subseteq [x'y']$. Since $A \neq B$, we have $[x^*y^*] \gg [xy]$ and $[x'y'] \gg [x^*y^*]$, so that $[x'y'] \gg [xy]$ by Lemma 4(c). But then $[x'y'] \geq_0 [xy]$ is false, and this contradicts $[xy]$, $[x'y'] \in A$. Therefore $\mathcal{M}(A) \neq \mathcal{M}(B)$. ∎

Along with $A > B$ iff $\mathcal{M}(A) \supset \mathcal{M}(B)$, we shall let

$$A^- = \{B \in \mathcal{N}_0 : A > B\}, \quad \text{for each} \quad A \in \mathcal{N}_0.$$

Thus, A^- is the set of all classes in $\mathcal{N}_0$ that are dominated by A. We shall say that t is an *end point* of $\mathcal{M}(A)$ if $t \in \mathcal{M}(A)$ and either $t \gtrsim x$ for all $x \in \mathcal{M}(A)$, or $x \gtrsim t$ for all $x \in \mathcal{M}(A)$. The following lemma indicates that end points play an important role in the preference structure.

LEMMA 9. *Suppose $A \in \mathcal{N}_0$. Then*

(a) $\mathcal{M}(A) = \mathcal{M}$ *iff $B > A$ for no $B \in \mathcal{N}_0$;*

(b) *If $A^- \neq \emptyset$ and if t is in $\mathcal{M}(A)$ but is not in any $\mathcal{M}(B)$ for $B \in A^-$, then t is an end point of $\mathcal{M}(A)$.*

Proofs. (a) Given $A \in \mathcal{N}_0$, suppose to the contrary of (a) that $B > A$ for no $B \in \mathcal{N}_0$, and $\mathcal{M}(A) \subset \mathcal{M}$. Fix $t \in \mathcal{M} \setminus \mathcal{M}(A)$ and $[xy] \in A$. Then

$t \notin [xy]$. Assume for definiteness that $t \succ x$. Then $[xy] \subset [ty]$ and, since $[ty] \notin A$, $[ty] \gg [xy]$. Let B be the class in $\mathcal{N}_0$ that contains $[ty]$. Then $B > A$ follows from Lemma 8, and this contradicts a supposition. Hence if $B > A$ for no $B \in \mathcal{N}_0$, then $\mathcal{M}(A) = \mathcal{M}$. Conversely, if $\mathcal{M}(A) = \mathcal{M}$, then $B > A$ for no $B \in \mathcal{N}_0$, for otherwise we get $\mathcal{M} \subset \mathcal{M}$ by Lemma 8.

(b) Let $\mathcal{M}(A^-) = \bigcup \{\mathcal{M}(B) : B \in A^-\}$, assume that $A^- \neq \emptyset$, and suppose that $t \in \mathcal{M}(A) \backslash \mathcal{M}(A^-)$. Then, given $A > B$, either $t \succ x$ for all $x \in \mathcal{M}(B)$, or $x \succ t$ for all $x \in \mathcal{M}(B)$. Assume for definiteness that

$$t \succ x \quad \text{for all} \quad x \in \mathcal{M}(B), \quad \text{with} \quad A > B.$$

We shall prove that if $t \succ w \succ x$ for all $x \in \mathcal{M}(B)$ then $w \in \mathcal{M}(C)$ for some $C \in A^-$. It then follows from this that $z \succ t$ for no $z \in \mathcal{M}(A)$, for otherwise we get $t \in \mathcal{M}(D)$ for some $D \in A^-$, which contradicts $t \notin \mathcal{M}(A^-)$. Thus, in the present case, t must be a most-preferred point in $\mathcal{M}(A)$.

With $t \succ w \succ x$ for all $x \in \mathcal{M}(B)$, we consider three exhaustive possibilities for $u^A(w)$, where u^A on $\mathcal{M}(A)$ satisfies the conditions in Lemma 7.

CASE 1. $u^A(w) = u^A(x)$ for some $x \in \mathcal{M}(B)$. Then $[rs] \gg [wx]$ for some $[rs] \in A$. With $[wx] \in C \in \mathcal{N}_0$, it follows from Lemma 8 that $A > C$.

CASE 2. $u^A(w) = u^A(t)$. Since $t \succ w$, there is an $[rs] \in A$ that includes $[tw]$ and has $[rs] \gg [tw]$ since $u^A(t) = u^A(w)$. Hence, with $[tw] \in C$, $A > C$. But then $t \in \mathcal{M}(A^-)$, a contradiction. Therefore this case cannot arise.

CASE 3. $u^A(t) > u^A(w) > u^A(x)$ for all $x \in \mathcal{M}(B)$. Let $0 < \alpha < 1$ be such that $u^A(w) = \alpha u^A(t) + (1 - \alpha)u^A(x) = u^A(t \alpha x)$ for all $x \in \mathcal{M}(B)$. [Since $A > B$, u^A is constant on $\mathcal{M}(B)$.] Since $t \alpha x \succ t \alpha y$ if $x, y \in \mathcal{M}(B)$ and $x \succ y$ (by A2), there is a point $t \alpha y$ for some $y \in \mathcal{M}(B)$ that is not indifferent to w but has the same u^A value as w. Let C be the equivalence class in $\mathcal{N}_0$ that contains the interval from w to $t \alpha y$. Then $A > C$. ∎

COROLLARY 1. If $A >_1 B$, $A >_1 C$ and $B \neq C$ then $\mathcal{M}(B) \cap \mathcal{M}(C) = \emptyset$; for any $B \in \mathcal{N}_0$, $A >_1 B$ for at most one $A \in \mathcal{N}_0$; if $A >_k B$ and $B >_j C$ then $A >_{k+j} C$; if $A > B$ then $A >_k B$ for at most one $k \in \{1, 2, \ldots\}$.

Proof. The first two parts of the corollary follow immediately from Lemma 8 and the definition of $>_1$ on $\mathcal{N}_0$. The third part, for $A >_{k+j} C$, follows from the definition of $>_k$ and induction. For the last part, let S_i be the proposition $\{$If $A >_i B$ then $A >_{i+j} B$ for no $j > 0\}$. S_1 is clearly true. Suppose S_i is true and, in addition, suppose S_{i+1} is false with

$A >_{i+1} B$, $A >_{i+1+j} B$ for some $j > 0$, and let C and D be such that $A >_1$ $C >_i B$ and $A >_1 D >_{i+j} B$. Since S_i is true, $C \neq D$. Hence $\mathcal{M}(C) \cap \mathcal{M}(D) = \emptyset$ by the first part of the corollary. But this is absurd since $C >_i B$ and $D >_{i+j} B$ require $\mathcal{M}(B) \subset \mathcal{M}(C)$ and $\mathcal{M}(B) \subset \mathcal{M}(D)$. Hence S_{i+1} must be true when S_i is true, and the desired result follows by induction on i. ∎

Theorem 3

Let axiom A3(n) hold for an $n > 1$. (If A3(1) holds then Theorem 3 is tantamount to Theorem 2.1(a, c).) By the remarks following the statement of A3(n), let A with $\mathcal{M}(A) = \mathcal{M}$ (Lemma 9(a)) have no $B \in \mathcal{N}_0$ for which $B > A$, and let $h(A) = 1$. Then for each $B \in \mathcal{N}_0$ for which $B \neq A$, there is a unique $k \leq n - 1$ for which $A >_k B$, and for such a B let $h(B) = k + 1$. If $B \neq C$ and either $h(B) = h(C)$ or else neither $B > C$ nor $C > B$, then $\mathcal{M}(B) \cap \mathcal{M}(C) = \emptyset$.

As indicated following the statement of Theorem 3, let u^B for each $B \in \mathcal{N}_0$ satisfy the conditions in Lemma 7, and define $u_1, \ldots, u_n$ by

$$u_k = u^B \text{ on } \mathcal{M}(B) \text{ when } h(B) = k;$$

$$u_k(x) = 0 \text{ when } x \notin \mathcal{M}(B) \text{ for all } B \text{ with } h(B) = k.$$

If $[xy] \in A$ with $h(A) = 1$, then $u_1(x) > u_1(y)$. If $[xy] \in B$ with $h(B) = k + 1$ then $u_{k+1}(x) > u_{k+1}(y)$ by Lemma 7; and $u_j(x) = u_j(y)$ for each $j \leq k$ since there are $B_1, \ldots, B_k = B$ with $A >_1 B_1 >_1 \cdots >_1 B_k$ and with $\mathcal{M}(A) \supset \mathcal{M}(B_1) \supset \cdots \supset \mathcal{M}(B_k)$ such that, by the construction of u^A and the u^{B_i}, each of these $(i < k)$ is constant on $\mathcal{M}(B)$. It then follows that, for all $x, y \in \mathcal{M}$,

$$x > y \quad \text{iff} \quad (u_1(x), \ldots, u_n(x)) >_L (u_1(y), \ldots, u_n(y)).$$

The quasilinearity of the u_k in Theorem 3 follows directly from linearity of the u^B in Lemma 7.

Theorem 4

We assume henceforth that $\mathcal{M}$ is a mixture space and that axiom A3(n) holds for a designated $n \geq 1$. The representation part of Theorem 4 for the designated n is

LEMMA 10. *There are linear functions $u_1, \ldots, u_n$ on $\mathcal{M}$ such that, for all $x, y \in \mathcal{M}$,*

$$x > y \quad \text{iff} \quad (u_1(x), \ldots, u_n(x)) >_L (u_1(y), \ldots, u_n(y)).$$

Proof. We shall prove this by induction on n. As already noted, Lemma 10 is true for $n = 1$. We assume henceforth that it is true for all positive integers less than $n > 1$ and prove that it is true also for n.

Let A be the unique element in $\mathcal{N}_0$ for which $\mathcal{M}(A) = \mathcal{M}$, with $A > B$ for all $B \in \mathcal{N}_0 \backslash \{A\}$. By Lemma 7 there is a linear function $u_1 = u^A$ on $\mathcal{M}$ such that, for all $x, y \in \mathcal{M}$,

$$[xy] \in A \Rightarrow u_1(x) > u_1(y)$$

$$x \succsim y \Rightarrow u_1(x) \geq u_1(y).$$

Fix $x_0, y_0 \in \mathcal{M}$ with $[x_0 y_0] \in A$, and transform u_1 linearly if necessary so that

$$u_1(x_0) = 1, \qquad u_1(y_0) = -1.$$

Next, let $A^{-1} = \{B \in \mathcal{N}_0 : A >_1 B\}$. By A3(n), $A^{-1} \neq \emptyset$. Also let

$$\mathcal{M}_1(c) = \{x \in \mathcal{M} : u_1(x) = c\}.$$

In particular, consider $\mathcal{M}_1(0) = \{x \in \mathcal{M} : u_1(x) = 0\}$. This subset of $\mathcal{M}$ is not empty since $u_1(x_0 \frac{1}{2} y_0) = 0$. Since $x_0 \succ x_0 \frac{1}{2} y_0 \succ y_0$, it follows from A3(n) and Lemmas 8 and 9 that there is a $B_0 \in A^{-1}$ with $x_0 \frac{1}{2} y_0 \in \mathcal{M}(B_0)$. By the definition of $>$ on $\mathcal{N}_0$, $\mathcal{M}(B_0) \subseteq \mathcal{M}_1(0)$. In fact,

$$\mathcal{M}(B_0) = \mathcal{M}_1(0),$$

for if $\mathcal{M}_1(0)$ contains a point not in $\mathcal{M}(B_0)$ then $A >_1 B_0$ would be false.

Thus, $A >_1 B_0$, and $u_1(x) = 0$ iff $x \in \mathcal{M}(B_0)$. By assumption, $\mathcal{M}(B_0)$ is a mixture space, and axioms A6 and A3$(n-1)$ hold within $\mathcal{M}(B_0)$. More specifically, if $\mathcal{N}_0(B_0)$ is the set of equivalence classes on the intervals in $\mathcal{M}(B_0)$ under $=_0$, then $B_0 > C$ and $C \in \mathcal{N}_0(B_0)$ imply that $B_0 >_i C$ for some $i \in \{1, ..., n-2\}$. (If $n = 2$ then $\mathcal{N}_0(B_0)$ has only one element.) This follows from the facts that $A >_1 B_0$, A3(n) holds for $\mathcal{M}$, and $B_0 > C$ when $>$ is defined from $\succ$ on $\mathcal{M}(B_0)$ as the starting point iff $B_0 > C$ when $>$ is defined from $\succ$ on $\mathcal{M}$ as the starting point.

Because Lemma 10 is assumed to be true at $n - 1$, there are linear functions $g_2, ..., g_n$ on $\mathcal{M}(B_0)$ such that, for all $x, y \in \mathcal{M}(B_0)$,

$$x \succ y \quad \text{iff} \quad (g_2(x), ..., g_n(x)) >_L (g_2(y), ..., g_n(y)).$$

Let the g_i be transformed linearly so that $g_i(x_0 \frac{1}{2} y_0) = 0$ for $i = 2, ..., n$, and define u_i on all of $\mathcal{M}$ from g_i on $\mathcal{M}_1(0)$ as follows:

$$u_i(x) = (1+c)g_i\left(y_0\frac{c}{1+c}x\right) \quad \text{for } x \in \mathcal{M}_1(c) \text{ when } c \geq 0,$$

$$u_i(x) = (1-d)g_i\left(x_0\frac{-d}{1-d}x\right) \quad \text{for } x \in \mathcal{M}_1(d) \text{ when } d \leq 0.$$

If $x \in \mathcal{M}_1(c)$ and $c \geq 0$ then $u_1(x) = c$ and $u_1(y_0(c/1+c)x) = (-c+c)/(1+c) = 0$ so that $y_0(c/1+c)x$ is in $\mathcal{M}_1(0)$, or $\mathcal{M}(B_0)$. Similarly, if $x \in \mathcal{M}_1(d)$ with $d \leq 0$, then $x_0(-d/1-d)x$ is in $\mathcal{M}_1(0)$. Moreover, $u_i(x) = g_i(x)$ if $x \in \mathcal{M}_1(0)$, and $u_i(y_0) = 2g_i(x_0\frac{1}{2}y_0) = 0$ and $u_i(x_0) = 2g_i(y_0\frac{1}{2}x_0) = 0$. Therefore each u_i for $i \geq 2$ is unambiguously defined on $\mathcal{M}$.

To complete the proof of Lemma 10, we show first that $>_L$ preserves $\succ$, and then verify that u_i as just defined is linear for each $i \geq 2$.

If $x \in \mathcal{M}_1(c)$ and $y \in \mathcal{M}_1(d)$ with $c \neq d$, then Lemma 7 gives $x \succ y$ iff $u_1(x) > u_1(y)$. If $c = d$, then $u_1(x) = u_1(y)$. In the latter case suppose for definiteness that $x, y \in \mathcal{M}_1(c)$ with $c \geq 0$. Then, by the definition of u_i for $i \geq 2$, and letting $\gamma = c/(1+c)$,

$$(u_2(t), \ldots, u_n(t)) = (1+c)(g_2(y_0\gamma t), \ldots, g_n(y_0\gamma t))$$

for $t \in \{x, y\}$. Moreover, by A6 and the $>_L$ result for $n-1$,

$$x \succ y \quad \text{iff} \quad y_0\gamma x \succ y_0\gamma y$$

$$\text{iff} \quad (g_2(y_0\gamma x), \ldots, g_n(y_0\gamma x)) >_L (g_2(y_0\gamma y), \ldots, g_n(y_0\gamma y))$$

$$\text{iff} \quad (u_2(x), \ldots, u_n(x)) >_L (u_2(y), \ldots, u_n(y)).$$

A similar analysis for $c < 0$ shows in general that

$$x \succ y \quad \text{iff} \quad (u_1(x), \ldots, u_n(x)) >_L (u_1(y), \ldots, u_n(y)),$$

for all $x, y \in \mathcal{M}$.

Linearity for u_i with $i \geq 2$ will be verified by considering cases for c and d and $\lambda c + (1-\lambda)d$ when $x \in \mathcal{M}_1(c)$ and $y \in \mathcal{M}_1(d)$.

CASE 1. $c \geq 0$, $d \geq 0$. Since $u_1(x\lambda y) = \lambda c + (1-\lambda)d$, $x\lambda y \in \mathcal{M}_1(\lambda c + (1-\lambda)d)$. Since $\lambda c + (1-\lambda)d \geq 0$,

$$u_i(x\lambda y) = [1 + \lambda c + (1-\lambda)d]g_i\left(y_0\frac{\lambda c + (1-\lambda)d}{1 + \lambda c + (1-\lambda)d}(x\lambda y)\right).$$

Using M6 (the special mixture space axiom) along with M2 and M3, we get

$$\left(y_0 \frac{c}{1+c} x\right) \frac{\lambda(1+c)}{1 + \lambda c + (1-\lambda)d} \left(y_0 \frac{d}{1+d} y\right)$$

$$= y_0 \frac{\lambda c}{1 + \lambda c + (1-\lambda)d} \left(x \frac{\lambda}{1 + (1-\lambda)d} \left(y_0 \frac{d}{1+d} y\right)\right) \qquad \text{(M6)}$$

$$= y_0 \frac{\lambda c}{1 + \lambda c + (1-\lambda)d} \left(y_0 \frac{(1-\lambda)d}{1 + (1-\lambda)d} (y(1-\lambda)x)\right) \qquad \text{(M2, M6)}$$

$$= y_0 \frac{\lambda c + (1-\lambda)d}{1 + \lambda c + (1-\lambda)d} (x \lambda y). \qquad \text{(M2, M3)}$$

When this is factored into the preceding expression for u_i,

$$u_i(x \lambda y) = [1 + \lambda c + (1-\lambda)d] g_i\left(\left(y_0 \frac{c}{1+c} x\right) \times \right.$$

$$\left. \times \frac{\lambda(1+c)}{1 + \lambda c + (1-\lambda)d} \left(y_0 \frac{d}{1+d} y\right)\right)$$

$$= \lambda(1+c) g_i\left(y_0 \frac{c}{1+c} x\right) + (1-\lambda)(1+d) g_i\left(y_0 \frac{d}{1+d} y\right)$$

$$= \lambda u_i(x) + (1-\lambda) u_i(y).$$

Hence u_i is linear when $c \geq 0$ and $d \geq 0$.

A similar proof applies if $c \leq 0$ and $d \leq 0$. *Henceforth, assume that* $c = u_1(x) > 0$ *and* $d = u_1(y) < 0$.

CASE 2. $\lambda c + (1-\lambda)d = 0$. Since $x \lambda y \in \mathcal{M}_1(0)$ and $u_i(y_0 \alpha x_0) = 0$ for all α, the preceding same-sign analysis gives

$$u_i(x \lambda y) = \frac{1}{1-\beta} u_i((y_0 \alpha x_0) \beta(x \lambda y)) \text{ for all } \beta \in [0, 1).$$

In particular, with $\beta = [\lambda c - (1-\lambda)d]/[1 + \lambda c - (1-\lambda)d]$ and $\alpha = \lambda c/[\lambda c - (1-\lambda)d]$, M6 and M2 give

$$(y_0 \alpha x_0) \beta(x \lambda y) = \left(y_0 \frac{c}{1+c} x\right) \frac{\lambda(1+c)}{1 + \lambda c - (1-\lambda)d} \left(x_0 \frac{-d}{1-d} y\right),$$

so that, with

$$\left(y_0\frac{c}{1+c}x\right)\in\mathcal{M}_1(0) \quad\text{and}\quad \left(x_0\frac{-d}{1-d}y\right)\in\mathcal{M}_1(0),$$

$$u_i(x\,\lambda\,y) = [1+\lambda c - (1-\lambda)d]g_i\left(\left(y_0\frac{c}{1+c}x\right)\frac{\lambda(1+c)}{1+\lambda c - (1-\lambda)d}\times\right.$$

$$\left.\times\left(x_0\frac{-d}{1-d}y\right)\right)$$

$$= \lambda(1+c)g_i\left(y_0\frac{c}{1+c}x\right) + (1-\lambda)(1-d)g_i\left(x_0\frac{-d}{1-d}y\right)$$

$$= \lambda u_i(x) + (1-\lambda)u_i(y).$$

CASE 3. $\lambda c + (1-\lambda)d > 0$. Since $(y(c/c-d)x)\in\mathcal{M}_1(0)$, the result for Case 2 gives

$$u_i\left(y\frac{c}{c-d}x\right) = \frac{c}{c-d}u_i(y) - \frac{d}{c-d}u_i(x).$$

Since $\lambda c + (1-\lambda)d > 0$, $1 > (1-\lambda)(c-d)/c$, and therefore, by (M2, M3), then the Case 1 result, and finally the result just stated from Case 2,

$$u_i(x\,\lambda\,y) = u_i\left(\left(x\frac{-d}{c-d}y\right)\frac{(1-\lambda)(c-d)}{c}x\right)$$

$$= \frac{(1-\lambda)(c-d)}{c}u_i\left(x\frac{-d}{c-d}y\right) + \frac{c-(1-\lambda)(c-d)}{c}u_i(x)$$

$$= \frac{(1-\lambda)(c-d)}{c}\left[\frac{-d}{c-d}u_i(x) + \frac{c}{c-d}u_i(y)\right] +$$

$$+ \frac{c-(1-\lambda)(c-d)}{c}u_i(x)$$

$$= \lambda u_i(x) + (1-\lambda)u_i(y).$$

CASE 4. $\lambda c + (1-\lambda)d < 0$. The proof of linearity here is similar to the proof for Case 3. Since this exhausts the different possibilities, the proof of Lemma 10 is complete. ■

We conclude with a proof of the uniqueness part of Theorem 4. Axiom A3(n) is presumed to hold.

LEMMA 11. *The representation of Lemma 10 holds for linear $v_1, \ldots, v_n$ on $\mathcal{M}$, given that it holds for the u_i, if and only if there are numbers $a_k > 0$, c_k and b_{kj} such that, for all $x \in \mathcal{M}$,*

$$v_k(x) = a_k u_k(x) + \sum_{j=1}^{k-1} b_{kj} u_j(x) + c_k \qquad (k = 1, \ldots, n).$$

Lemma 11 will be proved in two stages. The first stage verifies several fact about u_1 that are suggested by our proof of Lemma 10. These are summarized as follows.

LEMMA 12. *Suppose the representation of Lemma 10 holds, given that A3(n) holds, and let $A \in \mathcal{N}_0$ be such that $\mathcal{M}(A) = \mathcal{M}$. Then*
   (a) *If $A > B$ and $[xy] \in B$ then $u_1(x) = u_1(y)$;*
   (b) *If $[xy] \in A$ then $u_1(x) > u_1(y)$;*
   (c) *u_1 is a positive affine transformation of u^A as in Lemma 7.*

Proofs. (a) Suppose to the contrary that $A > B$, $[xy] \in B$ and $u_1(x) > u_1(y)$. There is some $z \in \mathcal{M}$ such that either $[xz]$ or $[zy]$ is in A. Assume for definiteness that $[zy] \in A$. Then, by Lemma 7, $u^A(z) > u^A(x) = u^A(y)$, and therefore $z \succ x$ by the same lemma. Then $u_1(z) \geq u_1(x)$ by Lemma 10. With $u_1(z) \geq u_1(x) > u_1(y)$, let λ satisfy $u_1(x) = \lambda u_1(z) + (1 - \lambda)u_1(y)$, and let μ satisfy $0 < \mu < \lambda$. Then J1 gives $z\lambda y \succ z\mu y$ so that, by Lemma 10,

$$u_1(z\lambda y) \geq u_1(z\mu y).$$

If equality holds here then $u_1(z) = u_1(y)$ by linearity, a contradiction. If inequality holds then $u_1(x) = \lambda u_1(z) + (1 - \lambda)u_1(y) > u_1(z\mu y)$, so that $x \succ z\mu y$ by Lemma 10. But, since $u^A(z) > u^A(x) = u^A(y)$, Lemma 7 requires $z\mu y \succ x$, and we get another contradiction. Hence $u_1(z\lambda y) \geq u_1(z\mu y)$ must be false, and therefore $u_1(x) > u_1(y)$ is impossible when $A > B$ and $[xy] \in B$. Thus, we get $u_1(y) \geq u_1(x)$ and then $u_1(x) = u_1(y)$ since Lemma 10 and $x \succ y$ require $u_1(x) \geq u_1(y)$.

   (b) Suppose to the contrary that $[xy] \in A$ and $u_1(x) = u_1(y)$. If $x \succsim z \succsim y$, then Lemma 10 requires $u_1(x) \geq u_1(z) \geq u_1(y)$, and therefore u_1 is constant on $[xy]$. Suppose $w \succ x$. Then $[wy] \in A$. If it is true also that $u_1(w) > u_1(y)$ then, for every $\lambda > 0$, $u_1(w\lambda y) > u_1(x)$ and therefore $w\lambda y \succ x$ by Lemma 10. However, since $u^A(w) \geq u^A(x) > u^A(y)$, $u^A(x) > \lambda u^A(w) + (1 - \lambda)u^A(y)$ for some $\lambda > 0$, and therefore $x \succsim w\lambda y$ by Lemma 7, a contradiction to $w\lambda y \succ x$. Therefore $u_1(w) = u_1(y)$ when $w \succ x$. Similarly, $u_1(w) = u_1(x)$ when $y \succ w$. Consequently, u_1 is constant on $\mathcal{M}$, and hence the representation of Lemma 10 reduces to

$$x \succ y \quad \text{iff} \quad (u_2(x), \ldots, u_n(x)) >_L (u_2(y), \ldots, u_n(y)),$$

for all $x, y \in \mathcal{M}$.

Let $A_1 >_1 A_2$, $A_2 >_1 A_3, \ldots, A_{n-1} >_1 A_n$ with $A = A_1$, as guaranteed by A3(n). By Lemma 12(a), u_1 is constant on $\mathcal{M}(A_2)$. Moreover, by re-applying Lemma 12(a) to $\mathcal{M}(A_2), \ldots, \mathcal{M}(A_{n-1})$ as the basic sets, we have that u_i is constant on $\mathcal{M}(A_{i+1})$ for $i = 2, \ldots, n-1$. But then, given the reduced representation for $\succ$ with $(u_2, \ldots, u_n)$, Lemma 12(a) implies that u_2 (which is now the initial u_i) is constant on $\mathcal{M}(A_2)$ and in fact that u_i is constant on $\mathcal{M}(A_i)$ for $i = 2, \ldots, n$. But since $\mathcal{M}(A_n) \subseteq \mathcal{M}(A_i)$ for all $i < n$, the reduced representation implies that $x \sim y$ when $[xy] \in A_n$, and this is obviously false.

Therefore, our original supposition of $u_1(x) = u_1(y)$ for $[xy] \in A$ must be false.

(c) By hypothesis, u_1 is linear and gives $u_1(x) \geq u_1(y)$ whenever $x \succsim y$. Moreover, $u_1(x) > u_1(y)$ when $[xy] \in A$, by Lemma 12(b). Thus, Lemma 7 implies that u_1 is a positive affine transformation of u^A. ∎

Proof of Lemma 11. We omit the straightforward proofs that the v_i are linear and satisfy $x \succ y$ iff $(v_1(x), \ldots, v_n(x)) >_L (v_1(y), \ldots, v_n(y))$ when they are related to the u_i as specified in Lemma 11. Assume henceforth that the v_i, like the u_i, are linear and satisfy the lexicographic representation.

As in the proof of Lemma 10, we use induction on n. Lemma 11 is true for $n = 1$. Assume then that it is true for all positive integers less than $n > 1$, and consider it at n with A3(n) holding. Let $A = A_1 >_1 A_2 >_1 \cdots >_1 A_n$ with $\mathcal{M}(A) = \mathcal{M}$. Since u_1 and v_1 are constant on $\mathcal{M}(A_2)$ by Lemma 12(a), it follows from Lemma 11 for $n - 1$ that there are numbers $a_k > 0, c_k^*$ and b_{kj} for $k \geq 2$ such that

$$v_k(x) = a_k u_k(x) + \sum_{j=2}^{k-1} b_{kj} u_j(x) + c_k^* \qquad (k = 2, \ldots, n)$$

for all $x \in \mathcal{M}(A_2)$. Moreover, by Lemma 12(c), there are $a_1 > 0$ and c_1 such that

$$v_1(x) = a_1 u_1(x) + c_1 \quad \text{for all} \quad x \in \mathcal{M}.$$

As in the proof of Lemma 10, fix $[x_0 y_0] \in A$ with $(x_0 \frac{1}{2} y_0) \in \mathcal{M}(A_2)$, and for convenience let $r_0 = x_0 \frac{1}{2} y_0$. By Lemma 12(b), $u_1(x_0) > u_1(r_0) > u_1(y_0)$ and, by linearity, $u_1(r_0) - u_1(y_0) = u_1(x_0) - u_1(r_0)$.

Now suppose that $x \gtrsim r_0$, and let $\lambda > 0$ satisfy $u_1(r_0) = \lambda u_1(x) + (1 - \lambda)u_1(y_0)$, so that $x\lambda y_0 \in \mathcal{M}(A_2)$. Then the relationships between v_k and u_k for $k \geq 2$ in $\mathcal{M}(A_2)$ give

$$v_k(x\lambda y_0) = a_k u_k(x\lambda y_0) + \sum_{j=2}^{k-1} b_{kj} u_j(x\lambda y_0) + c_k^*,$$

which can be rewritten with the aid of linearity as

$$v_k(x) = a_k u_k(x) + \left\{ \frac{a_k u_k(y_0) + \sum_{j=2}^{k-1} b_{kj} u_j(y_0) - v_k(y_0) + c_k^*}{u_1(r_0) - u_1(y_0)} \right\} u_1(x) +$$

$$+ \sum_{j=2}^{k-1} b_{kj} u_j(x) -$$

$$- \left\{ \frac{u_1(r_0)[a_k u_k(y_0) + \sum_{j=2}^{k-1} b_{kj} u_j(y_0) - v_k(y_0)] + c_k^* u_1(y_0)}{u_1(r_0) - u_1(y_0)} \right\}.$$

Suppose next that $r_0 \gtrsim x$, and let $\mu > 0$ be such that $u_1(r_0) = \mu u_1(x) + (1 - \mu)u_1(x_0)$, so that $x\mu x_0 \in \mathcal{M}(A_2)$. Then, by the approach of the preceding paragraph,

$$v_k(x) = a_k u_k(x) +$$

$$+ \left\{ \frac{a_k u_k(x_0) + \sum_{j=2}^{k-1} b_{kj} u_j(x_0) - v_k(x_0) + c_k^*}{u_1(r_0) - u_1(x_0)} \right\} u_1(x) +$$

$$+ \sum_{j=2}^{k-1} b_{kj} u_j(x) -$$

$$- \left\{ \frac{u_1(r_0)[a_k u_k(x_0) + \sum_{k=2}^{j-1} b_{kj} u_j(x_0) - v_k(x_0)] + c_k^* u_1(x_0)}{u_1(r_0) - u_1(x_0)} \right\}.$$

We have noted already that $v_1 = a_1 u_1 + c_1$. To obtain the relationship between v_k and the u_j for $j \leq k$ in Lemma 11 when $k \geq 2$, it suffices to show that the coefficients of $u_1(x)$ in the preceding two expressions are equal, and that the final expressions in braces in these two equations are equal. For the coefficients of $u_1(x)$, we subtract the latter from the former and multiply by $1/2$ to get

$$\frac{a_k u_k(r_0) + \sum_{j=2}^{k-1} b_{kj} u_j(r_0) - v_k(r_0) + c_k^*}{u_1(r_0) - u_1(y_0)},$$

which equals zero by the relationship in the second paragraph of this proof: since $r_0 \in \mathcal{M}(A_2)$, $v_k(r_0) = a_k u_k(r_0) + \Sigma + c_k^*$. Similarly, $1/2$ of the difference between the final braced expressions on the right-hand sides of the preceding $v_k(x)$ equations [one for $x \succsim r_0$, the other for $r_0 \succsim x$] is

$$\{ -u_1(r_0)[a_k u_k(r_0) + \Sigma b_{kj} u_j(r_0) - v_k(r_0)] - c_k^* u_1(r_0)\} / [u_1(r_0) - u_1(y_0)],$$

which also equals zero.

CHAPTER 5

LINEAR UTILITY FOR PARTIALLY ORDERED PREFERENCES

We have assumed thus far that the preference relation $\succ$ on $\mathcal{M}$ or $\mathcal{P}$ is an asymmetric weak order. We now relax this assumption and consider linear utilities for $\succ$ on $\mathcal{P}$ that preserve $\succ$ in one direction only: for all $p, q \in \mathcal{P}$,

$$p \succ q \Rightarrow u(p) > u(q).$$

This one-way representation does not require indifference $\sim$ to be transitive. It does not even force $\succ$ to be transitive although it does imply that $\succ$ is acyclic: if $p_1 \succ p_2, p_2 \succ p_3, \ldots, p_{n-1} \succ p_n$, then not $(p_n \succ p_1)$. Our ongoing assumption (Section 2.2) that $\succ$ is asymmetric is the $n = 2$ part of acyclicity.

The first section of the chapter presents conditions that are sufficient for one-way linear utility when $\mathcal{P}$ is convex. These conditions are a very weak independence axiom and a strong Archimedean axiom. The second section notes that a strong independence axiom along with a very weak Archimedean axiom imply the one-way representation when $\mathcal{C}$ is finite. We then discuss extensions to the expected-utility form.

5.1. AXIOMS FOR ONE-WAY LINEAR UTILITY

Throughout this section, $\mathcal{A}$ is a Boolean algebra of subsets of a set $\mathcal{C}$ of consequences, and $\mathcal{P}$ is a set of finitely additive probability measures on $\mathcal{A}$. The only special property for $\mathcal{P}$ that is used in the main part of the section is

C0. $\mathcal{P}$ is closed under finite convex combinations.

Stronger structural assumptions will be made later.

We consider first an independence and an Archimedean axiom that are sufficient for the basic one-way representation. These are numbered C2 and C3 in correspondence to previous numbering and to emphasize the absence of a transitivity axiom like A1.

C2.   *For all* $p, q, r, s \in \mathscr{P}$ *and all* $0 < \lambda < 1$, *if* $p \succ q$ *and* $r \succ s$ *then*
       $\lambda p + (1 - \lambda)r \succ \lambda q + (1 - \lambda)s$,
C3.   *For all* $p, q, r, s \in \mathscr{P}$, *if* $p \succ q$ *and* $r \succ s$ *then* $\alpha p + (1 - \alpha)s \succ \alpha q +$
       $+ (1 - \alpha)r$ *for some* $0 < \alpha < 1$.

THEOREM 1. *Suppose* C0, C2, *and* C3 *hold. Then there is a linear function* u *on* $\mathscr{P}$ *for which* $u(p) > u(q)$ *whenever* $p, q \in \mathscr{P}$ *and* $p \succ q$.

The Archimedean axiom C3 is stronger than A3 in the present context since it clearly implies A3, whereas A3 does not imply C3. For example, suppose $\mathscr{P} = \mathscr{P}_0(\mathscr{C})$ with $\mathscr{C} = \{b, c, d, e\}$, let x^* be the measure that assigns probability 1 to $\{x\}$, and assume that $\succ$ consists of (d^*, e^*) – i.e. $d^* \succ e^*$ – plus $(\lambda b^* + (1 - \lambda)e^*, \lambda c^* + (1 - \lambda)d^*)$ for all $\lambda \in (0, 1]$, plus all preference statements generated from these by C2. Then C2 and A3 hold, while C3 must fail since there is clearly no linear u on $\mathscr{P}$ that gives $u(p) > u(q)$ whenever $p \succ q$.

Although C3 is stronger than A3, it seems about as plausible as A3 since we would expect the conclusion of C3 to hold when α is near to 1. The independence axiom C2, which appeared before as J3 in Section 2.4, also seems very reasonable since it relies on a double incidence of strict preference $(p \succ q, r \succ s)$ to carry its conclusion. Although C2 is not necessary for the conclusion of Theorem 1, it is more elegant than the following necessary independence axiom:

C2*.   *For any positive integer* n, *if* $p_i, q_i \in \mathscr{P}$ *with* $p_i \succ q_i$ *and* $\lambda_i > 0$ *for*
       $i = 1, \ldots, n$ *along with* $\Sigma \lambda_i = 1$, *then* $\Sigma \lambda_i p_i \neq \Sigma \lambda_i q_i$.

This requires $\succ$ to be acyclic, for otherwise, with $p_1 \succ p_2, \ldots$, $p_{n-1} \succ p_n$ and $p_n \succ p_1$, we get $n^{-1}(p_1 + p_2 + \ldots + p_n) = n^{-1}(p_2 + \ldots + p_n + p_1)$, which violates the conclusion of C2*. And C2* is clearly necessary for the one-way representation. Moreover, a simple inductive proof shows that C2* is implied by C2. Therefore, Theorem 1 follows immediately from our later proof of

THEOREM 2. C0, C2*, *and* C3 *imply that there is a linear function* u *on* $\mathscr{P}$ *for which* $u(p) > u(q)$ *whenever* $p \succ q$.

Let $p \approx q$ mean that everything indifferent to one of p and q is indifferent also to the other:

$$p \approx q \quad \text{iff} \quad \{r \in \mathscr{P} : r \sim p\} = \{r \in \mathscr{P} : r \sim q\}.$$

By adding another axiom, we obtain a representation that lies between the basic one-way representation and the usual two-way representation of Chapter 2. The new representation preserves $\approx$ as well as $\succ$.

C2($\approx$). *For all $p, q, r, s \in \mathcal{P}$ and all $0 < \lambda < 1$, if $p \approx q$ then $\lambda p + (1 - \lambda)r \approx$* $\approx \lambda q + (1 - \lambda)r$, *and if $p \approx q$ and $r \succ s$ then $\lambda p + (1 - \lambda)r \succ \lambda q + (1 - \lambda)s$.*

THEOREM 3. *Suppose C0, C2, C2($\approx$), and C3 hold. Then there is a linear function u on $\mathcal{P}$ such that, for all $p, q \in \mathcal{P}$, $u(p) > u(q)$ whenever $p \succ q$, and $u(p) = u(q)$ whenever $p \approx q$.*

Unlike previous theorems under weak order, uniqueness properties for u will not be stated for the theorems in this section. In general, u here is not unique up to a positive affine transformation, and, when $p \sim q$, it may be possible to have $u(p) > u(q)$ in one representation while $u(q) > u(p)$ in another.

If $\mathcal{A}$ includes all singleton subsets of $\mathcal{C}$ and each one-point measure is in $\mathcal{P}$, then $u(p) = E(u, p)$ for all simple measures in $\mathcal{P}$ when u on $\mathcal{C}$ is defined in the usual fashion from u on the one-point measures. After discussing some special aspects of one-way theory for finite $\mathcal{C}$ in the next section, we shall consider $u(p) = E(u, p)$ for more general measures in Section 3. Proofs for Theorems 2 and 3 are outlined in Sections 4 and 5.

5.2. FINITE CONSEQUENCE SPACES

This section notes several variations on the one-way theme for the special case characterized by

D0.   *$\mathcal{C}$ is finite and $\mathcal{P} = \mathcal{P}_0(\mathcal{C})$.*

We shall first consider an alternative to the axioms of the preceding section, and then present a lexicographic version of the one-way representation. The axioms for the alternative are

D1.   *$\succ$ on $\mathcal{P}$ is transitive,*
D2.   *For all $p, q, r \in \mathcal{P}$ and all $0 < \lambda < 1$, $p \succ q$ if and only if $\lambda p + (1 - \lambda)r \succ \lambda q + (1 - \lambda)r$,*
D3.   *For all $p, q, r, s \in \mathcal{P}$, if $\alpha p + (1 - \alpha)r \succ \alpha q + (1 - \alpha)s$ for all $0 < \alpha \leq 1$, then not $(s \succ r)$.*

Out interest in these axioms lies in the fact that D3 is the weakest Archimedean axiom that will suffice for the one-way representation since

it is necessary for that representation: if $\alpha u(p) + (1 - \alpha)u(r) > \alpha u(q) +$
$+ (1 - \alpha)u(s)$ for all $\alpha > 0$, then $u(r) \geq u(s)$, and therefore $s \succ r$ cannot
hold. The price that we pay for the weak Archimedean axiom while
maintaining simple interpretability for the others is the strong independence axiom D2. This point is discussed at greater length in Fishburn
(1971b). Moreover, an example in Aumann (1962) shows that finiteness
of $\mathscr{C}$ is essential to the following theorem since the conclusion of the
theorem is false when $\mathscr{C}$ is denumerable.

THEOREM 4. *Suppose* D0, D1, D2, *and* D3 *hold. Then there is a linear
function u on $\mathscr{P}$ for which $u(p) > u(q)$ whenever $p, q \in \mathscr{P}$ and $p \succ q$.*

When no Archimedean assumption is made, we do not require the
strength of D1 and D2 to obtain a one-way lexicographic representation
since C2 will suffice for this purpose.

THEOREM 5. *Suppose* D0 *and* C2 *hold. Then, when $\mathscr{C}$ has $m > 1$ elements, there is an $n < m$ and linear functions $u_1, \ldots, u_n$ on $\mathscr{P}$ such that,
for all $p, q \in \mathscr{P}$,*

$$p \succ q \Rightarrow (u_1(p), \ldots, u_n(p)) >_L (u_1(q), \ldots, u_n(q)).$$

Because of the D0 context, $u_i(p) = E(u_i, p)$ under the usual definition
of u_i on $\mathscr{C}$. Within this context, Theorem 5 gets at the core of expected
utility theory since it demonstrates that $\succ$ can be preserved by an expected-utility form when only a very weak independence assumption
(along with the usual asymmetry) is made.

Proofs of Theorems 4 and 5 appear in Section 6.

5.3. EXPECTED UTILITY

We now consider extending the expected-utility form for simple probability measures that was noted at the end of Section 1 to more general
measures after the fashion of Chapter 3. To avoid complex questions of
integrability, it will be assumed that $\mathscr{A} = 2^{\mathscr{C}}$, the set of all subsets of $\mathscr{C}$.
This and our other structural presuppositions are summarized in

A0.3. $\mathscr{A} = 2^{\mathscr{C}}$, *and $\mathscr{P}$ includes all one-point measures and is closed
         under finite convex combinations and under the formation of
         conditional measures.*

Our initial result introduces no new preference axioms and mimics

Lemma 3.1. As usual, u on $\mathscr{C}$ for $E(u, p)$ is defined from the $u(p)$ values for one-point measures in $\mathscr{P}$. In addition, $\inf u(A) = \inf\{u(c): c \in A\}$, and $\sup u(A) = \sup\{u(c): c \in A\}$.

PROPOSITION 1. *Suppose A0.3 holds, u is a linear function on $\mathscr{P}$, and $\inf u(A) \leq u(p) \leq \sup u(A)$ whenever $p \in \mathscr{P}$ and $p(A) = 1$. Then, for all $p \in \mathscr{P}$ and all $A \in \mathscr{A}$:*
  (a) *$E(u, p) = u(p)$ if $p(A) = 1$ and $\inf u(A)$ and $\sup u(A)$ are finite;*
  (b) *$u(p) \geq E(u, p)$ if $p(A) = 1$ and $\inf u(A)$ is finite;*
  (c) *$E(u, p) \geq u(p)$ if $p(A) = 1$ and $\sup u(A)$ is finite;*
  (d) *$E(u, p)$ is well defined and finite.*

A key aspect of this technical result is the bounding condition that $\inf u(A) \leq u(p) \leq \sup u(A)$ when $p(A) = 1$. Within the context of our one-way representation, we identify two conditions that are sufficient for this bounding condition regardless of whether measures in $\mathscr{P}$ are countably additive. The first special condition is

C5.   (a) *If $p \in \mathscr{P}$, $p(A) = 1$, and $c \succ d \succ e$ for all $c \in A$ and some $d, e \in \mathscr{C}$, then for every $0 < \lambda < 1$ there are c^λ, $c_\lambda \in A$ such that $c^\lambda \succ \lambda p + (1 - \lambda)e^*$ and $p \succ \lambda c_\lambda^* + (1 - \lambda)e^*$;*
     (b) *If $p \in \mathscr{P}$, $p(A) = 1$, and $e \succ d \succ c$ for all $c \in \mathscr{C}$ and some $d, e \in \mathscr{C}$, then for every $0 < \lambda < 1$ there are $c_\lambda, c^\lambda \in A$ such that $\lambda c_\lambda^* + (1 - \lambda)e^* \succ p$ and $\lambda p + (1 - \lambda)e^* \succ c^\lambda$.*

Like A5 of Section 3.2, C5 looks rather complex, but is not so imposing on close examination. In both parts, d acts as a buffer between e and the consequences in A that is necessitated by the possibility of measures that are not countably additive. Consider part (b), where $e \succ d \succ c$ for all $c \in A$ with $p(A) = 1$, and fix λ strictly between 0 and 1. The axiom then asserts that there is some (relatively desirable) consequence c_λ in A such that the two-point measure $\lambda c_\lambda^* + (1 - \lambda)e^*$ is preferred to p, and there is some (relatively undesirable) consequence c^λ in A that is less preferred than $\lambda p + (1 - \lambda)e^*$.

The second special condition that we shall use for $\inf u(A) \leq u(p) \leq \sup u(A)$ is a plausible nontriviality-separation condition which concludes the hypotheses of the following theorem. Comments on the proofs of this theorem and Proposition 1 are given in Section 7.

THEOREM 6. *Suppose A0.3 and C5 hold, u on $\mathscr{P}$ satisfies the conclusion of Theorem 1, and there are $c_1, c_2, c_3, c_4 \in \mathscr{C}$ such that $c_1 \succ c_2 \succ c_3 \succ c_4$*

and for every $c \in \mathscr{C}$ either $c_2 \succ c$ or $c \succ c_3$. Then $\inf u(A) \le u(p) \le \sup u(A)$ *whenever $p \in \mathscr{P}$ and $p(A) = 1$.*

Thus, when the hypotheses of Theorem 6 hold along with C2 and C3, we know from Theorems 1 and 6 and Proposition 1 that there is a linear u on $\mathscr{P}$ that gives $u(p) > u(q)$ whenever $p \succ q$ and for which $E(u, p)$ is well defined and finite for all p, with $u(p) \ge E(u, p)$ when $p(A) = 1$ and $\inf u(A)$ is finite, and with $u(p) \le E(u, p)$ when $p(A) = 1$ and $\sup u(A)$ is finite. If it were true also that u on $\mathscr{C}$ were bounded, then we would have $u(p) = E(u, p)$ for all $p \in \mathscr{P}$.

Suppose, for example, that we enrich A0.3 by assuming that $\mathscr{P}$ is closed under countable convex combinations and that the following dominance axiom (cf. A4 and A4* in Chapter 3) holds for all countably additive measures in $\mathscr{P}$:

C4.   *If $p(A) = 1$ and $d \in \mathscr{C}$, then $p \succ d^*$ if $c \succ d$ for all $c \in A$, and $d^* \succ p$ if $d \succ c$ for all $c \in A$.*

It then follows easily from C4 and the hypotheses of Theorem 6 by a proof similar to the boundedness proof in Section 3.4 that u is bounded on $\mathscr{C}$. Hence, under C4 and the enriched A0.3, $u(p) = E(u, p)$ for all $p \in \mathscr{P}$.

The same conclusion is of course possible within the context of A0.3 as originally given and without forcing u to be bounded, but there are difficulties in stating an interpretable condition on $\succ$ that will yield $u(p) = E(u, p)$ throughout $\mathscr{P}$ for this case. By comparison with the discussion following the proof of Lemma 3.1, the type of technical condition needed to ensure $u(p) = E(u, p)$ when $p(A) = 1$, $u(A)$ is bounded below but unbounded above, and $p(\{c : u(c) > x\}) > 0$ for all real x, is $\inf\{p(\{c : u(c) > x\})[u(p_{\{c : u(c) > x\}}) - x] = 0$. In Chapter 3 we used axiom A5(a) to derive this condition, but I can see no simple analogue to that axiom for the present case in which $\succ$ is not assumed to be an asymmetric weak order.

5.4. CONES IN VECTOR SPACES

The purpose of this section is to define various terms and present results that will be used in the following section to prove Theorems 2 and 3. Several definitions will apply also to later developments.

A binary relation R on a nonempty set X is a *strict partial order* if it is asymmetric and transitive, and a *linear order* if it is asymmetric, transitive and complete $(x \ne y \Rightarrow xRy$ or $yRx)$. A nonempty subset Y of a linearly ordered set (X, R) has a *first element* y if $y \in Y$ and

yRx for all $x \in Y \setminus \{y\}$. Such a Y is *well ordered* if every nonempty subset of Y has a first element. A nonempty set X can be well ordered if there is a linear order on X that well orders X.

An axiom of set theory that we shall presume henceforth asserts that every nonempty set can be well ordered. One of the many equivalents (Kelley, 1955) of this well-ordering principle is known as

ZORN'S LEMMA. *Suppose R on X is a strict partial order, and for every nonempty subset Y of X that is linearly ordered by R there is an $x \in X$ such that $x = y$ or xRy for all $y \in Y$, i.e. x is the first element of $Y \cup \{x\}$. Then X contains an element x^* such that yRx^* for no $y \in X$.*

Depending on how we interpret R, x^* might be referred to either as a maximal element in (X, R) – e.g., when R is $\supset$, or as a minimal element in (X, R), as when R is $\subset$.

We turn now to consideration of vector spaces. A *vector space* over the reals (or real linear space) is a nonempty set $\mathscr{V}$ on which operations called addition $(+)$ and scalar multiplication $(\cdot)$ are defined such that: $\mathscr{V}$ is closed under addition and under scalar multiplication $(a \cdot x;\ a$ real, $x \in \mathscr{V})$; addition is commutative and associative; multiplication is associative $(a \cdot (b \cdot x) = (ab) \cdot x)$, distributive with respect to addition in $\mathscr{V}$, and distributive with respect to the addition of reals $((a + b) \cdot x = a \cdot x + b \cdot x$, where the latter $+$ is addition in $\mathscr{V}$); there is a unique origin $\mathbf{0}$ such that $x + \mathbf{0} = x$ for every $x \in \mathscr{V}$; every $x \in \mathscr{V}$ has a unique additive inverse $-x \in \mathscr{V}$ such $x + (-x) = \mathbf{0}$; and $1 \cdot x = x$ for all $x \in \mathscr{V}$. Common examples of vector spaces are provided by Euclidean spaces and certain function spaces.

A *linear function* F from a (real) vector space $\mathscr{V}$ to a (real) vector space $\mathscr{V}'$ is a mapping from $\mathscr{V}$ into $\mathscr{V}'$ such that $F(ax + by) = aF(x) + bF(y)$ for all $x, y \in \mathscr{V}$ and all real a and b. Here $ax + by$ adheres to $(+, \cdot)$ for $\mathscr{V}$, while $aF(x) + bF(y)$ adheres to $(+, \cdot)$ for $\mathscr{V}'$. The linear function F is a *linear functional* if $\mathscr{V}'$ is the real line with the usual definitions of addition and multiplication.

A *linearly ordered vector space* $(\mathscr{V}, >_0)$ is a vector space $\mathscr{V}$ that is linearly ordered by $>_0$ such that

   (i) $x >_0 \mathbf{0} \Rightarrow ax >_0 \mathbf{0}$ for all real positive a,
   (ii) $x >_0 \mathbf{0}$ and $y >_0 \mathbf{0} = x + y >_0 \mathbf{0}$,
   (iii) $x >_0 y$ iff $x - y >_0 \mathbf{0}$,

where $x - y = x + (-y)$. It follows easily that the set $\mathscr{V}^+ = \{x \in \mathscr{V} : x >_0 \mathbf{0}\}$ of 'positive' elements of a linearly ordered vector space $(\mathscr{V}, >_0)$

is a *convex cone* in $\mathscr{V}$, i.e. $ax + by \in \mathscr{V}^+$ whenever $x, y \in \mathscr{V}^+$ and a and b are positive reals. Moreover, $\mathscr{V}^+$ is a maximal cone that does not contain $\mathbf{0}$, for any other cone in $\mathscr{V}$ that properly includes $\mathscr{V}^+$ must contain the origin of $\mathscr{V}$.

Our purpose at this point is to formulate a theorem of Hausner and Wendel (1952) on representations of linearly ordered vector spaces. We shall then prove a corollary of their theorem that will be needed in the next section to prove Theorem 2. The Hausner–Wendel theorem is of interest beyond this application however. In particular, within the context of C0 and C2, it leads to a generalization of Theorem 5 for lexicographic representations of $\succ$ in the one-way mode. Their theorem can also be used as a base for general lexicographic representations of a non-Archimedean weak order on a set $\mathscr{P}$ or, more generally, on a mixture space $\mathscr{M}$ as defined in Hausner (1954). The definitions in the next two paragraphs, which are related in certain ways to definitions in the preceding chapter, are intended to apply in context to Theorem 7.

Given a linearly ordered vector space $(\mathscr{V}, >_0)$ with positive cone $\mathscr{V}^+$, let $\gg$ denote the dominance relation defined on $\mathscr{V}^+$ by

$$x \gg y \quad \text{iff} \quad x >_0 ay \text{ for all positive real } a.$$

It is easily verified that $\gg$ is an asymmetric weak order on $\mathscr{V}^+$ that is included in $>_0$. Therefore, with $\sim^+$ the symmetric complement of $\gg$ in $\mathscr{V}^+$, so that

$$x \sim^+ y \quad \text{iff} \quad ax >_0 y >_0 bx \text{ for some } a, b > 0,$$

$\sim^+$ is an equivalence relation on $\mathscr{V}^+$. Let $\mathscr{E} = \mathscr{V}^+/\sim^+$, the set of equivalence classes in $\mathscr{V}^+$ under $\sim^+$, and define the linear order $<^+$ on $\mathscr{E}$ by

$$E <^+ E' \quad \text{iff} \quad x \gg y \text{ for some (hence for all) } x \in E \text{ and } y \in E'.$$

One might read $E <^+ E'$ as "E comes before E' in the hierarchy induced by $\gg$". Given $(\mathscr{E}, <^+)$ as thus defined, let $\mathscr{V}(\mathscr{E})$ be the vector space of all real-valued functions f on $\mathscr{E}$ that have nonzero values only on well ordered subsets of $\mathscr{E}$. Addition and scalar multiplication for $\mathscr{V}(\mathscr{E})$ are defined in the usual manner. In addition, with $\mathbf{0} \in \mathscr{V}(\mathscr{E})$ the function that is zero for every $E \in \mathscr{E}$, let $f >_L \mathbf{0}$ for $f \in \mathscr{V}(\mathscr{E})$ mean that $f(E) > 0$ for the first E at which f does not vanish. Then $(\mathscr{V}(\mathscr{E}), >_L)$ is a linearly ordered vector space as defined previously.

Several more definitions are needed before we state the theorem. Given $(\mathscr{V}(\mathscr{E}), >_L)$ let f_E be the characteristic function for $E \in \mathscr{E}$ defined by $f_E(E) = 1$ and $f_E(E') = 0$ for all $E' \neq E$, and for each $E \in \mathscr{E}$ let $x(E)$ be a representative vector from $\mathscr{E}^+$ that is in E. (We can choose an $x(E)$ for each $E \in \mathscr{E}$ according to the axiom of choice, which is another equivalent of the well-ordering principle.) Finally, let T_E be the linear transformation which truncates every $f \in \mathscr{V}(\mathscr{E})$ at E, so that

$$T_E(f) = g \quad \text{if } g(E') = f(E') \text{ for all } E' <^+ E$$
$$\text{and if } g(E') = 0 \text{ otherwise.}$$

THEOREM 7 (Hausner-Wendel). *Suppose* $(\mathscr{V}, >_0)$ *is a linearly ordered vector space with positive cone* $\mathscr{V}^+$, *and* $x(E) \in E$ *for each* $E \in \mathscr{E}$. *Then there is a* 1–1 *linear function F from* $\mathscr{V}$ *into* $\mathscr{V}(\mathscr{E})$ *such that, for all* $x \in \mathscr{E}$ *and all* $E \in \mathscr{E}$:
(a) $x >_0 0$ *iff* $F(x) >_L 0$,
(b) $F(x(E)) = f_E$,
(c) *if* $f \in F(\mathscr{V})$, *then* $T_E(f) \in F(\mathscr{V})$.

For the following corollary, we define a convex cone C in a vector space $\mathscr{V}$ as *Archimedean* if for all $x, y \in C$ there exist positive real a and b such that $ax - y$ and $y - bx$ are in C.

COROLLARY 1. *Suppose C is an Archimedean convex cone in a real vector space* $\mathscr{V}$, *and the origin* 0 *of* $\mathscr{V}$ *is not in C. Then there is a linear functional u on* $\mathscr{V}$ *such that* $u(x) > 0$ *for all* $x \in C$.

Proof. Let C be as specified in the corollary, and let $\mathscr{U}$ be the set of convex cones $C' \subseteq \mathscr{V}$ with $C \subseteq C'$ and $0 \notin C'$. Since the union of the C' in any nonempty subset of $\mathscr{U}$ that is linearly ordered by $\supset$ is easily seen to be in $\mathscr{U}$ also, it follows from Zorn's lemma that $\mathscr{U}$ contains a maximal cone. To tie into the notation of Theorem 7, let $\mathscr{V}^+$ be a maximal cone in $\mathscr{U}$, and define $>_0$ on $\mathscr{V}$ by $x >_0 y$ iff $x - y \in \mathscr{V}^+$. A routine check then shows that $(\mathscr{V}, >_0)$ is a linearly ordered vector space.

Since C is Archimedean, it is included in one of the equivalence classes in $\mathscr{E} = \mathscr{V}^+/\sim^+$ as defined earlier. Let $E \in \mathscr{E}$ include C, and let F from $\mathscr{V}$ into $\mathscr{V}(\mathscr{E})$ have the properties specified in Theorem 7. For each $x \in \mathscr{V}$, $F(x)$ is a real-valued function on $\mathscr{E}$: its value at $E \in \mathscr{E}$ is $F(x)(E)$. Let

$$u(x) = F(x)(E) \quad \text{for all} \quad x \in \mathscr{V}.$$

Since F is a linear function, u is a linear functional. It remains to prove that $u(x) > 0$ for all $x \in C$. For this purpose, let $x(E)$ be the designated representative from E, with $F(x(E))(E) = 1$ [so $u(x(E)) = 1$] and $F(x(E))(E') = 0$ when $E' \in \mathscr{E} \setminus \{E\}$ by part (b) of Theorem 7. Suppose

$y \in E$ and $y \neq x(E)$. Then, by definition, $ay >_0 x(E) >_0 by$ for some $a, b > 0$: that is, $y \sim^+ x(E)$. Let E_y be the first class in $\mathscr{E}$ at which $F(y)$ does not vanish. We show that $E_y = E$.

Suppose first that $E <^+ E_y$. Then $F(ay - x(E))(E) = aF(y)(E) - F(x(E))$ $(E) = 0 - 1 = -1$, which contradicts part (a) of Theorem 7, which requires $F(ay - x(E))(E) > 0$ since $ay - x(E) >_0 \mathbf{0}$ and E is the first class at which $F(ay - x(E))$ is nonzero. Hence $E <^+ E_y$ is false. Suppose next that $E_y <^+ E$. Then, since $ay - x(E) >_0 \mathbf{0}$, we require $F(y)(E_y) > 0$ by Theorem 7(a): but this gives $F(x(E) - by)(E_y) < 0$, hence $by >_0 x(E)$, contrary to $x(E) >_0 by$. Therefore $E_y <^+ E$ is also false, so that $E_y = E$. Moreover, $F(y)(E) > 0$, for otherwise, if $F(y)(E) \leq 0$, we get $F(ay - x(E))(E) < 0$, contrary to $ay - x(E) >_0 \mathbf{0}$.

Therefore, u is a linear functional on $\mathscr{V}$ that is positive on E and therefore on C since $C \subseteq E$. ∎

5.5. PROOFS OF THEOREMS 2 AND 3

For Theorem 2, we show that C0, C2*, and C3 yield linear u on $\mathscr{P}$ for which $u(p) > u(q)$ whenever $p \succ q$. Let $\mathscr{V}$ be the vector space of all real valued functions on $\mathscr{A}$ with the usual operations of pointwise addition and scalar multiplication. Clearly $\mathscr{P} \subseteq \mathscr{V}$. Let $D = \{p - q : p, q \in \mathscr{P}$ and $p \succ q\}$, and let C be the convex cone in $\mathscr{V}$ generated by D:

$$C = \left\{ \sum_{i=1}^{n} a_i d_i : a_i > 0, d_i \in D \text{ for all } i; n \in \{1, 2, \ldots\} \right\}.$$

It follows immediately from C2* that $\mathbf{0} \notin C$. To show that C is Archimedean, we need to verify that $ax - y \in C$ and $y - bx \in C$ for some positive real a and b when $x, y \in C$. Let $x = \sum_{1}^{n} a_i(p_i - q_i)$ and $y = \sum_{1}^{m} b_j(r_j - s_j)$ with $p_i \succ q_i$ and $r_j \succ s_j$ for all i and j, and let $\lambda_{ij} \in (0, 1)$ be such that

$$\lambda_{ij} p_i + (1 - \lambda_{ij}) s_j \succ \lambda_{ij} q_i + (1 - \lambda_{ij}) r_j$$

as guaranteed by C3. Then, with $a_i' = \Sigma_j b_j \lambda_{ij} / [n(1 - \lambda_{ij})]$, summation over i and j of $\{b_j \lambda_{ij} / [n(1 - \lambda_{ij})]\}(p_i - q_i) - (b_j/n)(r_j - s_j)$, which is in C for all i and j, gives

$$\sum_i a_i'(p_i - q_i) - \sum_j b_j(r_j - s_j) \in C.$$

Take $a > \max\{a_i'/a_i\}$ and let $a_i'' = aa_i - a_i'$ so that $a_i''(p_i - q_i) \in C$ for all i. When these terms are added to the preceding displayed expression, we get

$$\sum_i (a_i' + a_i'')(p_i - q_i) - \Sigma b_j(r_j - s_j) \in C,$$

i.e. $ax - y \in C$. The proof that $y - bx \in C$ for some $b > 0$ is similar.

Therefore, C is an Archimedean convex cone in $\mathscr{V}$, and $0 \notin C$. Hence, by Corollary 1, there is a linear functional u on $\mathscr{V}$ such that $u(x) > 0$ for all $x \in C$. In particular, if $p \succ q$, then $u(p - q) = u(p) - u(q) > 0$, and the proof of Theorem 2 is complete.

We prepare for the proof of Theorem 3 by proving a lemma whose conclusion is like C2*.

LEMMA 1. *Suppose* C2 *and* C2($\approx$) *hold. If n is a positive integer, if $\lambda_i > 0$ and either $p_i \succ q_i$ or $p_i \approx q_i$ for $i = 1, ..., n$, and if $p_i \succ q_i$ for some $i \in \{1, ..., n\}$, then $\Sigma \lambda_i p_i \neq \Sigma \lambda_i q_i$.*

Proof. Given the hypotheses of the lemma for any specified n, let $I = \{i : p_i \succ q_i\}$ and $J = \{i : p_i \approx q_i\}$, and for convenience assume that $\Sigma \lambda_i = 1$. If $J = \emptyset$, then $\Sigma \lambda_i p_i \neq \Sigma \lambda_i q_i$ follows from C2 (cf. C2*), so suppose henceforth that $J \neq \emptyset$. Let $\alpha = \Sigma_I \lambda_i$, so $1 - \alpha = \Sigma_J \lambda_i$, and let $\lambda_i' = \lambda_i/\alpha$ for $i \in I$, and $\lambda_i' = \lambda_i/(1 - \alpha)$ for $i \in J$. Since $I \neq \emptyset$ by hypothesis, $0 < \alpha < 1$. Several applications of C2, as needed, give

$$\Sigma_I \lambda_i' p_i \succ \Sigma_I \lambda_i' q_i.$$

Since C2($\approx$) with $p \approx q$ and $r \approx s$ gives $\mu p + (1 - \mu)r \approx \mu q + (1 - \mu)r \approx \mu q + (1 - \mu)s$, hence $\mu p + (1 - \mu)r \approx \mu q + (1 - \mu)s$ by the transitivity of $\approx$, it follows by induction from this result that

$$\Sigma_J \lambda_i' p_i \approx \Sigma_J \lambda_i' q_i.$$

The other part of C2($\approx$) then yields

$$\alpha(\Sigma_I \lambda_i' p_i) + (1 - \alpha)(\Sigma_J \lambda_i' p_i) \succ \alpha(\Sigma_I \lambda_i' q_i) + (1 - \alpha)(\Sigma_J \lambda_i' q_i),$$

which is identical to $\Sigma \lambda_i p_i \succ \Sigma \lambda_i q_i$. Since $\succ$ is asymmetric, it follows that $\Sigma \lambda_i p_i \neq \Sigma \lambda_i q_i$. ∎

The proof of Theorem 3 follows the lines set forth in the proofs of Corollary 1 and Theorem 2. As in the proof of Theorem 2, let C be the convex cone in $\mathscr{V}$ generated by $\{p - q : p, q \in \mathscr{P} \text{ and } p \succ q\}$. In addition, let C_0 be the convex cone in $\mathscr{V}$ generated by $\{p - q : p, q \in \mathscr{P} \text{ and } p \approx q\}$. Then let

$$C^* = C - C_0 = \{x - y : x \in C \text{ and } y \in C_0\}.$$

Clearly, C^* is a convex cone in $\mathcal{V}$. Moreover, $\mathbf{0} \notin C^*$, for otherwise there are $p_i \succ q_i$ and $r_j \approx s_j$ along with positive a_i and b_j such that $\Sigma_i a_i(p_i - q) = \Sigma_j b_j(r_j - s_j)$, or $\Sigma_i a_i p_i + \Sigma_j b_j s_j = \Sigma_i a_i q_i + \Sigma_j b_j r_j$, and this contradicts Lemma 1. (Since $\mathbf{0} \notin C$, we would need one or more i and hence one or more j to generate the contradicted equality.) Since $\mathbf{0} \in C_0$, $C \subset C^*$.

In a slight modification of the proof of Corollary 1, let $\mathcal{U}$ be the set of convex cones $C' \subseteq \mathcal{V}$ with $C^* \subseteq C'$ and $\mathbf{0} \notin C'$. As before, $\mathcal{U}$ contains a maximal cone, say $\mathcal{V}^+$, and $(\mathcal{V}, >_0)$ is easily seen to be a linearly ordered vector space when $>_0$ is defined on $\mathcal{V}$ by $x >_0 y$ iff $x - y \in \mathcal{V}^+$. (Completeness of $>_0$, i.e. $x >_0 y$ or $y >_0 x$ whenever $x \neq y$, is guaranteed by maximality.)

With $\mathcal{V}^+$ thus defined, let $\mathscr{E} = \mathcal{V}^+ / \sim^+$ in the usual fashion. Since we know from the proof of Theorem 2 that C is Archimedean, with $C \subset \mathcal{V}^+$ by construction, C is included in one of the classes of $\mathscr{E}$, say E. As in the proof of Corollary 1, let u be defined on $\mathcal{V}$ by $u(x) = F(x)(E)$, so that u is linear with $u(x) > 0$ for all $x \in E$, hence $u(p) > u(q)$ whenever $p \succ q$.

It remains only to show that $u(y) = 0$ whenever $y \in C_0$, for then $u(p - q) = 0$, or $u(p) = u(q)$, whenever $p \approx q$. With $x(E)$ as the representative of E in Theorem 7, it follows from the symmetry of $\approx$ and our construction of C^* that, for any $y \in C_0$,

$$x(E) - ay >_0 \mathbf{0} \quad \text{and} \quad x(E) + ay >_0 \mathbf{0}$$

For all $a > 0$. Since $F(x(E))(E') = 0$ for $E' <^+ E$, part (a) of Theorem 2 and linearity of F require $F(y)(E') = 0$ for all $E' <^+ E$. Then, since $F(x(E))(E) = 1$, we get $F(x(E) - ay) >_L \mathbf{0}$ and $F(x(E) + ay) >_L \mathbf{0}$ for all $a > 0$, if and only if $F(y)(E) = 0$. Therefore $u(y) = 0$ for all $y \in C_0$, and the proof of Theorem 3 is complete.

5.6. PROOFS OF THEOREMS 4 AND 5

Therefore 4 and 5 will be proved using 'separation lemmas' in finite-dimensional Euclidean spaces. Let Re denote the real line, and let $\text{Re}^n = \{(x_1, \ldots, x_n) : x_i \in \text{Re for each } i\}$. For any $x, y \in \text{Re}^n$, let $x \cdot y = \sum_{i=1}^n x_i y_i$, the inner product of x and y. For any nonempty $C \subseteq \text{Re}^n$, let $-C = \{x \in \text{Re}^n : -x \in C\}$, and let $\bar{C}$ be the closure of $C : y \in \bar{C}$ iff inf $\{\text{Euclidean distance between } y \text{ and } x : x \in C\} = 0$. In addition, $\mathbf{0} = (0, \ldots, 0)$.

LEMMA 2. *Suppose C is a nonempty convex cone in Re^n and $\mathbf{0} \notin C$. Then there is a $w \in \text{Re}^n$ such that $w \cdot x > 0$ for some $x \in C$, and $w \cdot x \geq 0$ for all $x \in C$.*

LEMMA 3. *Suppose C is a nonempty convex cone in Re^n. Then there is a $w \in \mathrm{Re}^n$ such that $w \cdot x > 0$ for all $x \in C$ if, and only if, $\bar{C} \cap (-C) = \emptyset$.*

Proofs of Lemma 3 are given by Aumann (1962) and Fishburn (1970, Chapter 9), among others. A proof of Lemma 2 follows similar lines and can be based on Lemma 9.2 in Fishburn (1970).

For Theorems 4 and 5, we assume without loss in generality that $\succ \neq \emptyset$ and that $\mathscr{C}$ has $m \geq 2$ elements, enumerated as $c_1, \ldots, c_{m-1}, c_m$. The measure $p \in \mathscr{P}_0(\mathscr{C})$ is represented by the vector $(p(c_1), \ldots, p(c_{m-1}))$ in Re^{m-1}, and we take C as the convex cone in Re^{m-1} generated by $\{p - q : p \succ q\}$.

Consider Theorem 5 first. Since $\mathbf{0} \notin C$ follows from C2, there is a $w^1 \in \mathrm{Re}^{m-1}$ that satisfies the conclusion of Lemma 2. Let $C_1 = \{x \in \mathrm{Re}^{m-1} : w^1 \cdot x = 0\} \cap C$. If C_1 is not empty, then it is a nonempty convex cone in Re^{m-1} that does not contain $\mathbf{0}$ and whose dimensionality is less than the dimensionality of C since C_1 is included in the hyperplane $\{x \in \mathrm{Re}^{m-1} : w \cdot x = 0\}$. If $C_1 \neq \emptyset$, let $w^2 \in \mathrm{Re}^{m-1}$ satisfy the conclusion of Lemma 2 with C_1 in place of C: $w^2 \cdot x > 0$ for some $x \in C_1$; $w_2 \cdot x \geq 0$ for all $x \in C_1$. Let $C_2 = \{x \in \mathrm{Re}^{m-1} : w^2 \cdot x = 0\} \cap C_1$. If $C_2 \neq \emptyset$ we again use Lemma 2 to get w^3 for C_2 with $w^3 \cdot x > 0$ for some $x \in C_2$, and $w^3 \cdot x \geq 0$ for all $x \in C_2$. This process continues in the obvious way until we obtain an empty C_n, which must occur for $n \leq m - 1$ since the dimensionality is reduced at each step. We then have $(w^1 \cdot x, \ldots, w^n \cdot x) >_L \mathbf{0}$ for all $x \in C$. Define u_i on $\mathscr{P}_0(\mathscr{C})$ by $u_i(p) = \sum_{j \leq m-1} w_j^i p(c_j)$. Then, since $p - q \in C$ when $p \succ q$, we get $(u_1(p), \ldots, u_n(p)) >_L (u_1(q), \ldots, u_n(q))$ whenever $p \succ q$, and the proof of Theorem 5 is complete.

We now turn to Theorem 4. Suppose $w \in \mathrm{Re}^{m-1}$ satisfies the conclusion of Lemma 3 with $w \cdot x > 0$ for all $x \in C$. Then the conclusion of Theorem 4 holds when u on $\mathscr{P}_0(\mathscr{C})$ is defined as $u(p) = \sum_{j \leq m-1} w_j p(c_j)$. Thus, to prove Theorem 4, we need to show that $\bar{C} \cap (-C) = \emptyset$ when D1, D2, and D3 hold.

We note first that D1 and D2 imply that if $n \in \{2, 3, \ldots\}$, $\alpha_j > 0$ for $j = 1, \ldots, n$, $\Sigma \alpha_j = 1$, $p_j \succ q_j$ for $j = 1, \ldots, n-1$, and $\sum_1^n \alpha_j p_j = \sum_1^n \alpha_j q_j$, then $q_n \succ p_n$. Suppose $p \succ q$ and $r \succ s$. Then, by D2, $\lambda p + (1 - \lambda) r \succ \lambda q + (1 - \lambda) r \succ \lambda q + (1 - \lambda) s$, and therefore, by D1, $\lambda p + (1 - \lambda) r \succ \lambda q + (1 - \lambda) s$, given $0 < \lambda < 1$. Given the preceding hypotheses, with $p_j \succ q_j$ for $j \leq n - 1$, it then follows by induction that $\sum_{j \leq n-1} [\alpha_j / (1 - \alpha_n)] p_j \succ \sum_{j \leq n-1} [\alpha_j / (1 - \alpha_n)] q_j$. Hence, our assertion reduces to

$$[0 < \alpha < 1, p \succ q, \alpha p + (1 - \alpha) p_n = \alpha q + (1 - \alpha) q_n] \Rightarrow q_n \succ p_n.$$

By D2 and the hypotheses, $\alpha q + (1-\alpha)q_n = \alpha p + (1-\alpha)p_n \succ \alpha q + (1-\alpha)p_n$, so $\alpha q + (1-\alpha)q_n \succ \alpha q + (1-\alpha)p_n$. Then D2 in the other direction yields $q_n \succ p_n$.

The implication of D1 and D2 just established leads directly to the following conclusion through the definition of C:

I. $\qquad [p, q \in \mathscr{P}_0(\mathscr{C}), p - q \in C] \Rightarrow p \succ q.$

It then follows immediately from I and D3 that

II. $\qquad [\alpha(p-q) + (1-\alpha)(r-s) \in C \quad \text{for all} \quad 0 < \alpha \le 1] \Rightarrow s - r \notin C.$

For, if II fails, then I gives $\alpha p + (1-\alpha)r \succ \alpha q + (1-\alpha)s$ for all $\alpha \in (0, 1]$ along with $s \succ r$, which contradicts D3. Our next step is to show that II implies

III. $\qquad [\alpha x + (1-\alpha)y \in C \quad \text{for all} \quad 0 < \alpha \le 1] \Rightarrow - y \notin C.$

Suppose III fails with $\alpha x + (1-\alpha)y \in C$ for all $0 < \alpha \le 1$, and $-y \in C$. Using the definition of C, let $x = \sum a_i(p_i - q_i), y = \sum b_j(r_j - s_j)$, $a_i > 0$ and $p_i \succ q_i$ for all $i, b_j > 0$ and $s_j \succ r_j$ for all j, and, with $a = \sum a_i$ and $b = \sum b_j$, let $p = \sum (a_i/a)p_i, q = \sum (a_i/a)q_i, r = \sum (b_j/b)r_j$, and $s = \sum (b_j/b)s_j$. Clearly $p \succ q$ and $s \succ r$, so, in particular, $s - r \in C$. To show that II fails, hence that III must hold when II holds, we prove that

$$\alpha(p - q) + (1-\alpha)(r-s) \in C \quad \text{when} \quad \alpha \in (0, 1].$$

Given $\alpha x + (1-\alpha)y \in C$, we have $\alpha a(p-q) + (1-\alpha)b(r-s) \in C$. If $b \ge a$ then

$$(1/b)[\alpha a(p-q) + (1-\alpha)b(r-s)] + \alpha[(b-a)/b](p-q) \in C,$$

or $\alpha(p-q) + (1-\alpha)(r-s) \in C$. On the other hand, if $a > b$ then, with $\gamma \in (0, 1]$ and $k > 0$,

$$\alpha a(p-q) + (1-\alpha)b(r-s) + k[\gamma a(p-q) + (1-\gamma)b(r-s)] \in C,$$

since $\gamma x + (1-\gamma)y \in C$ by hypothesis. With γ near to zero and $k = \alpha(1-\alpha)(a-b)[\alpha b(1-\gamma) - \gamma a(1-\alpha)]$, the preceding expression equals a positive number times $\alpha(p-q) + (1-\alpha)(r-s)$, so that $\alpha(p-q) + (1-\alpha)(r-s) \in C$. Hence II fails if III fails, so II $\Rightarrow$ III.

Finally, we show that III implies that $\bar{C} \cap (-C) = \emptyset$. Assume that III holds. Suppose first that x is in the interior of C. Then, for any $y \in \bar{C}$, it can be shown that $\alpha x + (1-\alpha)y \in C$ for all $0 < \alpha \le 1$. Hence, by III, $-y \notin C$ and therefore $\bar{C} \cap (-C) = \emptyset$. Suppose next that C has an empty interior. It follows in this case that there is an $i \in \{1, \ldots, m-1\}$ such that x_i is uniquely determined by the other components of x for every $x \in C$. Assume for definiteness that $i = m - 1$, and let $C' = \{(x_1, \ldots, x_{m-2}) : x \in C\}$. Then C' is a convex cone in Re^{m-2} and the analogue of III holds for C'. Therefore, if C' has an interior point then $\bar{C}' \cap (-C') = \emptyset$ and hence $\bar{C} \cap (-C) = \emptyset$. If C' has no interior point, then similar reduction eventually gives a C'' with an interior point for which the analogue of III holds, and $\bar{C} \cap (-C) = \emptyset$ then follows from this.

5.7. PROOF COMMENTS FOR EXPECTED UTILITY

This section comments briefly on the proofs of Proposition 1 and Theorem 6 in Section 3.

Given the hypotheses of Proposition 1, define $\succ'$ on $\mathscr{P}$ by $p \succ' q$ iff $u(p) > u(q)$. Then A1, A2, A3, and A4 hold for $\succ'$ on $\mathscr{P}$. For example, A4 requires $p \succsim' q$ when $c \succ' q$ for all $c \in A$ and $p(A) = 1$. These hypotheses and those of Proposition 1 yield $u(p) \geq \inf u(A) \geq u(q)$, hence $p \succsim' q$. It is also clear that A0.3 implies A0.2 in the context of $\succsim'$, and therefore Proposition 1 follows directly from Lemma 3.1.

Given the hypotheses of Theorem 6, suppose $p \in \mathscr{P}$ and $p(A) = 1$. It then follows from the final hypothesis of the theorem that A can be partitioned into disjoint A_1 and A_2 such that $c_1 \succ c_2 \succ c$ for all $c \in A_1$, and $c \succ c_3 \succ c_4$ for all $c \in A_2$. Suppose $p(A_i) > 0$. Then, by C5 and the properties of u, it is easily seen that $\inf u(A_i) \leq u(p_{A_i}) \leq \sup u(A_i)$. If either $p(A_i)$ is zero, the desired result follows. If both $p(A_i)$ are positive, then $p = p(A_1)p_{A_1} + p(A_2)p_{A_2}$, and therefore $\inf u(A) \leq u(p) = p(A_1)u(p_{A_1}) + p(A_2)u(p_{A_2}) \leq \sup u(A)$.

CHAPTER 6

LINEAR UTILITIES ON PRODUCT SETS

Preceding chapters have concentrated on linear functions on $\mathcal{M}$ or $\mathcal{P}$ that preserve $\succ$ in specified ways. Apart from a few instances, no structural characteristics have been imposed on the set $\mathscr{C}$ of consequences. In this chapter we shall presume the usual linear utility model and focus on special forms for $u(c) = u(c_1, \dots, c_n)$ when $\mathscr{C}$ is the product of n others sets or a subset of this product. Thus, we are dealing here with situations in which the consequences have multiple 'dimensions' or attributes. The additive form $u(c) = u_1(c_1) + \dots + u_n(c_n)$ will be considered first. We then examine a general multiadditive decomposition for u on $\mathcal{P} = \mathcal{D} \times \mathscr{E}$.

It is assumed throughout the chapter that u is a linear function on $\mathcal{P}_0(\mathscr{C})$ such that, for all $p, q \in \mathcal{P}_0(\mathscr{C})$, $p \succ q$ iff $u(p) > u(q)$, and that u is defined on $\mathscr{C}$ by $u(c) = u(c^*)$ when c^* is the measure in $\mathcal{P}_0(\mathscr{C})$ that assigns probability 1 to c. The basic u could actually be defined on any set $\mathcal{P}$ that includes $\mathcal{P}_0(\mathscr{C})$, but it suffices to work with $\mathcal{P}_0(\mathscr{C})$ in axiomatizing the decompositions.

6.1. ADDITIVE UTILITIES

We assume in this section that $\mathscr{C}$ is a subset of $\mathscr{C}_1 \times \mathscr{C}_2 \times \cdots \times \mathscr{C}_n$ with $n \geq 2$, so that each consequence in $\mathscr{C}$ is an n-tuple $(c_1, c_2, \dots, c_n)$ with $c_i \in \mathscr{C}_i$ for every i. For each $p \in \mathcal{P}_0(\mathscr{C})$ and each $i \in \{1, \dots, n\}$, the *marginal measure* of p on $\mathscr{C}_i$ will be denoted by p_i: for all $c_i \in \mathscr{C}_i$,

$$p_i(c_i) = p(\{c \in \mathscr{C}: c_i \text{ is the } i\text{th component of } c\}).$$

Our basic axiom for additive utilities asserts that if p and q have the same marginal on $\mathscr{C}_i$ for $i = 1, \dots, n$, then they are indifferent:

A7.   *For all $p, q \in \mathcal{P}_0(\mathscr{C})$, if $(p_1, \dots, p_n) = (q_1, \dots, q_n)$ then $p \sim q$.*

This is a rather strong axiom since it prohibits preference interdependencies among the factors in the product set. As a simple example, suppose $n = 2$ with $\mathscr{C}_i$ potential salaries for an individual in year i. Year 1 is next year and year 2 is the year after that. Suppose that, with units in thousands of dollars,

$$p(30, 20) = p(20, 30) = \tfrac{1}{2}$$

$$q(20, 20) = q(30, 30) = \tfrac{1}{2}.$$

Since $p_1 = q_1$ (each is the 50–50 gamble for 20 or 30 next year) and $p_2 = = q_2$, A7 requires $p \sim q$. But, since p and q are substantially different, the individual may definitely prefer one to the other. For example, he might prefer p, which assures him at least one year at 30, to q, which has probability $\tfrac{1}{2}$ for each of the two-year income streams $(20, 20)$ and $(30, 30)$.

If utilities are additive, so that $u(c) = u_1(c_1) + \cdots + u_n(c_n)$ when $c = = (c_1, \ldots, c_n)$, then $u(p) = u_1(p_1) + \ldots + u_n(p_n)$ for each $p \in \mathcal{P}_0(\mathscr{C})$ where $u_i(p_i) = \sum_{\mathscr{C}_i} u_i(c_i) p_i(c_i)$. Consequently, if $(p_1, \ldots, p_n) = (q_1, \ldots, q_n)$ then $u(p) = u(q)$, and therefore $p \sim q$. Hence A7 is necessary for additive utilities. As we shall prove in Section 3, it is also sufficient.

THEOREM 1. *There are real-valued functions* u_i *on* $\mathscr{C}_i$ *for* $i = 1, \ldots, n$ *such that*

$$u(c_1, \ldots, c_n) = \sum_{i=1}^{n} u_i(c_i) \quad \text{for all} \quad (c_1, \ldots, c_n) \in \mathscr{C},$$

if and only if A7 *holds.*

Since $\mathscr{C}$ can be any nonempty subset of $\mathscr{C}_1 \times \cdots \times \mathscr{C}_n$, there is no simple uniqueness property for the u_i in Theorem 1. Indeed, the sufficiency proof given later is partly nonconstructive, and it appears that this is unavoidable. However, the picture changes dramatically if we suppose that $\mathscr{C}$ equals $\mathscr{C}_1 \times \cdots \times \mathscr{C}_n$. In this case, A7 can be replaced by a more specialized axiom and there is a nice uniqueness relationship among the u_i.

A7*. *For all* $p, q \in \mathcal{P}_0(\mathscr{C})$, *if* $p(c), q(c) \in \{0, \tfrac{1}{2}, 1\}$ *for all* $c \in \mathscr{C}$ *and* $(p_1, \ldots, p_n) = (q_1, \ldots, q_n)$, *then* $p \sim q$.

THEOREM 2. *Suppose* $\mathscr{C} = \mathscr{C}_1 \times \cdots \times \mathscr{C}_n$. *Then there are real-valued functions* u_i *on* $\mathscr{C}_i$ *for* $i = 1, \ldots, n$ *such that* $u(c_1, \ldots, c_n) = \sum u_i(c_i)$ *for all* $(c_1, \ldots, c_n) \in \mathscr{C}$ *if, and only if,* A7* *holds. Moreover, given* $u = \sum u_i$, *real-valued functions* v_i *on* $\mathscr{C}_i$ *satisfy* $u(c_1, \ldots, c_n) = \sum v_i(c_i)$ *for all* $(c_1, \ldots, c_n) \in \mathscr{C}$ *if and only if there are numbers* $b_1, \ldots, b_n$ *that sum to zero such that, for each* $i \in \{1, \ldots, n\}$,

$$v_i(c_i) = u_i(c_i) + b_i \quad \text{for all} \quad c_i \in \mathscr{C}_i.$$

Since linear u is itself unique up to a positive affine transformation for $p \succ q$ iff $u(p) > u(q)$, the uniqueness result in Theorem 2 for $\mathscr{C} = \mathscr{C}_1 \times \cdots \times \mathscr{C}_n$ says that linear u_i on the sets of marginal measures that satisfy $p \succ q$ iff $\sum u_i(p_i) > \sum u_i(q_i)$ are unique up to similar positive affine transformations. That is, if u_i satisfy $p \succ q$ iff $\sum u_i(p_i) > \sum u_i(q_i)$, then v_i satisfy $p \succ q$ iff $\sum v_i(p_i) > \sum v_i(q_i)$ if, and only if, there are numbers $a > 0$ and $b_1, \ldots, b_n$ such that, for each i, $v_i(p_i) = au_i(p_i) + b_i$ for all simple measures p_i on $\mathscr{C}_i$.

Although additive utilities deny preference interdependencies among the $\mathscr{C}_i$ as formulated here, Theorem 1 (but not Theorem 2) can be applied to interdependent situations under a suitable reformulation. To illustrate this, suppose $n \geq 3$ and the additive form is inappropriate due to interdependencies between each successive pair of factors. Suppose further that we can write $u(c_1, \ldots, c_n)$ as $u_{12}(c_1, c_2) + u_{23}(c_2, c_3) + \cdots + u_{n-1,n}(c_{n-1}, c_n)$. To axiomatize this interdependent-additive form, let $\mathscr{D}_i = \mathscr{C}_i \times \mathscr{C}_{i+1}$ for $i = 1, \ldots, n-1$. Then $\mathscr{C} \subseteq \mathscr{C}_1 \times \cdots \times \mathscr{C}_n$ corresponds to a subset $\mathscr{D} \subseteq \mathscr{D}_1 \times \cdots \times \mathscr{D}_{n-1}$ through the mapping that takes $(c_1, c_2, \ldots, c_n)$ into $((c_1, c_2), (c_2, c_3), \ldots, (c_{n-1}, c_n))$. We can then state A7 in the language of $\mathscr{P}_0(\mathscr{D})$, formulated in the obvious way, where p_i is the marginal of $p \in \mathscr{P}_0(\mathscr{D})$ on $\mathscr{D}_i$. Theorem 1 tells us that A7 holds under this reformulation if and only if there are real-valued u_i on $\mathscr{D}_i$ for $i = 1, \ldots, n-1$ such that $u(c_1, \ldots, c_n) = \sum u_i(c_i, c_{i+1})$ for all $(c_1, \ldots, c_n) \in \mathscr{C}$.

6.2. MULTIADDITIVE UTILITIES

We now consider a substantial generalization of additive utility developed by Fishburn and Farquhar (1979) for the two-factor situation in which $\mathscr{C} = \mathscr{D} \times \mathscr{E}$. The origins of this development lie in the concept of utility independence due to Keeney (1968) and Pollak (1967). A number of related developments in multiattribute utility theory are discussed by Keeney and Raiffa (1976) and Farquhar (1977).

Given $\mathscr{C} = \mathscr{D} \times \mathscr{E}$, we say that $\mathscr{D}$ is *utility independent* of $\mathscr{E}$ if the individual's preference relation over the gambles or simple measures in $\mathscr{P}_0(\mathscr{D})$ for a fixed $e \in \mathscr{E}$ does not depend on e. In other words, if we represent $p \in \mathscr{P}_0(\mathscr{C})$ as (p_1, e) when p_1 is the marginal of p on $\mathscr{D}$ and the marginal of p on $\mathscr{E}$ assigns probability 1 to e, then $\mathscr{D}$ is utility independent of $\mathscr{E}$ if $(p_1, e) \succ (q_1, e)$ iff $(p_1, e') \succ (q_1, e')$, for all $p_1, q_1 \in \mathscr{P}_0(\mathscr{D})$ and all $e, e' \in \mathscr{E}$. Similarly, with (d, p_2) representing the measure in $\mathscr{P}_0(\mathscr{C})$ whose marginal on $\mathscr{D}$ assigns probability 1 to $d \in \mathscr{D}$ and whose marginal on $\mathscr{E}$ is p_2, $\mathscr{E}$ is utility independent of $\mathscr{D}$ if $(d, p_2) \succ (d, q_2)$ iff $(d', p_2) \succ (d', q_2)$, for all $d, d' \in \mathscr{D}$ and all $p_2, q_2 \in \mathscr{P}_0(\mathscr{E})$.

It follows from the uniqueness part of Theorem 2.1 that $\mathscr{E}$ is utility independent of $\mathscr{D}$ if and only if there are real-valued functions f, g, and h on $\mathscr{D}, \mathscr{E}$, and $\mathscr{D}$, respectively such that f is positive and

$$u(d, e) = f(d)g(e) + h(d) \quad \text{for all} \quad (d, e) \in \mathscr{C}.$$

An analogous decomposition holds when $\mathscr{D}$ is utility independent of $\mathscr{E}$. If each of $\mathscr{D}$ and $\mathscr{E}$ is utility independent of the other, then it can be shown that u is either additive $-u(d, e) = u_1(d) + u_2(e)$, or can be written in a multiplicative form as $u(d, e) = u_1(d)u_2(e) + \text{constant}$.

Our generalization of utility independence is concerned with the multi-additive form

$$u(d, e) = \sum_{j=1}^{n} f_j(d)g_j(e) + h(d)$$

and with the related form obtained by interchanging the roles of d and e on the right-hand side, with no restrictions on the signs of the functions. Thus, we consider decompositions of u into finite sums of products of functions on the separate factors.

We shall characterize the multiadditive form in the preceding paragraph as follows on the basis of the indifference relation $\sim$ on $\mathscr{P}_0(\mathscr{C})$. For all $p_2, q_2 \in \mathscr{P}_0(\mathscr{E})$, all $d \in \mathscr{D}$ and all nonempty $D \subseteq \mathscr{D}$, define

$$p_2 \, \tilde{d} \, q_2 \quad \text{iff} \quad (d, p_2) \sim (d, q_2),$$

$$p_2 \, \tilde{D} \, q_2 \quad \text{iff} \quad (d, p_2) \sim (d, q_2) \quad \text{for all} \quad d \in D.$$

Thus, each $\tilde{d}$ and $\tilde{D}$ is an equivalence relation on $\mathscr{P}_0(\mathscr{E})$, and $\tilde{D} = \bigcap \{\tilde{d} : d \in D\}$. For convenience, we shall also let $\tilde{\emptyset} = \mathscr{P}_0(\mathscr{E}) \times \mathscr{P}_0(\mathscr{E})$. A nonempty subset D of $\mathscr{D}$ is said to be *independent* if $D \backslash \{d\} \not\subseteq \tilde{d}$ for each $d \in D$, and *spanning* if $\tilde{D} = \tilde{\mathscr{D}}$. If D is both independent and spanning, then it is called a *basis* of $\mathscr{D}$.

Thus D is a basis of $\mathscr{D}$ if $(d, p_2) \sim (d, q_2)$ for all $d \in D$ implies $(d, p_2) \sim \sim (d, q_2)$ for all $d \in \mathscr{D}$, and if for every $d \in D$ there is some pair $p_2, q_2 \in \mathscr{P}_0(\mathscr{E})$ such that $(d, p_2) \not\sim (d, q_2)$ while $(d', p_2) \sim (d', q_2)$ for all $d' \in \mathscr{D} \backslash \{d\}$, provided that $|D| \geq 2$. If $D = \{d\}$, then it is a basis if $\succ$ is not empty and $(d, p_2) \sim \sim (d, q_2)$ implies that $(d', p_2) \sim (d', q_2)$ for all $d' \in \mathscr{D}$.

Given that $\succ$ is not empty, $\mathscr{D}$ has a nonempty basis. Such a basis could be infinite, but we shall consider only finite bases in what follows, and say that $\mathscr{E}$ is *degree-n utility independent* of $\mathscr{D}$ if $\mathscr{D}$ includes an n-element basis. The definition of $\mathscr{D}$ being degree-n utility independent of $\mathscr{E}$ is analogous: just interchange the roles of $\mathscr{D}$ and $\mathscr{E}$ in the preceding discussion. The following axiom covers the finite cases for $\mathscr{E}$ vs $\mathscr{D}$. We assume that $n \in \{1, 2, \dots\}$.

A8(n). $\mathscr{D}$ *includes an n-element basis.*

THEOREM 3. *Axiom A8(n)* holds if and if there are real-valued functions $f_1, \dots, f_n, h$ on $\mathscr{D}$ and $g_1, \dots, g_n$ on $\mathscr{E}$ such that, for all $(d, e) \in \mathscr{C}$,

$$u(d, e) = \sum_{j=1}^{n} f_j(d) g_j(e) + h(d),$$

and u does not have an analogous form for any $n' < n$.

Proofs of Theorem 3 and related propositions appear in Section 4.

According to the final assertion in the theorem, A8(n) and A8(n') cannot both hold when $n \neq n'$. This says that if $\mathscr{D}$ includes some finite basis, then all bases of $\mathscr{D}$ have the same cardinality. Alternatively, if $\mathscr{E}$ is degree-n utility independent of $\mathscr{D}$, then $\mathscr{E}$ is not degree-n' utility independent of $\mathscr{D}$ when $n' \neq n$.

When the multiadditive form in Theorem 3 is viewed from the perspective of $\mathscr{D}$ vs. $\mathscr{E}$ rather than $\mathscr{E}$ vs. $\mathscr{D}$, it follows that if $\mathscr{E}$ is degree-n utility independent of $\mathscr{D}$, then $\mathscr{D}$ is degree-m utility independent of $\mathscr{E}$ for some $m \in \{n - 1, n, n + 1\}$. We use this fact to obtain an algebraic form for finite-degree independence that is based on conditional single-factor utility functions. For convenience, let

$$v_i(e) = u(d_i, e)$$

$$w_j(d) = u(d, e_j).$$

THEOREM 4. *Suppose A8(n)* holds with bases $\{d_1, \dots, d_n\}$ of $\mathscr{D}$ and $\{e_1, \dots, e_m\}$ of $\mathscr{E}$. Then there are real numbers a_{ij}, a_i, b_j and k such that, for all $(d, e) \in \mathscr{C}$,

$$u(d, e) = \sum_{i=1}^{n} \sum_{j=1}^{m} a_{ij} v_i(e) w_j(d) + \sum_{i=1}^{n} a_i v_i(e) + \sum_{j=1}^{m} b_j w_j(d) + k.$$

Thus, under the hypotheses of Theorem 4, u can be written in terms of n conditional utility functions on $\mathscr{E}$, m conditional utility functions on $\mathscr{D}$, and $(n + 1)(m + 1)$ scaling constants. When $n = m = 1$, it is easily shown that three constants suffice, with $a_1 = b_1$:

$$u(d, e) = a_{11} u(d, e_1) u(d_1, e) + a_1 [u(d, e_1) + u(d_1, e)] + k.$$

6.3. ADDITIVITY PROOFS

We begin with the proof of Theorem 2 since it will be used in completing the proof of Theorem 1. To show that A7* implies the additive form when $\mathscr{C} = \mathscr{C}_1 \times \cdots \times \mathscr{C}_n$, fix $c^0 = (c_1^0, \ldots, c_n^0)$ in $\mathscr{C}$, let $u_1(c_1^0), \ldots, u_n(c_n^0)$ be any numbers that sum to $u(c^0)$, and define u_i on $\mathscr{C}_i$ by

$$u_i(c_i) = u(c_1^0, \ldots, c_{i-1}^0, c_i, c_{i+1}^0, \ldots, c_n^0) - \sum_{j \neq i} u_j(c_j^0).$$

According to A7*, $u(c_1, \ldots, c_i, c_{i+1}^0, \ldots, c_n^0) + u(c_1^0, \ldots, c_i^0, c_{i+1}, c_{i+2}^0, \ldots, c_n^0) = u(c_1, \ldots, c_{i+1}, c_{i+2}^0, \ldots, c_n^0) + u(c^0)$ for all $i \leqslant n - 1$. When these are summed over i, we get

$$u(c_1, \ldots, c_n) = \sum_{i=1}^{n} u(c_1^0, \ldots, c_{i-1}^0, c_i, c_{i+1}^0, \ldots, c_n^0) - (n-1)u(c^0).$$

Since the right-hand side of this equals $\sum u_i(c_i)$ by the definitions of the u_i, additivity is verified.

If both the u_i and v_i satisfy the additive form with u fixed, then, with c^0 fixed as before, we have $v_i(c_i) = u_i(c_i) + b_i$ for all $c_i \in \mathscr{C}_i$ when b_i is defined as $\sum_{j \neq i} [u_j(c_j^0) - v_j(c_j^0)]$. Since the b_i sum to zero, the uniqueness part of Theorem 2 clearly holds.

We now turn to the sufficiency proof of Theorem 1. We are to show that u can be additively decomposed when A7 holds and $\mathscr{C} \subseteq \mathscr{C}_1 \times \cdots \times \mathscr{C}_n$. Our approach will be to extend u from $\mathscr{C}$ to all of $\mathscr{C}_1 \times \cdots \times \mathscr{C}_n$ in such a way that a condition on equal sums of u values that follows from A7 for $\mathscr{C}$ also holds for u extended on all of $\mathscr{C}_1 \times \cdots \times \mathscr{C}_n$. We then note that the extended u has an additive decomposition on $\mathscr{C}_1 \times \cdots \times \mathscr{C}_n$; hence the initial u has an additive decomposition on $\mathscr{C}$.

Given any subset $\mathscr{C}'$ of $\mathscr{C}_1 \times \cdots \times \mathscr{C}_n$, define $(c^1, \ldots, c^m)E(\mathscr{C}')(d^1, \ldots, d^m)$ if and only if m is a positive integer, c^j and d^j are in $\mathscr{C}'$ for each j, and, for $i = 1, \ldots, n, c_i^1, \ldots, c_i^m$ is a permutation of $d_i^1, \ldots, d_i^m$. In addition, let $(c^1, \ldots, c^m)E^0(\mathscr{C}')(d^1, \ldots, d^m)$ mean that $(c^1, \ldots, c^m)E(\mathscr{C}')(d^1, \ldots, d^m)$ and $\{c^1, \ldots, c^m\} \cap \{d^1, \ldots, d^m\} = \emptyset$.

We shall say that u *satisfies* $\mathscr{C}'$ if and only if $u(c)$ is defined for all $c \in \mathscr{C}'$ and

$$\sum_{j=1}^{m} u(c^j) = \sum_{j=1}^{m} u(d^j) \quad \text{whenever} \quad (c^1, \ldots, c^m)E(\mathscr{C}')(d^1, \ldots, d^m).$$

Because identical c^j and d^k can be cancelled here, the definition remains unchanged when $E^0(\mathscr{C}')$ is used instead of $E(\mathscr{C}')$. It is easily seen that A7 implies that u satisfies $\mathscr{C}$. In particular, with u defined on $\mathscr{C}$ at the outset, if $(c^1, \ldots, c^m)E(\mathscr{C})(d^1, \ldots, d^m)$, let p have probability k/m for c when c appears k times in $(c^1, \ldots, c^m)$, and let q have probability k/m for c when c appears k times in $(d^1, \ldots, d^m)$. It then follows that $(p_1, \ldots, p_n) = (q_1, \ldots, q_n)$ by the definition of $E(\mathscr{C})$, hence that $p \sim q$ by A7, so that $u(p) = u(q)$ which, by linearity, reduces to $\sum u(c^j) = \sum u(d^j)$.

Given that u satisfies $\mathscr{C}$, we show that it can be extended to $\mathscr{C}_1 \times \cdots \times \mathscr{C}_n$ in such a way that the extended u satisfies $\mathscr{C}_1 \times \cdots \times \mathscr{C}_n$. The first paragraph of this section then gives $u(c_1, \ldots, c_n) = \sum u_i(c_i)$ throughout $\mathscr{C}_1 \times \cdots \times \mathscr{C}_n$, so Theorem 1 is verified.

We extend u in two steps. First, let $\mathscr{U}$ be the set of all $\mathscr{C}'$ such that $\mathscr{C} \subseteq \mathscr{C}' \subseteq \mathscr{C}_1 \times \cdots \times \mathscr{C}_n$ and $(c^1, \ldots, c^m)E^0(\mathscr{C}')(d^1, \ldots, d^m)$ iff $(c^1, \ldots, c^m)$ $E^0(\mathscr{C})(d^1, \ldots, d^m)$. Since the union of the $\mathscr{C}'$ in any subset of $\mathscr{U}$ that is linearly ordered by $\supset$ is in $\mathscr{U}$, Zorn's lemma (Section 5.4) says that $\mathscr{U}$ contains a maximal $\mathscr{C}'$, say $\mathscr{C}^*$. Take $u(c) = 0$ (or anything else) on $\mathscr{C}^*\backslash\mathscr{C}$. Then u is defined on $\mathscr{C}^*$ and, since $\mathscr{C}^* \in \mathscr{U}$, u satisfies $\mathscr{C}^*$. Suppose henceforth that $\mathscr{C}^* \subset \mathscr{C}_1 \times \cdots \times \mathscr{C}_n$.

Our second step extends u from $\mathscr{C}^*$ to $\mathscr{C}_1 \times \cdots \times \mathscr{C}_n$. Since $\mathscr{C}^*$ is maximal in $\mathscr{U}$, $\mathscr{C}^* \cup \{c\} \notin \mathscr{U}$ for each $c \in (\mathscr{C}_1 \times \cdots \times \mathscr{C}_n)\backslash\mathscr{C}^*$. Hence for each such c there are $c^{k+1}, \ldots, c^m, d^1, \ldots, d^m$ in $\mathscr{C}^*$, and $0 < k < m$, such that

$$(kc, c^{k+1}, \ldots, c^m)E^0(\mathscr{C}_1 \times \cdots \times \mathscr{C}_n)(d^1, \ldots, d^m),$$

where kc is c repeated k times. We use this to extend u in the natural linear way:

$$u(c) = \left[\sum_{j=1}^{m} u(d^j) - \sum_{j=k+1}^{m} u(c^j) \right] \Big/ k.$$

To show that this $u(c)$ is well defined, suppose that c has another expression with elements from $\mathscr{C}^*$:

$$(hc, e^{h+1}, \ldots, e^M)E^0(\mathscr{C}_1 \times \cdots \times \mathscr{C}_n)(f^1, \ldots, f^M),$$

where $0 < h < M$ and the e^j and f^j are in $\mathscr{C}^*$. Then $(hkc, hc^{k+1}, \ldots, hc^m)$ $E^0(\mathscr{C}_1 \times \cdots \times \mathscr{C}_n)(hd^1, \ldots, hd^m)$ and $(khc, ke^{h+1}, \ldots, ke^M)E^0(\mathscr{C}_1 \times \cdots \times \mathscr{C}_n)$ $(kf^1, \ldots, kf^M)$, and therefore

$$(hd^1, \ldots, hd^m, ke^{h+1}, \ldots, ke^M)E(\mathscr{C}^*)(kf^1, \ldots, kf^M, hc^{k+1}, \ldots, hc^m).$$

Then, since u satisfies $\mathscr{C}^*$, we get

$$h \left[\sum_{j=1}^{m} u(d^j) - \sum_{j=k+1}^{m} u(c^j) \right] = k \left[\sum_{j=1}^{M} u(f^j) - \sum_{j=h+1}^{M} u(e^j) \right],$$

which shows that $u(c)$ defined from the e^j and f^j is the same as $u(c)$ defined from the c^j and d^j. Hence u is well defined on all of $\mathscr{C}_1 \times \cdots \times \mathscr{C}_n$.

Given u thus extended, suppose $(c^1, \ldots, c^m)E^0(\mathscr{C}_1 \times \cdots \times \mathscr{C}_n)(d^1, \ldots, d^m)$. It then follows easily from the linear extension for each c^j and d^j in $\mathscr{C}_1 \times \cdots \times \mathscr{C}_n \backslash \mathscr{C}^*$ and from the fact that u satisfies $\mathscr{C}^*$ that $\sum u(c^j) = = \sum u(d^j)$. Therefore u satisfies $\mathscr{C}_1 \times \cdots \times \mathscr{C}_n$.

6.4. MULTIADDITIVITY PROOFS

This section proves Theorem 3 and then Theorem 4. In the next few paragraphs we shall carry out some preliminary manipulations before axiom A8(n) is used.

Theorem 3

To prove Theorem 3, let

$$\mathscr{V} = \left\{ \sum_{i=1}^{n} a_i p_{2i} : a_i \text{ real}, p_{2i} \in \mathscr{P}_0(\mathscr{E}), n \text{ finite} \right\},$$

the vector space generated by $\mathscr{P}_0(\mathscr{E})$, and let $\mathscr{V}^2 = \mathscr{V} \times \mathscr{V}$, the vector space of ordered pairs of elements in $\mathscr{V}$. In addition, we shall let $\mathscr{L}$ and $\mathscr{L}_2$ denote the sets of real-valued linear functions on $\mathscr{V}$ and on $\mathscr{V}^2$, respectively.

With linear u on $\mathscr{P}_0(\mathscr{C})$ as given, we define u_d on $\mathscr{P}_0(\mathscr{E})$ by $u_d(p_2) = = u(d, p_2)$. Clearly, u_d is linear on $\mathscr{P}_0(\mathscr{E})$: we extend it linearly to all of $\mathscr{V}$ so that, with $x = \sum a_i p_{2i}$ in $\mathscr{V}$,

$$u_d(x) = \sum a_i u_d(p_{2i}).$$

The extended u_d is linear on $\mathscr{V}$, hence it is in $\mathscr{L}$. Next, we define a linear function $w_d \in \mathscr{L}_2$ for each $d \in \mathscr{D}$ by

$$w_d(x, y) = u_d(x) - u_d(y)$$

for all $(x, y) \in \mathscr{V}^2$. This is linear since $w_d(a(x, y) + b(x', y')) = = w_d((ax + bx', ay + by')) = u_d(ax + bx') - u_d(ay + by') = au_d(x) + + bu_d(x') - au_d(y) - bu_d(y') = aw_d(x, y) + bw_d(x', y')$.

The *null space* (kernel) of w_d is defined by

$$\mathscr{N}_d = \{(x, y) \in \mathscr{V}^2 : w_d(x, y) = 0\}.$$

Our motivation for this follows directly from the fact that if $p_2 \, \tilde{d} \, q_2$, or $(d, p_2) \sim (d, q_2)$, then $u_d(p_2) = u_d(q_2)$ and $w_d(p_2, q_2) = 0$. Hence $\tilde{d} \subseteq \mathscr{N}_d$.

Moreover, if $(d, p_2) \succ (d, q_2)$, then $(p_2, q_2) \notin \mathcal{N}_d$. Clearly, $\mathcal{N}_d = \mathcal{V}^2$ iff $\tilde{d} = \mathcal{P}_0(\mathcal{E}) \times \mathcal{P}_0(\mathcal{E})$, i.e. iff $(d, p_2) \sim (d, q_2)$ for all $p_2, q_2 \in \mathcal{P}_0(\mathcal{E})$. It follows from the definitions of Section 2 that if $\mathcal{N}_d = \mathcal{V}^2$ for all $d \in \mathcal{D}$ then no nonempty subset of $\mathcal{D}$ is independent and therefore axiom A8(n) is false for every positive integer n. In this case $u(d, e) = h(d)$ for all $(d, e) \in \mathcal{C}$ with h defined in the obvious way. Moreover, if this representation holds then $\mathcal{N}_d = \mathcal{V}^2$ for all $d \in \mathcal{D}$.

Now suppose that A8(n) holds for some positive integer n and that $\{d_1, \dots, d_n\}$ is a basis of $\mathcal{D}$. According to our earlier definitions, we then have $\mathcal{N}_d \subset \mathcal{V}^2$ for each $d \in \{d_1, \dots, d_n\}$ along with

$$\bigcap_{j \neq i} \mathcal{N}_{d_j} \nsubseteq \mathcal{N}_{d_i} \quad \text{for} \quad i = 1, \dots, n \text{ if } n > 1;$$

$$\bigcap_i \mathcal{N}_{d_i} = \bigcap_{d \in \mathcal{D}} \mathcal{N}_d.$$

According to a standard theorem on linear dependence, such as theorem 1.3 in Kelley, Namioka et al. (1963), a linear function (functional) w_0 is a linear combination of linear functions $w_1, \dots, w_n$ if and only if the null space of w_0 includes the intersection of the null spaces of $w_1, \dots, w_n$. Since our spanning equality says that $\mathcal{N}_d$ includes $\bigcap \mathcal{N}_{d_i}$ for every $d \in \mathcal{D}$, it follows that there are real-valued functions $f_1, \dots, f_n$ on $\mathcal{D}$ such that, with $w_i = w_{d_i}$,

$$w_d(x, y) = \sum_{i=1}^{n} f_i(d) w_i(x, y)$$

for all $(x, y) \in \mathcal{V}^2$. With $y = e_0$ fixed, $g_i(e) = u(d_i, e)$ and $h(d) = u(d, e_0) - \sum_i f_i(d) u(d_i, e_0)$, this gives

$$u(d, e) = \sum_{i=1}^{n} f_i(d) g_i(e) + h(d)$$

as required for Theorem 3. The same form cannot hold for $n' = 0$ [i.e., $u(d, e) = h(d)$ for all (d, e) must be false], so suppose it holds for some positive $n' < n$, say

$$u(d, e) = \sum_{i=1}^{n'} f_i'(d) g_i'(e) + h'(d).$$

Then, with g_i' defined linearly on $\mathcal{V}$ from g_i' on $\mathcal{E}$, we get

$$w_d(x, y) = \sum_{i=1}^{n'} f_i'(d) [g_i'(x) - g_i'(y)].$$

According to our independence condition for basis $\{d_1, \ldots, d_n\}$, for each $k \in \{1, \ldots, n\}$ there is a pair $(x_k, y_k) \in \mathscr{V}^2$ for which $w_k(x_k, y_k) \neq 0$ and $w_j(x_k, y_k) = 0$ for all $j \neq k$. However, this is impossible since the preceding expression with $n' < n$ implies that some w_k is a linear combination of the other w_k. Therefore, given A8(n), the desired form holds for n but for no $n' < n$.

Conversely, suppose the desired form holds for n but for no $n' < n$. If $\mathscr{D}$ includes an independent set with more than n elements, then any $n + 1$ of these yield a contradiction as in the last part of the preceding paragraph. Since $\mathscr{D}$ includes some nonempty independent set, every maximal independent set has n or fewer elements. But if some maximal independent set has $n' < n$ elements then it would form a basis with n' elements in contradiction to the first part of the preceding paragraph and our hypothesis that the multiadditive form holds for no $n' < n$. Therefore each maximal independent subset of $\mathscr{D}$ has n elements and, as is easily seen from maximality, each of these is spanning. Therefore A8(n) holds, and the proof of Theorem 3 is complete.

Theorem 4

Given that A8(n) holds with bases $\{d_1, \ldots, d_n\}$ of $\mathscr{D}$ and $\{e_1, \ldots, e_m\}$ of $\mathscr{E}$, with $n \geq 1$, $m \geq 1$ and $m \in \{n - 1, n, n + 1\}$, we are to show that u on $\mathscr{D} \times \mathscr{E}$ has the form displayed in Theorem 4. We shall assume with no loss in generality that $m \geq n$, and omit the simple proof for $m = n = 1$. Hence $m \geq 2$ in what follows.

By the preceding proof,

$$w_d(e, e_j) = \sum_{i=1}^{n} f_i(d) w_i(e, e_j) \quad j = 1, \ldots, m,$$

where $\quad w_d(e, e_j) = u(d, e) - u(d, e_j) = u(d, e) - w_j(d) \quad$ and $\quad w_i(e, e_j) = u(d_i, e) - u(d_i, e_j) = v_i(e) - u_{ij} \quad$ with $\quad u_{ij} = u(d_i, e_j)$. Set $e = e_1$ in the preceding equation to get

$$w_d(e_1, e_j) = \sum_{i=1}^{n} f_i(d) w_i(e_1, e_j) \quad j = 2, \ldots, m.$$

We now solve these equations in the usual reduction manner for the f_i, letting j be successively $2, 3, \ldots, m$. At each step, the current f_i solution is substituted into the original equation for any designated j and into the remaining $w_d(e_1, e_j)$ equations. Independence of $e_1, \ldots, e_m$ assures that (with a possible exception noted below for $m = n$) there is a viable f_i solution at each step.

To illustrate the process, set $j = 2$ in the preceding equation. Since $\{e_1, e_2\}$ is independent, $w_i(e_1, e_2) \neq 0$ for some i, say $i = n$. We then solve for f_n:

$$f_n(d) = \left[w_d(e_1, e_2) - \sum_{i=1}^{n-1} f_i(d) w_i(e_1, e_2) \right] \Big/ w_n(e_1, e_2).$$

If $n = 1$, we obtain the form required for Theorem 4 when this expression for $f_1(d)$ is substituted for $f_1(d)$ in one of the original equations, say in $w_d(e, e_1) = f_1(d) w_1(e, e_1)$.

Assume henceforth that $n \geq 2$, and suppose first that $m = n + 1$. After substituting for $f_n(d)$ into the $w_d(e_1, e_j)$ equations for $j \geq 3$, we solve the $j = 3$ equation for one of $f_1, \ldots, f_{n-1}$: since $\{e_1, e_2, e_3\}$ is independent, one of the coefficients of the f_i for $i \leq n - 1$ in the new $j = 3$ case must be nonzero. Continuing in the indicated manner, the penultimate step gives (with $j = m - 1$, and taking f_1 and f_2 as the remaining f_i)

$$f_2(d) = k f_1(d) + \sum_{j=2}^{n} k_j w_d(e_1, e_j),$$

where the k's are constants. When this is substituted into the current expression for $w_d(e_1, e_m)$, or $w_d(e_1, e_{n+1})$, it gives $w_d(e_1, e_{n+1}) = k' f_1(d) + \sum_{j>1} k'_j w_d(e_1, e_j)$. Since $\{e_1, \ldots, e_{n+1}\}$ is independent, $k' \neq 0$, so we can solve for f_1 and substitute back into one of the original equations, which is then devoid of the f_i and has the form required by Theorem 4.

Finally, suppose that $m = n$. Then the displayed equation in the preceding paragraph holds, but we have run out of j's and so do not get a final equation that isolates f_1. Instead, we use one of the original equations under the substitutions for the other f_i, which will have the form

$$u(d, e) = f_1(d) \left\{ \sum_{i=1}^{n} k v_i(e) + k \right\} + \sum_{i=2}^{n} \sum_{j=1}^{n} k v_i(e) w_j(d) +$$

$$+ \sum_{i=2}^{n} k v_i(e) + \sum_{j=1}^{n} k w_j(d),$$

where the k's are different constants. With $m = n$, a complete interchange in the roles of $\mathscr{D}$ and $\mathscr{E}$ yields say

$$u(d, e) = g_1(e) \left\{ \sum_{j=1}^{n} k w_j(d) + k \right\} + \sum_{i=1}^{n} \sum_{j=2}^{n} k v_i(e) w_j(d) +$$

$$+ \sum_{i=1}^{n} k v_i(e) + \sum_{j=2}^{n} k w_j(d).$$

The multiplier of $f_1(d)$ in braces in the first of these two equations must be nonzero for some $e_0 \in \mathscr{E}$, for otherwise there would be no $v_1(e)$ in that equation, which would imply that $\mathscr{E}$ was degree-n' utility independent of $\mathscr{D}$ for some $n' < n$. We therefore solve that equation for $f_1(d)$ with $e = e_0$ to get

$$f_1(d) = ku(d, e_0) + \sum_{j=1}^{n} kw_j(d) + k.$$

Since $u(d, e_0)$ is not in the expression of Theorem 4, we get rid of it with $e = e_0$ in the second equation above for $u(d, e)$, with $u(d, e_0) = g_1(e_0)\{\dots\}\dots$, or

$$u(d, e_0) = \sum_{j=1}^{n} kw_j(d) + k.$$

Appropriate substitutions into the first expression for $u(d, e)$ then yield the form stated in Theorem 4.

CHAPTER 7

MULTILINEAR UTILITY ON PRODUCTS OF MIXTURE SETS

In this chapter and the next, we shall assume that the preference relation $\succ$ applies to a product of mixture sets or sets of probability measures rather than to a single mixture set. The present chapter takes $\succ$ on $\mathcal{M}_1 \times \cdots \times \mathcal{M}_n$ and first gives axioms that are necessary and sufficient for a basic multilinear utility representation when each $\mathcal{M}_i$ is a mixture set as defined in Section 2.1. We then note how the mixture-set axioms can be replaced by indifference axioms, as in Section 2.3. The next chapter extends the multilinear form to an expected-utility integral representation when each $\mathcal{M}_i$ is a set of probability measures.

The difference between our present formulation and that of the preceding chapter should be carefully noted. In Chapter 6, the product structure was used 'internally' for the consequences, viewed as possible outcomes of probability measures on a subset $\mathcal{C}$ of $\mathcal{C}_1 \times \cdots \times \mathcal{C}_n$. In the rest of Part I, the product structure is applied 'externally' to a family of sets of probability measures or mixture sets.

7.1. MULTILINEARITY AND GAME THEORY

Let $\mathcal{M}_1, \ldots, \mathcal{M}_n$ be mixture sets with $n \geq 2$, and let $\mathcal{M}^* = \mathcal{M}_1 \times \cdots \times \mathcal{M}_n$ so that each $x \in \mathcal{M}^*$ is an n-tuple $(x_1, \ldots, x_n)$ with $x_i \in \mathcal{M}_i$ for each i. When we define $x \lambda y$ for $x = (x_1, \ldots, x_n)$ and $y = (y_1, \ldots, y_n)$ in $\mathcal{M}^*$ in the natural way as

$$x \lambda y = (x_1 \lambda y_1, \ldots, x_n \lambda y_n),$$

it is easily seen that $\mathcal{M}^*$ is a mixture set. There is, in principle, nothing that prevents us from applying the axioms of Chapter 2 to $\succ$ on $\mathcal{M}^*$, and we shall do this in Chapter 9, where it is proved that the earlier axioms yield linear functions u_i on $\mathcal{M}_i$ for $i = 1, \ldots, n$ such that

$$x \succ y \quad \text{iff} \quad \sum_{i=1}^{n} u_i(x_i) > \sum_{i=1}^{n} u_i(y_i).$$

This additive linear representation is considerably stronger than the multilinear representation that is axiomatized in the next section and which is – as will be explained momentarily – sufficient as a basis of expected utility in certain contexts.

To explicate the notion of multilinearity, let T_i be the binary relation on $\mathcal{M}^*$ defined by

$$x T_i y \quad \text{iff} \quad x_j = y_j \quad \text{for all} \quad j \neq i.$$

Hence $x T_i y$ when the components of x and y are identical for each j except perhaps for $j = i$. We then say that u is a *multilinear function* on $\mathcal{M}^*$ if u is a real-valued function on $\mathcal{M}^*$ such that, for all $i \in \{1, \dots, n\}$ and all $x, y \in \mathcal{M}^*$,

$$x T_i y \Rightarrow u(x \lambda y) = \lambda u(x) + (1 - \lambda) u(y).$$

Since $x T_i y$ gives $x \lambda y = (x_1, \dots, x_{i-1}, x_i \lambda y_i, x_{i+1}, \dots, x_n)$, this says that u is linear in each of the factors $\mathcal{M}_i$. If u were linear without qualification, then we would obtain the additive form $u(x) = \sum u_i(x_i)$ of the preceding paragraph. Clearly, linearity implies multilinearity, but not conversely. The axioms for $\succ$ on $\mathcal{M}^*$ in the next section use mixtures $x \lambda y$ only when $x T_i y$ for some i, thus avoiding the additive implication of unqualified linearity.

Our primary interest in multilinearity is its relevance to the theory of n-person games. Although it applies to other contexts that profess stochastic independence among factors, we discuss it only in the game-theoretic setting. In this setting let $\mathcal{C}_i$ denote the pure strategies available to player i, and let $\mathcal{M}_i = \mathcal{P}_0(\mathcal{C}_i)$, the set of simple mixed strategies of player i. Thus each $x \in \mathcal{M}^*$ is an n-tuple of mixed strategies for the n players. We assume that players choose strategies independently (simultaneously) although this is not essential for our interpretation. In any event, if $x = (x_1, \dots, x_n)$ is the n-tuple of strategies chosen by the players, then $x_1(c_1) x_2(c_2) \dots x_n(c_n)$ is the probability that $(c_1, \dots, c_n)$ will be the n-tuple of pure strategies resulting from their choices. Hence, if u is one player's utility function on $\mathcal{C}_1 \times \dots \times \mathcal{C}_n$, then his expected utility for $x = (x_1, \dots, x_n)$ is

$$\sum_{\mathcal{C}_1 \times \dots \times \mathcal{C}_n} u(c_1, c_2, \dots, c_n) x_1(c_1) x_2(c_2) \dots x_n(c_n).$$

It is easily seen that if $u(x_1, \dots, x_n)$ is defined as this sum, then u on $\mathcal{M}^*$

is multilinear. Conversely, if u on $\mathcal{M}^*$ is multilinear, then

$$u(x_1, \ldots, x_n) = \sum_{\mathcal{C}_1} u(c_1, x_2, \ldots, x_n) x_1(c_1)$$

$$= \sum_{\mathcal{C}_1} \left\{ \sum_{\mathcal{C}_2} u(c_1, c_2, x_3, \ldots, x_n) x_2(c_2) \right\} x_1(c_1)$$

$$\vdots$$

$$= \sum_{\mathcal{C}_1 \times \cdots \times \mathcal{C}_n} u(c_1, c_2, \ldots, c_n) x_1(c_1) x_2(c_2) \cdots x_n(c_n).$$

Therefore, multilinear u on $\mathcal{M}^*$ is the basic form that corresponds to expected utility in the game-theoretic setting.

In conjunction with this, it should be noted why the axioms of Chapter 2, or the presumption that u is linear on $\mathcal{M}^*$, is generally inappropriate for game theory. For simplicity, suppose $n = 2$, and consider the pair of mixed strategies $x = (x_1 \frac{1}{2} y_1, x_2 \frac{1}{2} y_2)$. According to our definition of mixtures in $\mathcal{M}^*$,

$$(x_1 \tfrac{1}{2} y_1, x_2 \tfrac{1}{2} y_2) = (x_1, x_2) \tfrac{1}{2} (y_1, y_2)$$

$$= (x_1, y_2) \tfrac{1}{2} (y_1, x_2).$$

If u were linear, then $u(x_1, x_2) + u(y_1, y_2) = u(x_1, y_2) + u(y_1, x_2)$, which would be absurd if the player with utility function u prefers (x_1, x_2) to (x_1, y_2) and also prefers (y_1, y_2) to (y_1, x_2). Multilinearity allows such preferences, but they are ruled out by linearity. In other words, multilinearity allows $\succ$ to be any asymmetric weak order on $\mathcal{C}_1 \times \cdots \times \mathcal{C}_n$, whereas linearity severely restricts the possibilities for $\succ$ on $\mathcal{C}_1 \times \cdots \times \mathcal{C}_n$.

It should also be mentioned that the traditional approach in game theory would apply $\succ$ to $\mathcal{P}_0(\mathcal{C}_1 \times \cdots \times \mathcal{C}_n)$ rather than to $\mathcal{M}^* = \mathcal{P}_0(\mathcal{C}_1) \times \cdots \times \mathcal{P}_0(\mathcal{C}_n)$. The traditional approach therefore obtains linear u on $\mathcal{P}_0(\mathcal{C}_1 \times \cdots \times \mathcal{C}_n)$, which does in fact allow $\succ$ to be any asymmetric weak order on $\mathcal{C}_1 \times \cdots \times \mathcal{C}_n$ and yields $\sum u(c_1, \ldots, c_n) x_1(c_1) \cdots x_n(c_n)$ as the expected utility that corresponds to the n-tuple $(x_1, \ldots, x_n)$ of mixed strategies. The problem with this approach is that most of the measures in $\mathcal{P}_0(\mathcal{C}_1 \times \cdots \times \mathcal{C}_n)$ do not correspond to entities that are actually available for choice in the situation, namely the $x \in \mathcal{M}^*$. For example, $p \in$ $\in \mathcal{P}_0(\{c_1, d_1\} \times \{c_2, d_2\})$ with $p(c_1, c_2) + p(c_1, d_2) + p(d_1, c_2) + p(d_1, d_2) =$ $= 1$ is easily seen to have the same probabilities on $\mathcal{C}_1 \times \mathcal{C}_2 = \{c_1, d_1\} \times$

$\times \{c_2, d_2\}$ as some $(x_1, x_2) \in \mathcal{M}^*$ if and only if $p(c_1, c_2)p(d_1, d_2) = = p(c_1, d_2)p(d_1, c_2)$, and this occurs with probability zero under Lebesgue measure on $\mathscr{P}_0(\mathscr{C}_1 \times \mathscr{C}_2)$.

7.2. AXIOMS FOR MULTILINEAR UTILITY

We shall use three axioms for $\succ$ on $\mathcal{M}^* = \mathcal{M}_1 \times \cdots \times \mathcal{M}_n$ along with M1, M2, and M3 for each $\mathcal{M}_i$ to characterize multilinear utility.

E1. $\succ$ on $\mathcal{M}^*$ is an asymmetric weak order,
E2.   For all $x, y, z, w \in \mathcal{M}^*$, all $i, j \in \{1, \ldots, n\}$, and all $0 < \lambda < 1$, if $x\, T_i\, z, y\, T_j\, w, x \succ y$ and $z \sim w$, then $x\lambda z \succ y\lambda w$,
E3.   For all $x, y, z \in \mathcal{M}^*$ and all $i \in \{1, \ldots, n\}$, if $x\, T_i\, z, x \succ y$ and $y \succ z$, then there are $\alpha, \beta \in (0, 1)$ such that $x\alpha z \succ y$ and $y \succ x\beta z$.

These are respectively similar to A1, A2, and A3 in Section 2.2, and in fact are equivalent to those earlier axioms when $n = 1$, with one exception. The exception is $z \sim w$ in E2, which is needed in the multilinear context to make interconnections between factors. Axiom A2 is the $n = 1$ simplification of E2 obtained by replacing $z \sim w$ with $z = w$.

The usual interpretations and criticisms of the earlier axioms apply to E1 through E3 with the obvious change in formulation. Axiom E2 is an independence axiom for the multilinearity setting, which with $i = 1$ and $j = 2$ says that if

$$(x_1, x_2, x_3, \ldots, x_n) \succ (y_1, y_2, y_3, \ldots, y_n)$$

and

$$(z_1, x_2, x_3, \ldots, x_n) \sim (y_1, w_2, y_3, \ldots, y_n),$$

then

$$(x_1\lambda z_1, x_2, x_3, \ldots, x_n) \succ (y_1, y_2\lambda w_2, y_3, \ldots, y_n).$$

This shows how $i \neq j$ in E2 effects comparisons between mixtures on different factors. The Archimedean axiom E3 for $i = 1$ says that if $(x_1, x_2, \ldots, x_n) \succ (y_1, y_2, \ldots, y_n) \succ (z_1, x_2, \ldots, x_n)$, then $(x_1\alpha z_1, x_2, \ldots, x_n) \succ \succ y \succ (x_1\beta z_1, x_2, \ldots, x_n)$ for some α, β in $(0, 1)$. All mixtures in E2 and E3 presume that the mixed elements differ in at most one factor.

THEOREM 1. *Suppose* $n \geq 2$ *and* $\mathcal{M}_1, \ldots, \mathcal{M}_n$ *are mixture sets. Then* E1, E2, *and* E3 *hold if and only if there is a multilinear function* u *on* $\mathcal{M}^* =$

$= \mathcal{M}_1 \times \ldots \times \mathcal{M}_n$ such that, for all x, $y \in \mathcal{M}^*$, $x \succ y$ iff $u(x) = u(y)$. In addition, such a u is unique up to a positive affine transformation.

Since the axioms are easily seen to be necessary for a multilinear order-preserving utility function, our proof of Theorem 1 in Section 4 focuses on sufficiency and uniqueness.

As noted in the preceding section, if $\mathcal{M}_i = \mathcal{P}_0(\mathcal{C}_i)$ for each i, then Theorem 1 and the usual definition of u on $\mathcal{C}_1 \times \cdots \times \mathcal{C}_n$ yield the expected-utility form

$$u(p_1, \ldots, p_n) = \sum_{\mathcal{C}_1 \times \cdots \times \mathcal{C}_n} u(c_1, \ldots, c_n) p_1(c_1) \ldots p_n(c_n)$$

for the product measure $p_1 \ldots p_n$ when $p_i \in \mathcal{P}_0(\mathcal{C}_i)$ for each i. This form is extended to general measures in the next chapter.

7.3. GENERALIZED MIXTURE AXIOMS

Fishburn and Roberts (1978) show how Theorem 1 can be generalized using indifference versions of the mixture axioms in a manner comparable to the replacement of M2 and M3 by M2($\sim$) and M3($\sim$) in Theorem 2.2. For the present generalization we define $(x \lambda y)^i$ as follows:

$$(x \lambda y)^i = (x_1, \ldots, x_{i-1}, x_i \lambda y_i, x_{i+1}, \ldots, x_n)$$

when $x T_i y$ with $y_j = x_j$ for all $j \neq i$. This form is used since we do not assume that $x_j \lambda x_j = x_j$ for $x_j \in \mathcal{M}_j$. Accordingly, the axioms for this case use $(x \lambda y)^i$ rather than $x \lambda y$ mixtures, and in a modification of our preceding definition, we shall say here that u on $\mathcal{M}^*$ is *multilinear* if

$$x T_i y \Rightarrow u((x \lambda y)^i) = \lambda u(x) + (1 - \lambda) u(y).$$

Axioms E2 and E3 are modified as follows to reflect the change from $x \lambda y$ to $(x \lambda y)^i$:

E2*. *For all* $x, y, z, w \in \mathcal{M}^*$, *all* $i, j \in \{1, \ldots, n\}$, *and all* $0 < \lambda < 1$, *if* $x T_i z$, $y T_j w$, $x \succ y$ *and* $z \sim w$, *then* $(x \lambda z)^i \succ (y \lambda w)^j$,

E3*. *For all* $x, y, z \in \mathcal{M}^*$ *and all* $i \in \{1, \ldots, n\}$, *if* $x T_i z$, $x \succ y$ *and* $y \succ z$, *then there are* $\alpha, \beta \in (0, 1)$ *such that* $(x \alpha z)^i \succ y$ *and* $y \succ (x \beta z)^i$.

Mixture axioms M2 and M3 are modified as follows for all $i \in \{1, \ldots, n\}$ and all $x, y \in \mathcal{M}^*$:

M2($\sim$)*. *If* $x T_i y$ *then* $(x \lambda y)^i \sim (y(1 - \lambda) x)^i$,
M3($\sim$)*. *If* $x T_i y$ *then* $((x \mu y)^i \lambda y)^i \sim (x(\lambda \mu) y)^i$.

Given $x\,T_1\,y$, M3($\sim$)* says that $((x_1\,\mu\,y_1)\lambda y_1, x_2, \ldots, x_n)$ is indifferent to $(x_1(\lambda\mu)y_1, x_2, \ldots, x_n)$, and M2($\sim$)* says that $(x_1\lambda y_1, x_2, \ldots, x_n) \sim$ $\sim (y_1(1-\lambda)x_1, x_2, \ldots, x_n)$.

THEOREM 2. *Suppose $n \geq 2$; for each $i \in \{1, \ldots, n\}$, $\mathcal{M}_i$ is a set that contains $x_i\lambda y_i$ for any λ and any $(x_i, y_i) \in \mathcal{M}_i \times \mathcal{M}_i$; and $\succ$ is a binary relation on $\mathcal{M}^* = \mathcal{M}_1 \times \cdots \times \mathcal{M}_n$ that satisfies M2($\sim$)*, M3($\sim$)*, E1, E2*, and E3*. Then there is a multilinear function u on $\mathcal{M}^*$ such that, for all $x, y \in \mathcal{M}^*$, $x \succ y$ iff $u(x) > u(y)$, and such a u is unique up to a positive affine transformation.*

A proof of Theorem 2 appears in Section 5.

7.4. PROOF OF THEOREM 1

It is assumed throughout this section that $n \geq 2$, each $\mathcal{M}_i$ is a mixture set, and E1, E2, and E3 hold. Our proof of the existence of a multilinear order-preserving function u on $\mathcal{M}^* = \mathcal{M}_1 \times \cdots \times \mathcal{M}_n$ that is unique up to a positive affine transformation proceeds in several steps, as indicated in Fishburn (1976). Our construction of u will be preceded by implications of the axioms that are similar to J1 through J5 in Section 2.4. As proved in that section, M4 and M5, i.e. $x_i\lambda x_i = x_i$ and $(x_i\beta y_i)\alpha(x_i\gamma y_i) = x_i(\alpha\beta + (1-\alpha)\gamma)y_i$, hold for each $\mathcal{M}_i$. We shall use the manipulations allowed by the mixture-set axioms freely, in most cases without special note.

Some Implications of the Axioms

K1. $(x\,T_i\,y, x \succ y, \lambda > \mu) \Rightarrow x\lambda y \succ x\mu y$,
K2. $(x\,T_i\,z, x \succsim y \succsim z, x \succ z) \Rightarrow y \sim x\lambda z$ for a unique λ,
K3. $(x\,T_i\,y, x \sim y) \Rightarrow x \sim x\lambda y$,
K4. $(x\,T_i\,z, y\,T_j\,w, x \sim y, z \sim w) \Rightarrow x\lambda z \sim y\lambda w$,
K5. $(x \succ y \succ z) \Rightarrow$ there are $s, t \in \mathcal{M}^*$ such that $s\,T_i\,t$ for some i and $x \succsim s \succ y \succ t \succsim z$.

Since the proofs of K1, K2, and K3 are similar respectively to the proofs of J1, J2, and J4, only K4 and K5 will be proved here.

K4. Assume that $0 < \lambda < 1$, since otherwise the conclusion is obvious. If $x \sim z$ along with the hypotheses of K4, then K3 gives $x\lambda z \sim x$ and $y \sim y\lambda w$ and $x\lambda z \sim y\lambda w$ by the transitivity of $\sim$ (E1). Suppose henceforth that $x \succ z$. (The proof for $z \succ x$ is similar.) Given $x \succ z$, K1 implies $x \lambda z \succ z$. Suppose the conclusion of K4 fails, with $y \lambda w \succ x \lambda z$. Then, since $x \lambda z \succ w$ by K1 and transitivity, K2 gives a unique α in $(0, 1)$ such that $x \lambda z \sim (y \lambda w) \alpha w = y(\lambda \alpha) w$ (by M3 for $\mathcal{M}_j$). But, since $x \succ z$, $y \succ w$ also, and therefore K1 gives $x \sim y \succ y \alpha w$, or $x \succ y \alpha w$. Since $w \sim z$, apply E2 to get $x \lambda z \succ (y \alpha w) \lambda w = y(\lambda \alpha) w$, which contradicts $x \lambda z \sim y(\lambda \alpha)w$ as obtained previously. Therefore $y \lambda w \succ x \lambda z$ is false. A similar proof shows that $x \lambda z \succ y \lambda w$ is false, and therefore $x \lambda z \sim y \lambda w$.

K5. Given $x \succ y \succ z$, it suffices to show that $s \succ y \succ t$ for some s, t for which $s\,T_i\,t$ for some i, for if $z \succ t$ or $s \succ x$ then K2 can be used to get $z \sim s \gamma t = t'$ or $x \sim s \delta t = s'$, and $(s$ or $s')\,T_i\,(t$ or $t')$. Thus, given $x \succ y \succ z$, we are to prove that $s \succ y \succ t$ for some $s\,T_i\,t$. Let $x = (x_1, \ldots, x_n)$ and $z = (z_1, \ldots, z_n)$. The desired result holds if either $(x_1, z_2, \ldots, z_n) \succ y \succ z$, for $(x_1, z_2, \ldots, z_n)\,T_1\,z$, or $x \succ y \succ (z_1, x_2, \ldots, x_n)$, for $x\,T_1\,(z_1, x_2, \ldots, x_n)$. Hence the desired result fails only if

$$(z_1, x_2, \ldots, x_n) \succsim y \succsim (x_1, z_2, \ldots, z_n).$$

Assume that this is true. Then, given $0 < \lambda < 1$, E1 and K1 imply that

$$(z_1 \lambda x_1, x_2, \ldots, x_n) \succ y \succ (z_1 \lambda x_1, z_2, \ldots, z_n).$$

Working with the second factor instead of the first, the desired result holds unless it is true that

$$(z_1 \lambda x_1, z_2, x_3, \ldots, x_n) \succsim y \succsim (z_1 \lambda x_1, x_2, z_3, \ldots, z_n),$$

in which case the preceding displayed expression and K1 imply that

$$(z_1 \lambda x_1, z_2 \lambda x_2, x_3, \ldots, x_n) \succ y \succ (z_1 \lambda x_1, z_2 \lambda x_2, z_3, \ldots, z_n).$$

If the desired results fail to hold as each new factor is brought into play, then we eventually conclude that $z \lambda x \succ y \succ z \lambda x$, which contradicts E1.

MAP Functions

For convenience in the ensuing construction, we shall refer to an order-preserving multilinear function on a subspace of $\mathcal{M}^*$ that is unique up to a positive affine transformation on this subspace as a *MAP function*. Since the theorem clearly holds if $\succ$ is empty, it is assumed henceforth that $\succ$ is not empty. It follows that there are $x, y \in \mathcal{M}^*$ such that $x \succ y$ and $x\,T_i\,y$ for some i, for otherwise we would have $x \sim (y_1, x_2, \ldots, x_n) \sim$

$\sim (y_1, y_2, x_3, \ldots, x_n) \sim \cdots \sim (y_1, \ldots, y_{n-1}, x_n) \sim y$ and therefore $x \sim y$ for all $x, y \in \mathcal{M}^*$.

As in the construction part of the proof of Theorem 2.1, we shall let

$$[xy] = \{z \in \mathcal{M}^* : x \succsim z \succsim y\},$$

the closed preference interval between x and y. Our initial result establishes the existence of MAP functions on certain preference intervals. Here, and later, we shall write

$$x \, T \, y \quad \text{iff} \quad x \, T_i \, y \text{ for some } i.$$

LEMMA 1. *If $x \succ y$ and xTy, then $[xy]$ is closed under mixtures between elements in $[xy]$ that stand in the relation T to one another, and there is a MAP function on $[xy]$.*

Proof. Results K1 and K3 imply that $z \lambda w \in [xy]$ whenever $z, w \in [xy]$ and $z \, T \, w$. For each $z \in [xy]$ let $f(z)$ be the unique number in $[0, 1]$ that, by K2, satisfies

$$z \sim x f(z) y,$$

with $f(x) = 1$ and $f(y) = 0$. To show that f is a MAP function on $[xy]$, suppose first that $z, w \in [xy]$ and $f(z) > f(w)$. Then K1 and E1 imply $z \succ w$; and if $f(z) = f(w)$, then $z \sim w$ by transitivity of $\sim$. Therefore f is order preserving on $[xy]$. To establish multilinearity, we wish to show that $f(z \lambda w) = \lambda f(z) + (1 - \lambda) f(w)$ whenever $z, w \in [xy]$ and $z \, T \, w$. Given $z \, T \, w$ and $z, w \in [xy]$, we have $z \lambda w \in [xy]$ by closure, and therefore the definition of f gives

$$z \lambda w \sim x f(z \lambda w) y.$$

In addition, $z \sim x f(z) y$ and $w \sim x f(w) y$. Then, since $z \, T \, w$ and $(xf(z)y) T (xf(w)y)$, the latter by $x \, T \, y$ in the hypotheses of the lemma, K4 implies that

$$z \lambda w \sim (x f(z) y) \lambda (x f(w) y) = x(\lambda f(z) + (1 - \lambda) f(w)) y,$$

where the equality follows from M5. The two preceding expressions then give $x f(z \lambda w) y \sim x(\lambda f(z) + (1 - \lambda) f(w)) y$ by transitivity of $\sim$, so, by K1 and E1, $f(z \lambda w) = \lambda f(z) + (1 - \lambda) f(w)$. Hence f is multilinear on $[xy]$.

To verify uniqueness up to a positive affine transformation, it suffices to show that if f and g are order preserving and multilinear on $[xy]$ with $f(x) = g(x)$ and $f(y) = g(y)$, then $f = g$ on $[xy]$. Since the given hypotheses with $z \sim x\lambda y$ imply that $f(z) = f(x\lambda y) = \lambda f(x) + (1-\lambda)f(y) = \lambda g(x) + (1-\lambda)g(y) = g(x\lambda y) = g(z)$, the proof of the lemma is complete. ∎

Interconnecting MAP Functions

We now prove a central lemma for interconnecting MAP functions that will be used later in conjunction with Lemma 1.

LEMMA 2. *If* $x \succ y, z \succ w, [xy] \cap [zw] \neq \emptyset$, *and if there are MAP functions on each of* $[xy]$ *and* $[zw]$, *then there is a MAP function on* $[xy] \cup [zw]$.

Proof. Given the hypotheses of the lemma, the conclusion is obvious if either $[xy]$ or $[zw]$ is included in the other preference interval. Moreover, if the intervals overlap without inclusion, say with $x \succ z \succ y \succ w$, then $[zw]$ can be replaced by $[yw]$, which yields MAP functions on the intersecting domains $[xy]$ and $[yw]$. Hence we need only consider the case in which $x \succ y \succ w$ with f a MAP function on $[xy]$ and g a MAP function on $[yw]$. Given f and g, take $f(y) = g(y) = 0$ for convenience (by positive affine transformations) and define h on $[xy] \cup [yw] = [xw]$ by

$$h(t) = k[f(t)] \quad \text{for} \quad t \in [xy]$$

$$h(t) = g(t) \qquad \text{for} \quad t \in [yw],$$

with $k > 0$ to be determined. By definition, h preserves $\succ$ on $[xw]$. In the next part of this proof, we show that k is uniquely determined for h to be multilinear on $[xw]$. Since f and g are presumed to be MAP functions, it will then follow that h is a MAP function on $[xw]$.

To determine k for multilinearity, let

$$\mathcal{N}^* = \{(r, s) : r \, T \, s \text{ and } x \succsim r \succ y \succ s \succsim w\}.$$

By K5, $\mathcal{N}^*$ is not empty. Given $(r, s), (z, t) \in \mathcal{N}^*$, K2 implies that there are unique $\alpha, \beta \in (0, 1)$ such that

$$r\alpha s \sim y \quad \text{and} \quad z\beta t \sim y.$$

These give $h(r\alpha s) = 0 = h(z\beta t)$. Therefore, h can be multilinear only if $\alpha h(r) + (1-\alpha)h(s) = 0 = \beta h(z) + (1-\beta)h(t)$, i.e.

$$\alpha k f(r) + (1-\alpha)g(s) = 0$$

$$\beta k f(z) + (1-\beta)g(t) = 0.$$

Each of these equations determines a positive value for k, and they yield the same k value if and only if

$$\frac{(1-\alpha)\beta}{\alpha(1-\beta)} = \frac{f(r)g(t)}{f(z)g(s)}.$$

After verifying this equality, we shall show that h with k thus determined is generally multilinear, then conclude the proof of Lemma 2 by noting that an order-preserving multilinear function on $[xw] = [xy] \cup [yw]$ is unique up to a positive affine transformation.

To verify the preceding equality, assume without loss in generality that $r \gtrsim z$ with (r, s), $(z, t) \in \mathcal{N}^*$ as specified. We consider two cases, depending on whether $s > t$ or $t \gtrsim s$. Suppose first that $t \gtrsim s$. Then $r \gtrsim z > y \sim r\alpha s > t \gtrsim s$, and, by K2, there are unique $\alpha_1 > 0$ and $\beta_1 > 0$ such that

$$z \sim r\alpha_1 (r\alpha s)$$

$$t \sim s\beta_1 (r\alpha s).$$

Multilinearity of f and g then gives

$$f(z) = \alpha_1 f(r)$$

$$g(t) = \beta_1 g(s)$$

since $r\ T\ (r\alpha s)$, $s\ T\ (r\alpha s)$ and $f(r\alpha s) = g(r\alpha s) = 0$. Thus

$$\frac{f(r)g(t)}{f(z)g(s)} = \frac{\beta_1}{\alpha_1}.$$

Moreover, since $z\ T\ t$ and

$$r\alpha_1(r\alpha s) = \{r[\alpha_1 + (1-\alpha_1)\alpha]s\}\ T\ \{r[\alpha(1-\beta_1)]s\} = s\beta_1(r\alpha s),$$

K4 applied to $z \sim r\alpha_1(r\alpha s)$ and $t \sim s\beta_1(r\alpha s)$, along with $r\alpha s \sim y \sim z\beta t$ and M5, gives

$$r\alpha s \sim z\beta t \sim \{r[\alpha_1 + (1-\alpha_1)\alpha]s\}\beta\{r[\alpha(1-\beta_1)]s\}$$
$$= r\{\beta[\alpha_1 + (1-\alpha_1)\alpha] + (1-\beta)[\alpha(1-\beta_1)]\}s.$$

The transitivity of $\sim$, and K1, then require

$$\alpha = \beta[\alpha_1 + (1-\alpha_1)\alpha] + (1-\beta)[\alpha(1-\beta_1)],$$

which reduces to

$$\frac{(1-\alpha)\beta}{\alpha(1-\beta)} = \frac{\beta_1}{\alpha_1}.$$

Since both $f(r)g(t)/[f(z)g(s)]$ and $(1-\alpha)\beta/[\alpha(1-\beta)]$ equal β_1/α_1, we obtain

$$\frac{(1-\alpha)\beta}{\alpha(1-\beta)} = \frac{f(r)\,g\,(t)}{f(z)\,g\,(s)}$$

when $t \gtrsim s$.

For the second case, with $s \succ t$, we have $r \gtrsim z \succ r\alpha s \sim y \sim z\beta t \succ s \succ t$. Then K2 implies that there are unique $\alpha_1 > 0$ and $0 < \beta_2 < 1$ such that

$$z \sim r\alpha_1\,(r\alpha s)$$
$$s \sim t\beta_2(z\beta t).$$

Multilinearity of f and g then gives

$$f(z) = \alpha_1 f(r)$$
$$g(s) = \beta_2\,g(t)$$

so that $f(r)g(t)/[f(z)g(s)] = 1/(\alpha_1\beta_2)$. In addition, K4 applied to $z \sim r\alpha_1\,(r\alpha s)$ and $t\beta_2\,(z\beta t) \sim s$ yields

$$z\tau[t\beta_2\,(z\beta t)] \sim [r\alpha_1\,(r\alpha s)]\tau s$$

for all τ. Select τ so that each side of the preceding $\sim$ statement is indifferent to y: since $r\alpha s \sim y \sim z\beta t$, this means that $\alpha = \tau[\alpha_1 + \alpha(1-\alpha_1)]$ and $\beta = \tau + (1-\tau)(1-\beta_2)\beta$, or

$$\alpha = \tau[\alpha_1 + \alpha(1-\alpha_1)]$$
$$\beta\beta_2 = \tau[1 - (1-\beta_2)\beta].$$

Together, these imply that $(1-\alpha)\beta/[\alpha(1-\beta)] = 1/(\alpha_1\beta_2)$, and therefore we again see that $(1-\alpha)\beta/[\alpha(1-\beta)] = f(r)g(t)/[f(z)g(s)]$.

The two preceding paragraphs show that, when k is determined in the indicated manner on the basis of $(r, s) \in \mathcal{N}^*$, the same $k > 0$ results for every $(r, s) \in \mathcal{N}^*$. Moreover, for h to be multilinear, this value of k must be used. To prove that h is multilinear on $[xw]$, we need to show that $h(r\lambda s) = \lambda h(r) + (1-\lambda)h(s)$ whenever $(r, s) \in \mathcal{N}^*$ and $0 < \lambda < 1$. If $r\lambda s \sim y$, then the desired result is immediate from the preceding analysis for k. Suppose that $\lambda > \alpha$ with $r\alpha s \sim y$. Then $r \succ r\lambda s \succ r\alpha s \sim y$ by K1, and, with $\mu = (\lambda - \alpha)/(1-\alpha)$, so that $\lambda = \mu + (1-\mu)\alpha$, we get

$$h(r\lambda s) = kf(r\lambda s)$$
$$= kf(r\mu(r\alpha s))$$
$$= k\mu f(r)$$
$$= \mu h(r).$$

In addition, since $\alpha k f(r) + (1 - \alpha)g(s) = 0$ and $h(s) = g(s)$,

$$\lambda h(r) + (1 - \lambda)h(s) = \lambda h(r) - (1 - \lambda)\alpha k f(r)/(1 - \alpha)$$
$$= [\lambda - (1 - \lambda)\alpha/(1 - \alpha)]h(r)$$
$$= \mu h(r),$$

and therefore $h(r \lambda s) = \lambda h(r) + (1 - \lambda)h(s)$. A similar proof yields the same result when $\alpha > \lambda$, and hence h is multilinear on $[xw]$.

For uniqueness, let h be as defined above. Clearly, every positive affine transformation of h is order preserving and multilinear. To go the other way, let h' be any order-preserving multilinear function on $[xw]$. Then, since f on $[xy]$ and g on $[yw]$ are MAP functions, the restrictions of h' on $[xy]$ and $[yw]$ must relate to f and g as

$$h'(t) = a_1 f(t) + b_1 \quad \text{for} \quad t \in [xy], a_1 > 0;$$
$$h'(t) = a_2 g(t) + b_2 \quad \text{for} \quad t \in [yw], a_2 > 0.$$

Since $f(y) = g(y) = 0$, these require $b_1 = b_2$, so that

$$h'(t) = a_1 f(t) + b_1 = a_1 h(t)/k + b_1 \quad \text{on} \quad [xy]$$
$$h'(t) = a_2 g(t) + b_1 = a_2 h(t) \quad + b_1 \quad \text{on} \quad [yw].$$

Given $(r, s) \in \mathcal{N}^*$ with $r \alpha s \sim y$, order preservation and multilinearity for h' yield $b_1 = h'(y) = h'(r \alpha s) = \alpha h'(r) + (1 - \alpha)h'(s) = \alpha[a_1 h(r)/k + b_1] + (1 - \alpha)[a_2 h(s) + b_1]$, so that

$$\alpha a_1 h(r)/k + (1 - \alpha)a_2 h(s) = 0.$$

This and $\alpha h(r) + (1 - \alpha)h(s) = 0$ then imply $a_1 = a_2 k$, and therefore $h'(t) = a_2 h(t) + b_1$ for all $t \in [xw]$. Hence h is a MAP function on $[xw]$. ∎

Proof Completion

Two more steps are needed to complete the proof of Theorem 1. The first of these is the proof of

LEMMA 3. *If $x \succ y$ then there is a MAP function on $[xy]$.*

Proof. Given $x \succ y$, consider the set of nonempty and nondegenerate preference intervals that are contained in

$$\{[x(y_1, x_2, \ldots, x_n)], [(y_1, x_2, \ldots, x_n) \times$$
$$\times (y_1, y_2, x_3, \ldots, x_n)], \ldots, [(y_1, \ldots, y_{n-1}, x_n)y)]\}.$$

Each such interval has a MAP function according to Lemma 1. Since the set of intervals covers $[xy]$, successive applications of Lemma 2 imply that there is a MAP function on an interval that includes $[xy]$. Hence $[xy]$ itself has a MAP function. ∎

Finally, we use Lemma 3 to obtain a MAP function on all of $\mathcal{M}^*$. Since $\succ$ is presumed to be nonempty, take $x_0 \succ y_0$ and let f be a MAP function on $[x_0 y_0]$ as guaranteed by Lemma 3. If $[x_0 y_0] \subseteq [xy]$, let g be a MAP function on $[xy]$ aligned with f so that $g(x_0) = f(x_0)$ and $g(y_0) = f(y_0)$. Lemma 2 ensures that any two such g, say for $[xy]$ and $[x'y']$ that include $[x_0 y_0]$, are identical on $[xy] \cap [x'y']$. Then, with $u(z)$ the common value of $g(z)$ for every $[xy]$ that contains z and includes $[x_0 y_0]$, it follows that u is well defined on $\mathcal{M}^*$, where it is order preserving and multilinear.

Every positive affine transformation of this u is order preserving and multilinear. Conversely, if v is order preserving and multilinear on $\mathcal{M}^*$, then v is a positive affine transformation of u, for otherwise Lemma 3 would be contradicted for some interval $[xy]$ with $x \succ y$. Hence axioms E1, E2 and E3 imply that there is a MAP function on $\mathcal{M}^*$.

7.5. PROOF OF THEOREM 2

Our proof of Theorem 2 is a modification of the proof in the preceding section. We assume here that the hypotheses of Theorem 2 hold, i.e. each $\mathcal{M}_i$ for $i = 1, \ldots, n$ with $n \geq 2$ is closed under 'mixtures' $x_i \lambda y_i$, and $\succ$ on $\mathcal{M}^*$ satisfies M2($\sim$)*, M3($\sim$)*, E1, E2*, and E3*. The first step towards establishing the existence of an order-preserving multilinear function on $\mathcal{M}^*$ that is unique up to a positive affine transformation is to prove assertions similar to K1 through K5 along with indifference versions of M1, M4 and M5:

M1($\sim$)*. $x \, T_i y \Rightarrow (x \, 1 \, y)^i \sim x$,

M4($\sim$)*. $(x \lambda x)^i \sim x$,

M5($\sim$)*. $x \, T_i y \Rightarrow ((x \beta y)^i \alpha (x \gamma y)^i)^i \sim (x(\alpha + (1-\alpha)\gamma)y)^i$;

K1*. $\quad (x \, T_i y, x \succ y, \lambda > \mu) \Rightarrow (x \lambda y)^i \succ (x \mu y)^i$,

K2*. $\quad (x \, T_i z, x \succsim y \succsim z, x \succ z) \Rightarrow y \sim (x \lambda z)^i$ for a unique λ,

K3*. $\quad (x \, T_i y, x \sim y) \Rightarrow x \sim (x \lambda y)^i$,

K4*. $(x.T_i z, y\ T_j w, x \sim y, z \sim w) \Rightarrow (x \lambda z)^i \sim (y \lambda w)^j$,

K5*. $(x \succ y \succ z) \Rightarrow$ there are $s, t \in \mathcal{M}^*$ such that $s\ T_i\ t$ for some i and $x \succsim s \succ y \succ t \succsim z$.

These can be verified in the following order: M1($\sim$)*, M4($\sim$)*, K1*, K2*, K3*, K4*, K5*, and M5($\sim$)*. In doing this, use is made of the fact that $x\ T_i\ y$ implies $(x \lambda y)^i\ T_i\ y$, $((x \beta y)^i \alpha (x \gamma y)^i)^i\ T_i\ ((x \lambda y)^i \mu y)^i$, and so forth. The proofs of M1($\sim$)* and M4($\sim$)* are similar to the proofs of M1($\sim$) and M4($\sim$) in Section 2.5, and the proofs of K1* through K5* are similar to the proofs of K1 through K5 with the obvious contextual changes. The proof of M5($\sim$)* follows the pattern shown for M5 and M5($\sim$) in Chapter 2. Since the present proofs are so similar to their predecessors, they will not be detailed.

The proof of Theorem 2 follows the steps used for Theorem 1 in the preceding section. The only significant changes are the use of $(x \lambda y)^i$ in place of $x \lambda y$, and replacement of several $=$ statements by $\sim$ statements. For example, $(xf(z)y) \lambda (xf(w)y) = x(\lambda f(z) + (1 - \lambda) f(w))y$ in the midst of the proof of Lemma 1 is replaced by $((xf(z)y)^i \lambda (xf(w)y)^i)^i \sim (x(\lambda f(z) + (1 - \lambda) f(w))y)^i$ when $x\ T_i\ y$, and this change is justified by M5($\sim$)*. Another example occurs in the proof of Lemma 2 where $\{r[\alpha_1 + (1 - \alpha_1)\alpha]s\}\ \beta\ \{r[\alpha(1 - \beta_1)]s\} = r\{\beta[\alpha_1 + (1 - \alpha_1)\alpha] + (1 - \beta) \times [\alpha(1 - \beta_1)]\}s$ with $r\ T_i\ s$ is replaced by $((r[\alpha_1 + (1 - \alpha_1)\alpha]s)^i \times \beta(r[\alpha(1 - \beta_1)]s)^i)^i \sim (r(\beta[\alpha_1 + (1 - \alpha_1)\alpha] + (1 - \beta)[\alpha(1 - \beta_1)])s)^i$, and $r\alpha_1(r\alpha s) = r[\alpha_1 + (1 - \alpha_1)\alpha]s$ is replaced by $(r\alpha_1(r\alpha s)^i)^i \sim (r[\alpha_1 + (1 - \alpha_1)\alpha]s)^i$. The first of these follows from M5($\sim$)*, and the second follows from M1($\sim$)*, M2($\sim$)*, M3($\sim$)*, and K4*.

CHAPTER 8

MULTILINEAR UTILITY FOR PROBABILITY MEASURES

We conclude Part I of the book by extending the multilinear form of the preceding chapter to

$$u(p) = \int_{\mathscr{C}_1} \cdots \int_{\mathscr{C}_n} u(c_1, \ldots, c_n)\, dp_n(c_n) \ldots dp_1(c_1)$$

for all p in the set $\mathscr{P}^* = \mathscr{P}_1 \times \cdots \times \mathscr{P}_n$ of n-tuples of probability measures, where $\mathscr{P}_i$ is a convex set of measures defined on a Boolean algebra of subsets of $\mathscr{C}_i$. As in Chapter 3, we consider the general finite additivity case first and then note changes allowed by countable additivity for the measures in the $\mathscr{P}_i$.

Throughout this chapter, $\mathscr{A}_i$ is a Boolean algebra for $\mathscr{C}_i$ that contains the singleton subset $\{c_i\}$ for each $c_i \in \mathscr{C}_i$, and $\mathscr{P}_i$ is a set of probability measures on $\mathscr{A}_i$ that contains every one-point measure. Moreover, $\mathscr{P}^* = \mathscr{P}_1 \times \cdots \times \mathscr{P}_n$, and c_i^* denotes the measure in $\mathscr{P}_i$ that assigns probability 1 to $\{c_i\}$. As usual, $(c_1, \ldots, c_n) \succ (d_1, \ldots, d_n)$ means that $(c_1^*, \ldots, c_n^*) \succ (d_1^*, \ldots, d_n^*)$. Additional notation will be specified as we proceed.

8.1. AXIOMS WITH FINITE ADDITIVITY

The basic structural axiom that will be used for the case in which not all measures in $\mathscr{P}_i$ are assumed to be countably additive is an extension of A0.2 in Section 3.2. Because this extension uses conditional preference intervals from the $\mathscr{C}_i$ we shall let

$$\mathscr{P}_{(i)} = \mathscr{P}_1 \times \cdots \times \mathscr{P}_{i-1} \times \mathscr{P}_{i+1} \times \cdots \times \mathscr{P}_n$$

with $p_{(i)}$ a generic element in $\mathscr{P}_{(i)}$. For convenience, we often write $p = (p_1, \ldots, p_n)$ as $(p_i, p_{(i)})$, where $p_{(i)} = (p_1, \ldots, p_{i-1}, p_{i+1}, \ldots, p_n)$. For a given $p_{(i)} \in \mathscr{P}_{(i)}$, $\succ$ on $\mathscr{P}^*$ induces a conditional preference relation $(\succ, p_{(i)})$ on $\mathscr{P}_i$ in the natural manner: $p_i(\succ, p_{(i)})q_i$ iff $(p_i, p_{(i)}) \succ (q_i, p_{(i)})$. A subset A_i of $\mathscr{C}_i$ is a *preference interval conditional on* $p_{(i)} \in \mathscr{P}_{(i)}$ if $d_i \in A_i$ whenever $c_i, e_i \in A_i$ and $(c_i^*, p_{(i)}) \succsim (d_i^*, p_{(i)})$ and $(d_i^*, p_{(i)}) \succsim (e_i^*, p_{(i)})$. Furthermore, $A_i \subseteq \mathscr{C}_i$ is called a *conditional preference interval in* $\mathscr{C}_i$ if there is a $p_{(i)} \in \mathscr{P}_{(i)}$ for which A_i is a preference interval conditional on $p_{(i)}$.

As in Chapter 3, $\mathscr{P}_i$ is closed under finite convex combinations if $\lambda p_i + (1 - \lambda)q_i \in \mathscr{P}_i$ whenever p_i, $q_i \in \mathscr{P}_i$ and $\lambda \in [0, 1]$, and $\mathscr{P}_i$ is closed under the formation of condition measures if $p_{iA} \in \mathscr{P}_i$ whenever $A \in \mathscr{A}_i$, $p_i \in \mathscr{P}_i$ and $p_i(A) > 0$, where $p_{iA}(B) = p_i(A \cap B)/p_i(A)$ for all $B \in \mathscr{A}_i$.

Our extension of A0.2 for the multilinear case is

E0.   *For each $i \in \{1, \dots, n\}$, $\mathscr{A}_i$ contains every conditional preference interval in $\mathscr{C}_i$, and $\mathscr{P}_i$ is closed under finite convex combinations and under the formation of conditional measures. Moreover, $n \geq 2$.*

Along with E0 and E1, E2 and E3 for $\succ$ on $\mathscr{P}^*$, we shall use two more axioms that are related to A4 and A5 in Section 3.2. The first of these mimics A4 for each i:

E4.   *If $i \in \{1, \dots, n\}$, p_i, $q_i \in \mathscr{P}_i$, $p_{(i)} \in \mathscr{P}_{(i)}$, $A \in \mathscr{A}_i$ and $p_i(A) = 1$, then $(p_i, p_{(i)}) \succsim (q_i, p_{(i)})$ if $(c_i^*, p_{(i)}) \succ (q_i, p_{(i)})$ for all $c_i \in A$, and $(q_i, p_{(i)}) \succsim \succsim (p_i, p_{(i)})$ if $(q_i, p_{(i)}) \succ (c_i^*, p_{(i)})$ for all $c_i \in A$.*

The first part of this axiom says that, with $p_{(i)}$ fixed, if c_i is preferred to the measure q_i for all c_i in an $\mathscr{A}_i$-measurable subset of $\mathscr{C}_i$ on which p_i has probability 1, then p_i as a whole is conditionally as preferable as q_i. Generally speaking, E4 is an appealing dominance principle.

Our final axiom for the case at hand uses conditional preference intervals defined as follows:

$$\langle p_{(i)}; c_i \rangle = \{d_i \in \mathscr{C}_i : (c_i^*, p_{(i)}) \succ (d_i^*, p_{(i)})\}$$

$$\langle p_{(i)}; c_i] = \{d_i \in \mathscr{C}_i : (c_i^*, p_{(i)}) \succsim (d_i^*, p_{(i)})\}$$

$$(c_i; p_{(i)}\rangle = \{d_i \in \mathscr{C}_i : (d_i^*, p_{(i)}) \succ (c_i^*, p_{(i)})\}$$

$$[c_i; p_{(i)}\rangle = \{d_i \in \mathscr{C}_i : (d_i^*, p_{(i)}) \succsim (c_i^*, p_{(i)})\}.$$

For example, $d_i \in \langle p_{(i)}; c_i \rangle$ if the n-tuple $(c_i^*, p_{(i)})$ is preferred to the n-tuple $(d_i^*, p_{(i)})$.

E5.   (a) *If $i \in \{1, \dots, n\}$, $p_{(i)} \in \mathscr{P}_{(i)}$, p_{i0} and p_{i1} are simple measures in $\mathscr{P}_i$ for which $(p_{i1}, p_{(i)}) \succ (p_{i0}, p_{(i)})$, and if $p_i \in \mathscr{P}_i$ is such that*

$$p_i([c_i; p_{(i)}\rangle) = 1 \quad \text{for some} \quad c_i \in \mathscr{C}_i,$$

$$p_i((c_i; p_{(i)}\rangle) > 0 \quad \text{for every} \quad c_i \in \mathscr{C}_i,$$

$$p_i(\langle p_{(i)}; c_i]) > 0 \quad \text{for some} \quad c_i \in \mathscr{C}_i,$$

then there is a $d_i \in \mathscr{C}_i$ with $A = (d_i; p_{(i)}\rangle$ such that

$$p_i(A)(d_i^*, p_{(i)}) + [1 - p_i(A)](p_{i1}, p_{(i)}) \succsim$$

$$\succsim p_i(A)(p_{iA}, p_{(i)}) + [1 - p_i(A)](p_{i0}, p_{(i)});$$

(b) *If $i \in \{1, \ldots, n\}$, $p_{(i)} \in \mathscr{P}_{(i)}$, p_{i0} and p_{i1} are simple measures in $\mathscr{P}_i$ for which $(p_{i1}, p_{(i)}) \succ (p_{i0}, p_{(i)})$, and if $p_i \in \mathscr{P}_i$ is such that*

$$p_i(\langle p_{(i)}; c_i]) = 1 \quad for \ some \quad c_i \in \mathscr{C}_i,$$

$$p_i(\langle p_{(i)}; c_i)) > 0 \quad for \ every \quad c_i \in \mathscr{C}_i,$$

$$p_i([c_i; p_{(i)}\rangle) > 0 \quad for \ some \quad c_i \in \mathscr{C}_i,$$

then there is an $e_i \in \mathscr{C}_i$ with $B = \langle p_{(i)}; e_i)$ such that

$$p_i(B)(p_{iB}, p_{(i)}) + [1 - p_i(B)](p_{i1}, p_{(i)}) \succsim$$

$$\succsim p_i(B)(e_i^*, p_{(i)}) + [1 - p_i(B)](p_{i0}, p_{(i)}).$$

Like similar axioms used earlier, E5 is rather long-winded, but it is essential in deriving multilinear expected utilities in the presence of finite additivity without forcing u to be bounded. Given fixed $p_{(i)}$, the three hypotheses for p_i in E5(a) say that it has a conditional preference interval support that is bounded below but unbounded above, and that it has positive probability on a bounded-above preference interval. Given the hypotheses of E5(a), including the conditional preference of p_{i1} to p_{i0}, its conclusion says that there is some open and unbounded-above interval $A = (d_i; p_{(i)}\rangle$ such that, with $\lambda = p_i(A)$, the mixture $\lambda d_i^* + (1 - \lambda)p_{i1}$ (with $p_{(i)}$ fixed) is as preferable as the mixture $\lambda p_{iA} + (1 - \lambda)p_{i0}$. This is a straightforward extension of A5(a) to the conditional context. As discussed in Fishburn (1980), E5(a) is a type of Archimedean axiom that for a given i comes into play only if $u(\cdot, p_{(i)})$ on $\mathscr{P}_i$ is unbounded above, and in this case $p_i(A)$, or λ, must approach 0 as d_i becomes more desirable. When this occurs, it does not seem unreasonable that some λ sufficiently close to 0 will give $\lambda d_i^* + (1 - \lambda)p_{i1}(\succsim, p_{(i)})\lambda p_{iA} + (1 - \lambda)p_{i0}$.

Axiom E5(b) is the natural dual of E5(a) for measures in $\mathscr{P}_i$ that are unbounded below with respect to conditional preference.

THEOREM 1. *Suppose E0 holds. Then there is a real valued function u on $\mathscr{C} = \mathscr{C}_1 \times \cdots \times \mathscr{C}_n$ such that $\int_\mathscr{C} u(c_1, \ldots, c_n) \, dp_n(c_n) \ldots dp_1(c_1)$ is well defined* *and finite for all $p \in \mathscr{P}^*$, and such that, for all $p, q \in \mathscr{P}^*$,*

$$p \succ q \quad \text{iff} \quad \int_{\mathscr{C}} u(c) \, dp_n(c_n) \ldots dp_1(c_1) > \int_{\mathscr{C}} u(c) \, dq_n(c_n) \ldots dq_1(c_1),$$

if and only if E1 through E5 hold for $\succ$ on $\mathscr{P}^*$.

This theorem for multilinear expected utility is a more-or-less natural generalization of Theorem 3.2 for ordinary expected utility. It may be noted that, with $p \, T_i \, q$ iff $p_{(i)} = q_{(i)}$, the axioms of Theorem 1 never use a mixture of the form $\lambda p + (1 - \lambda)q$ unless $p \, T_i \, q$ for some i. In particular, the convex combinations in E5 adhere to this restriction along with the mixtures for E2 and E3 in Section 7.2.

In view of Theorem 7.1, it should be obvious that u on $\mathscr{C}$ in Theorem 1 above is unique up to a positive affine transformation. Moreover, the order of integration in the theorem is immaterial, as will be evident from the proof that appears in Section 3.

8.2. AXIOMS WITH COUNTABLE ADDITIVITY

When each $\mathscr{A}_i$ is assumed to be a Borel algebra of subsets of $\mathscr{C}_i$, and all measures in $\mathscr{P}_i$ are presumed to be countably additive, axioms E4 and E5 can be replaced by the following conditions.

E4*.   If $i \in \{1, \ldots, n\}$, $p_{(i)} \in \mathscr{P}_{(i)}$, $p_i \in \mathscr{P}_i$, $A \in \mathscr{A}_i$, $p_i(A) = 1$, and $d_i \in \mathscr{C}_i$,
then $(p_i, p_{(i)}) \succsim (d_i^*, p_{(i)})$ if $(c_i^*, p_{(i)}) \succsim (d_i^*, p_{(i)})$ for all $c_i \in A$, and
$(d_i^*, p_{(i)}) \succsim (p_i, p_{(i)})$ if $(d_i^*, p_{(i)}) \succsim (c_i^*, p_{(i)})$ for all $c_i \in A$.

E5*.   If $i \in \{1, \ldots, n\}$, $p_{(i)} \in \mathscr{P}_{(i)}$, $p_i \in \mathscr{P}_i$, and p_{io} is a simple measure in
$\mathscr{P}_i$, then $(p_{iA}, p_{(i)}) \succsim (p_{io}, p_{(i)})$ for some $d_i \in \mathscr{C}_i$ with $A = \langle p_{(i)} ; d_i]$
if $(p_i, p_{(i)}) \succ (p_{io}, p_{(i)})$, and $(p_{io}, p_{(i)}) \succsim (p_{iB}, p_{(i)})$ for some $e_i \in \mathscr{C}_i$
with $B = [e_i ; p_{(i)} \rangle$ if $(p_{io}, p_{(i)}) \succ (p_i, p_{(i)})$.

These axioms are tantamount to A4* and A5* respectively of Section 3.3 applied to conditional preferences on each $\mathscr{P}_i$. Axiom E4* is a dominance axiom for each coordinate, and E5* is an Archimedean axiom for each coordinate that forces extreme preferences to be 'well behaved'. For example, the last part of E5* says that if $p_{io}(\succ, p_{(i)})p_i$, then p_{io} is at least as preferable as a truncation p_{iB} of p_i so that the preference for p_{io} over p_i is not due solely to 'extremely undesirable' elements in $\mathscr{C}_i$. Axiom E5* requires $p_i(A) > 0$ and $p_i(B) > 0$ for the conditional measures p_{iA} and p_{iB} to be well defined, and the existence of such A and B is guaranteed by the stronger structural hypotheses that are used in the present case.

THEOREM 2. *Suppose E0 holds and, for each i, $\mathscr{A}_i$ is a Borel algebra and all measures in $\mathscr{P}_i$ are countably additive. Then the conclusion of Theorem 1 holds when E4 and E5 are replaced there by E4* and E5*.*

Comments on the proof of Theorem 2 are given in the next section.

8.3. PROOFS

Almost all the developments needed to prove Theorems 1 and 2 have been set forth in previous chapters. The necessity of the axioms in each case is easily demonstrated: in particular, see the subsection on necessity in Section 3.5 with regard to E4, E4*, E5, and E5*.

The sufficiency proof for Theorem 1 goes as follows. Assume that E0 through E5 hold for $\succ$ on $\mathscr{P}^* = \mathscr{P}_1 \times \cdots \times \mathscr{P}_n$. Since $\mathscr{P}^*$ is the product of mixture sets, Theorem 7.1 implies that there is an order-preserving multilinear function u on $\mathscr{P}^*$ that is unique up to a positive affine transformation. Given any $i \in \{1, \ldots, n\}$ and any $(p_i, p_{(i)}) \in \mathscr{P}^*$, it follows from Theorem 3.2 applied to the ith coordinate here that

$$u(p_i, p_{(i)}) = \int_{\mathscr{C}_i} u(c_i^*, p_{(i)}) \, dp_i(c_i).$$

Therefore, for any $p = (p_1, \ldots, p_n)$ in $\mathscr{P}^*$,

$$u(p) = \int_{\mathscr{C}_1} u(c_1^*, p_2, \ldots, p_n) \, dp_1(c_1)$$

$$= \int_{\mathscr{C}_1} \left\{ \int_{\mathscr{C}_2} u(c_1^*, c_2^*, p_3, \ldots, p_n) \, dp_2(c_2) \right\} dp_1(c_1)$$

$$\vdots$$

$$= \int_{\mathscr{C}_1} \cdots \int_{\mathscr{C}_n} u(c_1^*, \ldots, c_n^*) \, dp_n(c_n) \cdots dp_1(c_1).$$

The desired conclusion follows with $u(c) = u(c^*)$. Obviously, any order of integration could be used in the multiple integral.

The sufficiency proof for Theorem 2 is similar. In this case, Theorem 3.4 is used instead of Theorem 3.2.

PART II

SUBJECTIVE EXPECTED UTILITY

CHAPTER 9

SUBJECTIVE LINEAR UTILITY ON
PRODUCTS OF MIXTURE SETS

In Part II of the book, S is a set of states of the world, and $\mathscr{S}$ is a Boolean algebra of subsets of S. We refer to $A \in \mathscr{S}$ as an *event*. As usual, $\emptyset$ will denote the empty event. In general, we reserve the phrase *null event* to denote any event that the individual believes to be impossible, i.e. an event that cannot possibly obtain or which the individual feels cannot contain a state that describes the true nature of the world about which the individual is uncertain.

The individual's uncertainty about the world will often be characterized numerically by a finitely additive probability measure P on $\mathscr{S}$, with $P(A)$ the individual's personal or subjective probability for event A. This measure is not given *a priori*, but is derived from the axioms for $\succ$. Null events are usually defined on the basis of the symmetric complement $\sim$ of $\succ$, and it turns out that A is null if and only if $P(A) = 0$.

Our interpretations in much of Part II recognize two potentially different sources of uncertainty. The first of these is S, which we presume is so formulated that the individual believes that one and only one state in S obtains or will obtain. The second source arises from chance mechanisms that generate the 'extraneous scaling probabilities' used in our formulation of certain types of gambles and acts. As in Part I, these probabilities are taken as given and, unlike the $P(A)$, appear explicitly in the axioms. Apart from the extraneous scaling probabilities, which are often denoted $\lambda, \alpha, \beta, \dots$, it is tacitly assumed that S covers all possibilities about which the individual is uncertain. Moreover, by means of the axioms, it is assumed that the individual's degrees of belief in the various events, i.e. his $P(A)$'s, do not depend on the acts. In other words, his subjective probability for event A will be the same whether he 'does' f or 'does' g.

Apart from the final chapter, where $\succ$ is applied to $\mathscr{M} \times (\mathscr{S} \setminus \{\emptyset\})$, we shall apply $\succ$ to a set of functions $f, g, \dots$, each of which assigns an element in a mixture set $\mathscr{M}(s)$ to each state s in S. The extraneous-scaling-probability interpretation comes into play when we view $\mathscr{M}(s)$ as the set $\mathscr{P}_0(\mathscr{C}(s))$ of simple probability measures on the set $\mathscr{C}(s)$ of consequences that are relevant for state s. In this case, the probabilities used for the gambles in $\mathscr{P}_0(\mathscr{C}(s))$ are to be thought of as being generated by chance mechanisms such as roulette wheels, balanced dice, and so forth.

An act f that assigns a gamble over $\mathscr{C}(s)$ to each state $s \in S$ is sometimes referred to as a *horse lottery* (Anscombe and Aumann, 1963; Fishburn, 1970). The flavor of this language is imparted by a horse race in which the states correspond to the horses: state s obtains iff horse s wins the race. An act or horse lottery f assigns a gamble $p(s) \in \mathscr{P}_0(\mathscr{C}(s))$ to each s. If the individual chooses f then things proceed as follows. The race is run and the winner, say s', is determined. A random device whose probabilities correspond to those for $p(s')$ is then activated to determine a particular $c \in \mathscr{C}(s')$ according to the given probabilities. For example, if $p(s')$ assigns probability 1/3 to "win \$10" and probability 2/3 to "get a free pass to the track for the next week", then the individual either gets the \$ 10 or the free pass according to the stated probabilities.

Since our basic concern for decision theory in the states context is with acts that assign sure consequences (rather than nondegenerate gambles) to the states, it should be noted that extraneous scaling probabilities are used merely to provide sufficient structure for constructing well-behaved utilities and subjective probabilities in the subjective expected utility models. Savage (1954) avoids this approach by postulating very rich structures for S and $\mathscr{S}$. Indeed, as Savage himself recognized, our approach can be embedded within his formulation by forming a new set of states that combine S with events associated with chance mechanisms. Then P applies to the new set, and the individual's subjective probabilities for events in (the original) $\mathscr{S}$ can be recovered from P. Related comments on this point are given by Fishburn (1981).

In the present chapter, we shall focus on countable state sets. The next two sections work with $\mathscr{M}^* = \mathscr{M}_1 \times \cdots \times \mathscr{M}_n$, and Section 3 considers $\mathscr{M}^\infty = \mathscr{M} \times \mathscr{M} \times \cdots$. With $\mathscr{M}(s) = \mathscr{M}$ for all s, the next chapter generalizes our approach to arbitrary state sets.

9.1. ADDITIVE LINEAR UTILITIES

This section discusses the theorem advertised in the first paragraph of Section 7.1. The theorem is a basic result for additive linear utilities that does not involve subjective probabilities as such but which underlies later developments in Part II. Subjective probabilities will appear in the next section.

With $\mathscr{M}^* = \mathscr{M}_1 \times \cdots \times \mathscr{M}_n$, we shall say here that i *is null* if $x \sim y$

whenever $x_j = y_j$ for all $j \neq i$. Thus, i is null if a change in the ith component of $x = (x_1, \ldots, x_n)$ does not affect preference. The following theorem is a direct generalization of Theorem 2.1; its axioms are stated in Section 2.2; its proof appears later in Section 4.

THEOREM 1. *Suppose* $\mathscr{M}^* = \mathscr{M}_1 \times \cdots \times \mathscr{M}_n$ *and each* $\mathscr{M}_i$ *is a mixture set. Then the following three statements are mutually equivalent*:

(a) A1, A2, *and* A3 *hold for* $\succ$ *on* $\mathscr{M}^*$;
(b) B1, B2, *and* B3 *hold for* $\succ$ *on* $\mathscr{M}^*$;
(c) *For each* $i \in \{1, \ldots, n\}$ *there is a linear function* u_i *on* $\mathscr{M}_i$ *such that, for all* $x, y \in \mathscr{M}^*$,

$$x \succ y \quad iff \quad \sum_{i=1}^{n} u_i(x_i) > \sum_{i=1}^{n} u_i(y_i).$$

Given (c), u_i *is constant on* $\mathscr{M}_i$ *if an only if* i *is null, and linear functions* v_i *on the* $\mathscr{M}_i$ *satisfy* (c) *in place of the* u_i *if and only if there are numbers* $a > 0$ *and* $b_1, \ldots, b_n$ *such that, for all* i *and all* $x_i \in \mathscr{M}_i$,

$$v_i(x_i) = au_i(x_i) + b_i.$$

The uniqueness assertion which concludes the theorem says that – in terms defined after Theorem 6.2 – the u_i for (c) are unique up to similar positive affine transformations. In a sense, this is the key to the emergence of subjective probabilities for the various i in the next section, where we replace u_i by $P(\{i\})u$ or, more simply by $\rho_i u$ with $\sum \rho_i = 1$. Since u_i is constant iff i is null, null states will be taken account of later by $\rho_i = 0$.

Suppose that $\mathscr{M}_i = \mathscr{P}_0(\mathscr{C}_i)$, where $\mathscr{C}_i$ is a set of consequences relevant to i. Then, with E denoting expectation as defined in Section 3.1, and with $u_i(c_i) = u_i(x_i)$ when x_i assigns probability 1 to c_i, the additive form in Theorem 1(c) gives

$$\sum_{i=1}^{n} u_i(x_i) = \sum_{i=1}^{n} E(u_i, x_i).$$

When x and y in (c) stand for basic acts of the form $c = (c_1, \ldots, c_n)$ and $d = (d_1, \ldots, d_n)$, where $c_i \in \mathscr{C}_i$ is the consequence that occurs when c is used and state i obtains, we have

$$c \succ d \quad iff \quad \sum_{i=1}^{n} u_i(c_i) > \sum_{i=1}^{n} u_i(d_i),$$

which of course is formally the same as the representation for preferences between consequences formulated as n-tuples in Theorem 6.2. As explained in Chapter 7, however, the application of $\succ$ differs significantly in the two contexts, for in Chapter 6 we took $\succ$ on $\mathcal{P}_0(\mathcal{C}_1 \times \cdots \times \mathcal{C}_n)$ whereas $\succ$ is applied to $\mathcal{P}_0(\mathcal{C}_1) \times \cdots \times \mathcal{P}_0(\mathcal{C}_n)$ in the present context.

Theorem 1 is stated in a generality that leaves open the interpretation of the different i. In Chapter 7, i referred to a player in a game situation (in the prevailing interpretation used there), while now we intend to view i as a state. Because of this change, a somewhat different reading of the axioms results. In particular, our argument against linearity of u towards the end of Section 7.1 in the game-theoretic setting is an argument against A2 or B2 when Theorem 1 is viewed in that setting. However, these independence axioms seem much more reasonable when $\{1, \ldots, n\}$ is a set of states of the world. For example, if you prefer (x_1, x_2) to (y_1, y_2) in a two-horse race with $S = \{1, 2\}$, then it seems most likely that you will also prefer $\frac{1}{2}(x_1, x_2) + \frac{1}{2}(z_1, z_2) = (\frac{1}{2}x_1 + \frac{1}{2}z_1, \frac{1}{2}x_2 + \frac{1}{2}z_2)$ to $\frac{1}{2}(y_1, y_2) + \frac{1}{2}(z_1, z_2) = (\frac{1}{2}y_1 + \frac{1}{2}z_1, \frac{1}{2}y_2 + \frac{1}{2}z_2)$.

9.2. SUBJECTIVE PROBABILITIES

In this section we replace $u_i(x_i)$ in the representation of Theorem 1(c) by $\rho_i u(x_i)$, where u is a function on $\bigcup_{i=1}^n \mathcal{M}_i$ that is linear on each $\mathcal{M}_i$ for nonnull i, and ρ_i is the individual's subjective probability for state i. A primary concern in effecting this change is the degree of overlap among the $\mathcal{M}_i$. We illustrate with two extreme cases.

The first extreme case has $\mathcal{M}_i \cap \mathcal{M}_j = \emptyset$ whenever $i \neq j$, so that the $\mathcal{M}_i$ have nothing in common. Because of this, we can define the ρ_i to be any nonnegative numbers that sum to unity, restricted only by $\rho_i > 0$ when i is not null, and let u be defined on $\bigcup \mathcal{M}_i$ so that $u(x_i) = u_i(x_i)/\rho_i$ whenever $\rho_i > 0$. Then, given the representation of Theorem 1(c), we get $x \succ y$ iff $\sum \rho_i u(x_i) > \sum \rho_i u(y_i)$, and no new axioms are needed for this. The obvious shortcoming in this case is that the ρ_i are arbitrary and cannot be said to reflect the individual's beliefs about the likelihoods of the various states obtaining.

The other extreme case has $\mathcal{M}_i = \mathcal{M}_j$ for all i, j, so that the $\mathcal{M}_i$ are identical. In this case, additional axioms are needed to get $u_i = \rho_i u$, and the ρ_i will be unique, subject to $\sum \rho_i = 1$. Although we shall use this approach in later sections, it has one glaring deficiency. Namely, there is no particular reason to suppose that different states have identical consequences, as can be seen by contemplating the possible consequences of a planned winter vacation at a ski resort when $S = \{\text{snow, no snow}\}$. In other words, it would seem to be the rule rather than the exception that, for most realistic decision situations, $\mathscr{C}(s) \neq \mathscr{C}(t)$ when $s \neq t$.

Our approach here will be to take a middle course between the two extremes by requiring enough overlap among the $\mathscr{M}_i$ to produce unique ρ_i without requiring the $\mathscr{M}_i$ to be identical. The requisite overlap is stated in the first of the following two axioms. The second axiom, which is neutral with respect to the overlap question and will be trivially true when the $\mathscr{M}_i$ are mutually disjoint, is an independence axiom among the states. It might also be referred to as an interstate monotonicity axiom.

B4.   *There are $x_*, x^* \in \mathscr{M}_i$ for all i such that $(x^*, \dots, x^*) \succ (x_*, \dots, x_*)$,*

B5.   *For all $i, j \in \{1, \dots, n\}$, all $x \in \mathscr{M}^*$, and all $a, b \in \bigcup \mathscr{M}_i$, if i and j are not null and $a, b \in \mathscr{M}_i \cap \mathscr{M}_j$, then $(x \text{ with } x_i \text{ replaced by } a) \succ$ $\succ (x \text{ with } x_i \text{ replaced by } b)$ iff $(x \text{ with } x_j \text{ replaced by } a) \succ (x \text{ with } x_j \text{ replaced by } b)$.*

To illustrate B5, again consider the horse-race situation with $a = $ "win $ 10" and $b = $ "get a free pass to the track for the next week". Since the horse lotteries $(x$ with x_1 replaced by $a)$ and $(x$ with x_1 replaced by $b)$ yield the same x_i if any horse other than horse 1 wins, a preference judgment between the two should come down to whether the individual would rather have a or b if horse 1 wins. Suppose he prefers a to b. Then, since a comparison between $(x$ with x_2 replaced by $a)$ and $(x$ with x_2 replaced by $b)$ ought to be based on what ensues if horse 2 wins, it is natural to expect that $(x$ with x_2 replaced by $a)$ will be preferred to $(x$ with x_2 replaced by $b)$. Hence the conclusion of B5 is very appealing, except when one of i and j is null and the other is not null. (If you believe that horse 2 has absolutely no chance of winning, then you would presumably be indifferent between x and y when $x_i = y_i$ for all $i \neq 2$.)

THEOREM 2. *Suppose $\mathscr{M}^* = \mathscr{M}_1 \times \cdots \times \mathscr{M}_n$, each $\mathscr{M}_i$ is a mixture set, either A1, A2, and A3 or B1, B2, and B3 hold for $\succ$ on $\mathscr{M}^*$, and B4 and B5 hold. Then there is a real-valued function u on $\bigcup_i \mathscr{M}_i$ that is linear on each $\mathscr{M}_i$ for which i is not null, and ρ_i with $\sum_i \rho_i = 1$ such that, for all $x, y \in \mathscr{M}^*$,*

$$x \succ y \quad \text{iff} \quad \sum_{i=1}^{n} \rho_i u(x_i) > \sum_{i=1}^{n} \rho_i u(y_i),$$

with $\rho_i = 0$ iff i is null. In this representation, the ρ_i are unique and the *restriction of u on the union of the $\mathcal{M}_i$ for which i is not null is unique up to a positive affine transformation.*

Since $\rho_i = 0$ if i is null, we can let u be defined in any way we wish on elements that are in $\mathcal{M}_i$ but no $\mathcal{M}_j$ for $j \neq i$, and this will not affect the representation. Clearly, if $\mathcal{M}_i = \mathcal{P}_0(\mathscr{C}_i)$ for all i, then $\sum \rho_i u(x_i) = \sum \rho_i E(u, x_i)$ when u on $\bigcup \mathscr{C}_i$ is defined in the usual way, and $\sum \rho_i u(c_i)$ is obtained as the subjective expected utility of basic act $(c_1, \ldots, c_n)$.

Given x_* and x^* as in B4, Theorem 2 shows how to determine the relative magnitudes of ρ_i and ρ_j for nonnull states i and j, with $i \neq j$. Let x^1, x^2, and x^3 have $x_k^1 = x_k^2 = x_k^3$ for all $k \notin \{i, j\}$ along with

$$(x_i^1, x_j^1) = (x_*, x_*)$$

$$(x_i^2, x_j^2) = (x^*, x_*)$$

$$(x_i^3, x_j^3) = (x^*, x^*)$$

so that $x^3 \succ x^2 \succ x^1$. Let λ satisfy $x^2 \sim x^3 \lambda x^1$. It then follows from the representation of Theorem 2 that $\rho_i/\rho_j = \lambda/(1 - \lambda)$.

A proof of Theorem 2 appears in Section 4.

9.3. A DENUMERABLE CASE

Before we look at the general S case in the next chapter, we shall consider the denumerable-states situation in which $\succ$ is applied to

$$\mathcal{M}^\infty = \{(x_1, x_2, \ldots) : x_i \in \mathcal{M} \text{ for } i = 1, 2, \ldots \},$$

where $\mathcal{M}$ is a mixture set. Our interest here is in extending the form of Theorem 2 to $\sum_{i=1}^\infty \rho_i u(x_i)$, with $\sum \rho_i = 1$, so that the ρ_i serve as the point probabilities for a countably additive probability measure P on the set of all subsets of $S = \{1, 2, \ldots \}$.

We approach the desired form in two steps, the first of which extends the additive linear form in Theorem 1 for $\mathcal{M}_i = \mathcal{M}$ for $i = 1, \ldots, n$ to $\sum_{i=1}^\infty u_i(x_i)$. The second step then replaces $u_i(x_i)$ by $\rho_i u(x_i)$. The axioms used in both steps are as follows. For B5*, i is *null* if $x \sim y$ whenever $x_j = y_j$ for all $j \neq i$, and in B6

$$x^{(n)} = (x_1, \ldots, x_n, x_0, x_0, \ldots)$$

so that $x^{(n)}$ duplicates x through the nth component and is constant thereafter with $x_i^{(n)} = x_0$ for all $i > n$.

B4*. There are $x_*, x^* \in \mathcal{M}$ such that $(x^*, x^*, \dots) \succ (x_*, x_*, \dots)$,

B5*. For all $i, j \in \{1, 2, \dots\}$, all $x \in \mathcal{M}^\infty$, and all $a, b \in \mathcal{M}$, if i and j are not null then $(x$ with x_i replaced by $a) \succ (x$ with x_i replaced by $b)$ iff $(x$ with x_j replaced by $a) \succ (x$ with x_j replaced by $b)$,

B6. For some $x_0 \in \mathcal{M}$, all $x, y \in \mathcal{M}^\infty$ and all $\lambda < 1$, if $x \succ y$ then there is an $n(\lambda) \in \{1, 2, \dots\}$ such that $x^{(n)} \succsim x \lambda y$ for all $n \geq n(\lambda)$, and if $y \succ x$ then there is an $n(\lambda) \in \{1, 2, \dots\}$ such that $x \lambda y \succsim x^{(n)}$ for all $n \geq n(\lambda)$.

Although the nontriviality axiom B4* is not strictly necessary for the desired representation, both B5* and B6 are implied by the representation. The new axiom, B6, is a continuity-convergence condition which has the effect of forcing $U(x^{(n)})$ to $U(x)$ as $n \to \infty$. Here U is an order-preserving linear function on the mixture set $\mathcal{M}^\infty$ as obtained through A1, A2, and A3 applied to $\succ$ on $\mathcal{M}^\infty$. If $z \succ x \succ y$ and $\lambda < 1$, our earlier axioms imply that $x \lambda z \succ x \succ x \lambda y$, with $x \lambda z$ and $x \lambda y$ 'nearly indifferent' to x if λ is nearly 1. Axiom B6 then implies that $x \lambda z \succsim x^{(n)} \succsim x \lambda y$ for all suitably large n. Thus B6 asserts that $x^{(n)}$ will be virtually indifferent to x when n is large.

One would expect B6 to hold in the following type of situation. A (possibly loaded) die is to be rolled until a 1 or 6 appears on the up face. State i obtains if the first 1 or 6 occurs on the ith roll. Suppose $\mathcal{C}$ is a finite set of prizes or a bounded interval of monetary prizes, and $\mathcal{M} = \mathcal{P}_0(\mathcal{C})$. Take x_0 as the "win nothing, lose nothing" consequence in $\mathcal{C}$. Then it seems quite reasonable that, if you prefer x to y and if $\lambda < 1$, you will prefer $(x_1, \dots, x_n, x_0, x_0, \dots)$ to $x \lambda y$ for large n.

The first step in our two-step approach uses B6 but not B5* since the additive linear form $\sum u_i(x_i)$ makes no ordering presumption about how the different u_i on $\mathcal{M}$ might be related to one another. To forestall uncertainty about the meaning of $\sum_{i=1}^\infty u_i(x_i)$, we note that this countable sum is defined as (1) the real number r if for every $\varepsilon > 0$ there is an $n(\varepsilon) \in \{1, 2, \dots\}$ such that $|\sum_{i=1}^n u_i(x_i) - r| < \varepsilon$ for all $n \geq n(\varepsilon)$, or as (2) ∞ if for every real number M there is an $n(M)$ such that $\sum_{i=1}^n u_i(x_i) > M$ for all $n \geq n(M)$, or as (3) $-\infty$ if for every real number M there is an $n(M)$ such that $\sum_{i=1}^n u_i(x_i) < M$ for all $n \geq n(M)$. If none of (1), (2), and (3) is true, then $\sum_{i=1}^\infty u_i(x_i)$ is not well defined.

THEOREM 3. Suppose $\mathcal{M}$ is a mixture set and B1, B2, B3, and B6 hold for $\succ$ on $\mathcal{M}^\infty$. Then for each $i \in \{1, 2, \dots\}$ there is a linear function u_i on

$\mathscr{M}$ such that $\sum_{i=1}^{\infty} u_i(x_i)$ is well defined and finite for all $x \in \mathscr{M}^{\infty}$, and such that, for all $x, y \in \mathscr{M}^{\infty}$,

$$x \succ y \quad \text{iff} \quad \sum_{i=1}^{\infty} u_i(x_i) > \sum_{i=1}^{\infty} u_i(y_i).$$

Moreover, u_i is constant if and only if i is null, and linear v_i on $\mathscr{M}$ satisfy the representation in place of the u_i if and only if there are numbers $a > 0$ and b_i with $\sum_{i=1}^{\infty} b_i$ well defined and finite such that, for all i and all $x_i \in \mathscr{M}$, $v_i(x_i) = au_i(x_i) + b_i$.

Since $\sum u_i(x_i)$ is finite for all x, almost all u_i have images $u_i(\mathscr{M})$ within a small neighborhood of 0, with $u_i(\mathscr{M}) \to \{0\}$ as $i \to \infty$. This is reflected by the boundedness statement in the following theorem.

THEOREM 4. Suppose the hypotheses of Theorem 3 hold along with B4* and B5*. Then there is a linear function u on $\mathscr{M}$, and ρ_i for $i = 1, 2, \dots$ with $\sum_{i=1}^{\infty} \rho_i = 1$ and $\rho_i = 0$ iff i is null, such that $\sum_{i=1}^{\infty} \rho_i u(x_i)$ is well defined and finite for all $x \in \mathscr{M}^{\infty}$, and such that, for all $x, y \in \mathscr{M}^{\infty}$,

$$x \succ y \quad \text{iff} \quad \sum_{i=1}^{\infty} \rho_i u(x_i) > \sum_{i=1}^{\infty} \rho_i u(y_i).$$

Moreover, in this representation the ρ_i are unique, u is unique up to a positive affine transformation, and u is bounded if $\rho_i > 0$ for more than a finite number of i.

Let $P(\{i\}) = \rho_i$. Then the ρ_i can be viewed as the point probabilities of a countably additive probability measure P on the set of all subsets of $S = \{1, 2, \dots\}$. If we then define u_x on S for $x \in \mathscr{M}^{\infty}$ by $u_x(i) = u(x_i)$, the representation of Theorem 4 can be expressed as

$$x \succ y \quad \text{iff} \quad E(u_x, P) > E(u_y, P).$$

We shall use essentially this format in the next chapter for arbitrary S. Given the preceding representation for $S = \{1, 2, \dots\}$, it should be noted that it does *not* imply the representation of Theorem 4. For example, since P generally denotes a finitely additive probability measure, it could happen that $P(A) = 0$ for all finite A included in S, in which case if the ρ_i were defined by $P(\{i\})$ they would all equal 0.

The key axiom of Theorem 4 that renders P countably additive, and thus allows one to use either the ρ_i or P representation, is the continuity condition B6. Although we shall comment on countable additivity in the next chapter, our basic axiom system will not use a correspondent of B6.

Proofs for Theorems 3 and 4 are given in Section 5.

9.4. PROOFS OF THEOREMS 1 AND 2

Assume throughout this section that each $\mathcal{M}_i$ is a mixture set and $\mathcal{M}^* = = \mathcal{M}_1 \times \cdots \times \mathcal{M}_n$. We prove Theorem 1 first, then Theorem 2.

Since $\mathcal{M}^*$ is a mixture set, Theorem 2.1 says that (a) and (b) of Theorem 1 are equivalent, and both are equivalent to the existence of linear U on $\mathcal{M}^*$ that preserves $\succ$ and is unique up to a positive affine transformation. If (c) of Theorem 1 holds, then U defined by $U(x) = \sum u_i(x_i)$ is linear and preserves $\succ$. Conversely, given order-preserving and linear U, fix $z \in \mathcal{M}^*$, let $x^i = (z_1, \ldots, z_{i-1}, x_i, z_{i+1}, \ldots, z_n)$, and define u_i on $\mathcal{M}_i$ by

$$u_i(x_i) = U(x^i) - \frac{n-1}{n} U(z).$$

We show that u_i is linear, and $\sum u_i = U$. Since U is linear,

$$u_i(x_i \lambda y_i) = U(x^i \lambda y^i) - \frac{n-1}{n} U(z)$$

$$= \lambda U(x^i) + (1 - \lambda) U(y^i) - \frac{n-1}{n} U(z)$$

$$= \lambda \left[U(x^i) - \frac{n-1}{n} U(z) \right] + (1 - \lambda) \left[U(y^i) - \frac{n-1}{n} U(z) \right]$$

$$= \lambda u_i(x_i) + (1 - \lambda) u_i(y_i),$$

so that u_i is linear. Since $\sum u_i(x_i) = \sum U(x^i) - (n-1)U(z)$ by the definition of u_i and summation, $\sum u_i(x_i) = U(x)$ if and only if

$$\sum \frac{1}{n} U(x^i) = \frac{1}{n} U(x) + \frac{n-1}{n} U(z).$$

This is obviously true for $n \leq 2$. For larger n we have, by the mixture-set operations and linearity of U,

$$\sum_{i=1}^{n} \frac{1}{n} U(x^i)$$

$$= \frac{2}{n} \left[\tfrac{1}{2} U(x^1) + \tfrac{1}{2} U(x^2) \right] + \sum_{i=3}^{n} \frac{1}{n} U(x^i)$$

$$= \frac{2}{n} U(x^1 \tfrac{1}{2} x^2) + \sum_{i=3}^{n} \frac{1}{n} U(x^i)$$

$$= \frac{2}{n} U((x_1 \tfrac{1}{2} z_1, x_2 \tfrac{1}{2} z_2, z_3, \ldots, z_n)) + \sum_{i=3}^{n} \frac{1}{n} U(x^i)$$

$$= \frac{3}{n} \left[\tfrac{2}{3} U(x_1 \tfrac{1}{2} z_1, x_2 \tfrac{1}{2} z_2, z_3, \ldots, z_n) + \tfrac{1}{3} U(x^3) \right] + \sum_{i \geq 4} \frac{1}{n} U(x^i)$$

$$= \frac{3}{n} \left[U((x_1 \tfrac{1}{2} z_1) \tfrac{2}{3} z_1, (x_2 \tfrac{1}{2} z_2) \tfrac{2}{3} z_2, z_3 \tfrac{2}{3} x_3, z_4, \ldots, z_n) \right] +$$

$$+ \sum_{i \geq 4} \frac{1}{n} U(x^i)$$

$$= \frac{3}{n} U(x_1 \tfrac{1}{3} z_1, x_2 \tfrac{1}{3} z_2, x_3 \tfrac{1}{3} z_3, z_4, \ldots, z_n) + \sum_{i \geq 4} \frac{1}{n} U(x^i)$$

$$\vdots$$

$$= U\left(x_1 \frac{1}{n} z_1, \ldots, x_n \frac{1}{n} z_n \right)$$

$$= U\left(x \frac{1}{n} z \right)$$

$$= \frac{1}{n} U(x) + \frac{n-1}{n} U(z).$$

Given (c), it is obvious from the definition that u_i is constant on $\mathcal{M}_i$ if and only if i is null. If linear v_i on $\mathcal{M}_i$ also satisfy (c) then, with $U(x) = \sum u_i(x_i)$ and $V(x) = \sum v_i(x_i)$, $V = aU + b$ with $a > 0$ by Theorem 2.1. With all x_j fixed for $j \neq i$, it follows that $v_i = au_i + b_i$. Since these affine transformations preserve $x \succ y$ iff $\sum v_i(x_i) > \sum v_i(y_i)$, given (c), the u_i are unique up to similar positive affine transformations. This completes the proof of Theorem 1.

For Theorem 2, we begin with the representation in Theorem 1(c) and let $N = \{i : i \in \{1, \ldots, n\}$ and i is *not* null$\}$. By B4, $N \neq \emptyset$. If the representation of Theorem 2 is to hold then $\rho_i u$ must be a positive affine transformation of u_i on $\mathcal{M}_i$. Moreover, since u is not constant on $\mathcal{M}_i$, with $u(x^*) > u(x_*)$ by B4, we require $\rho_i = 0$ iff i is null.

If N has only one element i, the desired result follows with $\rho_i = 1$, $u(t) = u_i(t)$ for all $t \in \mathcal{M}_i$, and $\rho_j = 0$ for all $j \neq i$. Suppose henceforth that $|N| \geq 2$. Given $i, j \in N$, let $\mathcal{M}_{ij} = \mathcal{M}_i \cap \mathcal{M}_j$. According to B5, $u_i(t) > u_i(t')$ iff $u_j(t) > u_j(t')$ for all $t, t' \in \mathcal{M}_{ij}$. It then follows from B4 and Theorem 2.1(c), in view of the fact that $\mathcal{M}_{ij}$ is a mixture set, that there is a unique $r_{ij} > 0$ such that

$$u_i(t) - u_i(x_*) = r_{ij}[u_j(t) - u_j(x_*)] \quad \text{for all} \quad t \in \mathcal{M}_{ij}.$$

Fix $k \in N$ and define ρ_i on N and u on $\bigcup_N \mathcal{M}_i$ by

$$\rho_i = r_{ik} / \sum_{i \in N} r_{ik}$$

$$u(t) = [u_i(t) - u_i(x_*)] / \rho_i \quad \text{for all} \quad t \in \mathcal{M}_i$$

for each $i \in N$. For completeness, let $\rho_j = 0$ when $j \notin N$, and set $u(t) = 0$ when $t \notin \bigcup_N \mathcal{M}_i$. To show that u is well defined on $\bigcup_N \mathcal{M}_i$, we need to verify

$$[u_i(t) - u_i(x_*)]/r_{ik} = [u_j(t) - u_j(x_*)]/r_{jk}$$

whenever $i, j \in N$ and $t \in \mathcal{M}_{ij}$. By the characterization for r_{ij}, along with $u(x^*) > u(x_*)$, we have $r_{ik}/r_{jk} = ([u_i(x^*) - u_i(x_*)]/[u_k(x^*) - u_k(x_*)])/ ([u_j(x^*) - u_j(x_*)]/[u_k(x^*) - u_k(x_*)]) = [u_i(x^*) - u_i(x_*)]/[u_j(x^*) - u_j(x_*)] = = r_{ij}$ which, in conjunction with $u_i(t) - u_i(x_*) = r_{ij}[u_j(t) - u_j(x_*)]$, validates the preceding equality. Substitution then gives

$$\sum_{i=1}^{n} u_i(x_i) > \sum_{i=1}^{n} u_i(y_i)$$

$$\text{iff} \quad \sum_N u_i(x_i) > \sum_N u_i(y_i)$$

$$\text{iff} \quad \sum_N [\rho_i u(x_i) + u_i(x_*)] > \sum_N [\rho_i u(y_i) + u_i(x_*)]$$

$$\text{iff} \quad \sum_N \rho_i u(x_i) > \sum_N \rho_i u(y_i)$$

$$\text{iff} \quad \sum_{i=1}^{n} \rho_i u(x_i) > \sum_{i=1}^{n} \rho_i u(y_i),$$

as desired for Theorem 2.

By definition, u is linear on each $\mathcal{M}_i$ for $i \in N$. It follows easily from $u(x^*) > u(x_*)$ and the uniqueness assertions of Theorem 1 that the ρ_i with $\sum \rho_i = 1$ are unique, and that u on $\bigcup_N \mathcal{M}_i$ is unique up to a positive affine transformation.

9.5. PROOFS OF THEOREMS 3 AND 4

As in Theorem 3, assume that B1, B2, B3, and B6 hold for $\succ$ on $\mathcal{M}^\infty$. By Theorem 2.1, let U be a linear order-preserving function on $\mathcal{M}^\infty$.

In addition, let $x_0 \in \mathscr{M}$ be as supposed in B6, transform U linearly so that $U(x_0, x_0, \dots) = 0$, and for every $i \in \{1, 2, \dots\}$ and every $t \in \mathscr{M}$, define linear u_i on $\mathscr{M}$ by

$$u_i(t) = U(x_0, \dots, x_0, t, x_0, x_0, \dots),$$

where t is the ith component of $(x_0, \dots, x_0, t, x_0, x_0, \dots)$. By definition, $u_i(x_0) = 0$ for all i. Moreover, since for any $x \in \mathscr{M}^\infty$ the mixture set axioms imply that

$$(x_1, \dots, x_i, x_0, x_0, \dots) \tfrac{1}{2} (x_0, \dots, x_0, x_{i+1}, x_0, x_0, \dots)$$
$$= (x_1, \dots, x_i, x_{i+1}, x_0, x_0, \dots) \tfrac{1}{2} (x_0, x_0, \dots)$$

for $i = 1, 2, \dots$, linearity of U gives

$$U(x_1, \dots, x_i, x_0, \dots) + u_{i+1}(x_{i+1}) = U(x_1, \dots, x_{i+1}, x_0, \dots).$$

When these are added from $i = 1$ to $i = n - 1$, we get

$$\sum_{i=1}^{n} u_i(x_i) = U(x_1, \dots, x_n, x_0, x_0, \dots).$$

Suppose $z \succ x \succ y$ for some $y, z \in \mathscr{M}^\infty$, and let $x^{(n)} = (x_1, \dots, x_n, x_0, x_0, \dots)$ as in B6. With $\varepsilon > 0$ small and $\lambda = 1 - \varepsilon$, linearity and B6 imply that

$$|U(x) - U(x^{(n)})| \le \varepsilon [\max \{U(z) - U(x), U(x) - U(y)\}]$$

for all large n, and it follows that $\sum_{i=1}^\infty u_i(x_i) = U(x)$. Suppose next that $x \succ y$ for some $y \in \mathscr{M}^\infty$, and $x \succsim z$ for all $z \in \mathscr{M}^\infty$. Then, by the first part of B6 along with $U(x) \ge U(z)$ for all $z \in \mathscr{M}^\infty$, we get

$$0 \le U(x) - U(x^{(n)}) \le \varepsilon [U(x) - U(y)]$$

for any given $\varepsilon > 0$ for suitably large n, so again $\sum_{i=1}^\infty u_i(x_i) = U(x)$. The same result obtains if $z \succ x$ and if $y \succsim x$ for all $y \in \mathscr{M}^\infty$, or if $x \sim y$ for all $y \in \mathscr{M}^\infty$. Hence $\sum_{i=1}^\infty u_i(x_i) = U(x)$ for all x, and therefore, since U preserves $\succ$, we have $x \succ y$ iff $\sum_{i=1}^\infty u_i(x_i) > \sum_{i=1}^\infty u_i(y_i)$. Clearly, u_i is constant if and only if i is null.

To complete the proof of Theorem 3, suppose that the u_i on $\mathscr{M}$ satisfy the initial conclusions of the theorem and that $v_1, v_2, \dots$ are also linear functions on $\mathscr{M}$. If $v_i = a u_i + b_i$ with $a > 0$ and $\sum b_i$ finite, then it is obvious that $x \succ y$ iff $\sum v_i(x_i) > \sum v_i(y_i)$, with v_i constant iff i is null. Conversely, suppose that the v_i satisfy $x \succ y$ iff $\sum v_i(x_i) > \sum v_i(y_i)$, with all sums finite, and let $V(x) = \sum v_i(x_i)$. Then, since V is linear and order preserving, Theorem 2.1 implies that, for all $x \in \mathcal{M}^\infty$, $V(x) = aU(x) + b$ for some numbers $a > 0$ and b. In particular, $v_i(x_i) + \sum_{j \neq i} v_j(x_0) = au_i(x_i) + + a\sum_{j \neq i} u_j(x_0) + b$, so that $v_i(x_i) = au_i(x_i) + b_i$ with $b_i = b + a\sum_{j \neq i} u_j(x_0) - - \sum_{j \neq i} v_j(x_0)$. Hence each b_i is well specified, and addition over i gives

$$\sum_{i=1}^n b_i = nb + a\left[nU(x_0, x_0, \dots) - \sum_{i \leq n} u_i(x_0) \right] -$$

$$- \left[nV(x_0, x_0, \dots) - \sum_{i \leq n} v_i(x_0) \right]$$

$$= - a \sum_{i \leq n} u_i(x_0) + \sum_{i \leq n} v_i(x_0).$$

Since $\sum_{i=1}^\infty u_i(x_0)$ and $\sum_{i=1}^\infty v_i(x_0)$ are well defined and finite by hypothesis, equalling $U(x_0, x_0, \dots)$ and $V(x_0, x_0, \dots)$ respectively, we have $\sum_{i \leq n} u_i(x_0) \to U(x_0, x_0, \dots)$ and $\sum_{i \leq n} v_i(x_0) \to V(x_0, x_0, \dots)$, so that $\sum_{i \leq n} b_i \to - aU(x_0, x_0, \dots) + V(x_0, x_0, \dots) = b$.

This completes the proof of Theorem 3, whose conclusions are now presumed in the proof of Theorem 4 with $U(x) = \sum u_i(x_i)$. As before, take $U(x_0, x_0, \dots) = 0$ with $u_i(x_0) = 0$ for each i, and let $N = \{i : i \text{ is not null}\} = = \{i : u_i(t) \neq 0 \text{ for some } t \in \mathcal{M}\}$. Since $U(x^*, x^*, \dots) > U(x_*, x_*, \dots)$ by B4*, N is not empty. It then follows from B5* and Theorem 2.1 that for all $i, j \in N$ there are $r_{ij} > 0$ such that

$$u_i(t) = r_{ij}u_j(t) \quad \text{for all} \quad t \in \mathcal{M}.$$

Consequently, with $k \in N$ fixed, $r_i = r_{ik}$ and $u = u_k$,

$$U(x) = \sum_{i \in N} r_i u(x_i) \quad \text{for all} \quad x \in \mathcal{M}^\infty.$$

Since $U(x^*, x^*, \dots) = u(x^*)\sum_N r_i$ and $U(x_*, x_*, \dots) = u(x_*)\sum_N r_i$, B4* assures us that $\sum_N r_i$ is well defined and finite. Hence, with ρ_i defined as $r_i/\sum_N r_i$ for $i \in N$ and zero otherwise, $\sum \rho_i = 1$ and, for all $x, y \in \mathcal{M}^\infty$,

$$x \succ y \quad \text{iff} \quad \sum_{i=1}^\infty \rho_i u(x_i) > \sum_{i=1}^\infty \rho_i u(y_i).$$

This proves the first part of Theorem 4.

If $\rho_i > 0$ for more than a finite number of i, and if u is unbounded either above or below, then we can construct $x \in \mathcal{M}^\infty$ for which $\sum \rho_i u(x_i)$ is infinite. Hence u must be bounded if $\rho_i > 0$ for a denumerable number of i.

Finally, suppose the representation holds both for $\{\rho_i, u\}$ and $\{\rho'_i, v\}$. Let $\mathscr{M}'$ be the set of all constant elements in $\mathscr{M}^\infty$, so that $x \in \mathscr{M}'$ iff $x_i = x_j$ for all i, j. Then $\mathscr{M}'$ is a mixture set, and, since $\sum \rho_i = \sum \rho'_i = 1, u(t) > u(t')$ iff $v(t) > v(t')$ for all $t, t' \in \mathscr{M}$. Hence, by Theorem 2.1, v is a positive affine transformation of u. [Since $\{\rho_i, au + b\}$ satisfies the representation when $\{\rho_i, u\}$ does ($a > 0$), it follows that u is unique up to a positive affine transformation.] Since $v = au + b$ with $a > 0$ when both $\{\rho_i, u\}$ and $\{\rho'_i, v\}$ satisfy the representation, we have

$$\sum \rho_i u(x_i) > \sum \rho_i u(y_i) \quad \text{iff} \quad \sum \rho'_i u(x_i) > \sum \rho'_i u(y_i),$$

for all $x, y \in \mathscr{M}^\infty$, with $\sum \rho_i = \sum \rho'_i = 1$ and $\rho_i = 0$ iff $\rho'_i = 0$ iff i is null. We noted earlier that $N \neq \emptyset$. If $N = \{i\}$ then $\rho_i = \rho'_i = 1$, and the proof is complete. If $i, j \in N$ with $i \neq j$, let x^1, x^2, and x^3 be defined in the fashion indicated in the penultimate paragraph of Section 2 where $x^3 \succ x^2 \succ x^1$ and $x^2 \sim$ $\sim x^3 \lambda x^1$. Then, with $(x_i^1, x_j^1) = (x_*, x_*), (x_i^2, x_j^2) = (x^*, x_*)$, and $(x_i^3, x_j^3) = (x^*, x^*)$, we get $\rho_i(1 - \lambda) = \rho_j \lambda$ and $\rho'_i(1 - \lambda) = \rho'_j \lambda$, so that $\rho_i/\rho_j = \rho'_i/\rho'_j$. Since this is true for all distinct $i, j \in N$, it follows that $\rho_i = \rho'_i$ for all $i \in N$. Hence the ρ_i are unique.

CHAPTER 10

SUBJECTIVE EXPECTED UTILITY FOR
ARBITRARY STATE SETS

This chapter generalizes the subjective expected utility model of the preceding chapter to situations in which the set S of states is any nonempty set. The finite and denumerable cases considered earlier implicitly took $\mathscr{S}$ as the set of all subsets of S. Here we let $\mathscr{S}$ denote any Boolean algebra of subsets of S, with the set of all subsets of S denoted by 2^S. A partition of S is said to be *measurable* if each subset A of S in the partition is an element in $\mathscr{S}$. Hence, when $\mathscr{S} = 2^S$, all partitions of S are measurable.

In the present chapter, acts are functions $f, g, \ldots$ which map S into a mixture set $\mathscr{M}$, with $f(s)$ the element in $\mathscr{M}$ assigned to state s by act f. Elements in $\mathscr{M}$ will be denoted as $x, y, x_1, x_2, \ldots$ as well as by $f(s), g(s)$, and so forth. Hence, unlike Chapter 9, x does not denote a list $(x_1, x_2, \ldots)$: it is simply an element in $\mathscr{M}$. The most inclusive set of acts that will be considered is

$$\mathscr{F} = \{f : f \text{ is a function from } S \text{ into } \mathscr{M} \text{ that is constant on each element in some measurable partition of } S\}.$$

Thus if $f \in \mathscr{F}$ then there is a family of nonempty and mutually disjoint subsets of S whose union equals S such that, for each event A in the family, $A \in \mathscr{S}$ and $f(s) = f(s')$ for all $s, s' \in A$. If there were acts not in $\mathscr{F}$ that were felt to be relevant, then $\mathscr{S}$ could be expanded to accommodate such acts within the new $\mathscr{F}$ based on the expansion of $\mathscr{S}$.

It is assumed throughout the chapter that u is a linear function on $\mathscr{F}$ such that, for all $f, g \in \mathscr{F}, f \succ g$ iff $u(f) > u(g)$. In other words, since $\mathscr{F}$ is clearly a mixture set under the usual definition that $(f \lambda g)(s) = f(s) \lambda g(s)$ for all $s \in S$, we assume that $\succ$ on $\mathscr{F}$ satisfies A1, A2, and A3 or B1, B2, and B3 of Section 2.2. By Theorem 2.1(c), u is unique up to a positive affine transformation. We extend u to $\mathscr{M}$ in the usual way: for each $x \in \mathscr{M}$, $u(x) = u(f)$ when $f(s) = x$ for all $s \in S$.

Our basic concern in ensuing sections involves further conditions for $\succ$ on $\mathscr{F}$ which imply that $u(f) = \int_S u(f(s)) \, dP(s)$ for all f in some designated subset of $\mathscr{F}$, where P is a finitely additive probability measure on $\mathscr{S}$. Equivalently, with u_f the function on S defined by

$$u_f(s) = u(f(s)),$$

we will be concerned with conditions that yield $u(f) = E(u_f, P)$ for various types of acts in $\mathscr{F}$.

Because of the general nature of $\mathscr{S}$ that is adopted in this chapter, it will be necessary to pay close attention to notions of measurability and integrability when considering $E(u_f, P)$. This will be done in Section 2 after we note in the next section that $u(f) = E(u_f, P)$ for all simple acts in $\mathscr{F}$ when axioms that are closely related to B4 and B5 of the preceding chapter are assumed for $\succ$. Section 3 considers countable additivity for P.

10.1. SIMPLE ACTS

The set of *simple acts* in $\mathscr{F}$ is defined as

$$\mathscr{F}_0 = \{f \in \mathscr{F} : f \text{ is constant on each element in some } \textit{finite}$$
$$\text{measurable partition of } S\}.$$

Although the image $f(S)$ of simple $f \in \mathscr{F}_0$ is finite, it is not generally true that $f \in \mathscr{F}$ and $f(S)$ finite imply $f \in \mathscr{F}_0$. For example, if $S = \{1, 2, \ldots\}$ and $\mathscr{S} = \{A \subseteq S : \text{either } A \text{ or } S \backslash A \text{ is finite}\}$, then the set of odd positive integers is not in $\mathscr{S}$, nor is its complement (the set of even positive integers). Hence, if $f(s) = x$ for all $s \in \{1, 3, 5, \ldots\}$ and $f(s) = y$ for all $s \in \{2, 4, 6, \ldots\}$, then $f \in \mathscr{F}$ and $|f(s)| = 2$, but f is not in $\mathscr{F}_0$.

Here, and later, we shall say that $f = g$ on A iff $f(s) = g(s)$ for all $s \in A$; that $f = x$ on A for $f \in \mathscr{F}$ and $x \in \mathscr{M}$ iff $f(s) = x$ for all $s \in A$; that $x \succ y$ iff $f \succ g$ when $f = x$ and $g = y$ on S; and that $x \succ f$ iff $g \succ f$ when $g = x$ on S. The set of *null events* in $\mathscr{S}$ is denoted by $\mathscr{N}$ and defined by

$$\mathscr{N} = \{A \in \mathscr{S} : f \sim g \text{ whenever } f, g \in \mathscr{F} \text{ and } f = g \text{ on } S \backslash A\}.$$

Thus, if any two acts in $\mathscr{F}$ that are identical on the complement of A are indifferent, then A is null.

The two axioms that are used to obtain $u(f) = E(u_f, P)$ for all $f \in \mathscr{F}_0$ are

F4.   *There are $x, y \in \mathscr{M}$ such that $x \succ y$,*

F5.   *For all $A \in \mathscr{S} \backslash \mathscr{N}$, all $f, g \in \mathscr{F}$, and all $x, y \in \mathscr{M}$, if $f = x$ on A, $g = y$ on A and $f = g$ on $S \backslash A$, then $f \succ g$ iff $x \succ y$.*

Axiom F5 is a straightforward generalization of B5 and B5* for nonnull events. It says that if f and g yield the same element in $\mathscr{M}$ for every state outside A, and if A is nonnull and f and g are constant on A, with $f = x$ and

$g = y$ on A, then act f is preferred to act g if and only if x is preferred to y. In other words, preferences on nonnull events correspond monotonically to preferences on S for constant acts. Although $\mathscr{F}$ in F5 could be replaced by $\mathscr{F}_0$ for the following theorem, we state the theorem for F5 as given since it will be used later for subsets of $\mathscr{F}$ that include the simple acts.

THEOREM 1. *Suppose* F4 *and* F5 *hold. Then there is a unique finitely additive probability measure* P *on* $\mathscr{S}$ *such that* $P(A) = 0$ *iff* $A \in \mathscr{N}$, *and* $u(f) = E(u_f, P)$ *for all* $f \in \mathscr{F}_0$.

A proof of Theorem 1 appears in Section 4.

By definition, when $f \in \mathscr{F}_0$ and $\{A_1, \ldots, A_n\}$ is an n-part partition of S with $A_i \in \mathscr{S}$ and $f = x_i$ on A_i for $i = 1, \ldots, n$, then

$$E(u_f, P) = \sum_{i=1}^{n} P(A_i)u(x_i).$$

Given $A \in \mathscr{S}$, $x \succ y$, $f = x$ and $h = y$ on S, $g = x$ on A, $g = y$ on $S \backslash A$, and $g \sim f \lambda h$, it follows that $P(A)u(x) + [1 - P(A)]u(y) = \lambda u(x) + (1 - \lambda)u(y)$, so that

$$P(A) = \lambda.$$

Thus there is a conceptually simple way of determining P under the hypotheses of Theorem 1.

Generally speaking, F4 and F5 do not imply $u(f) = E(u_f, P)$ for $f \in \mathscr{F} \backslash \mathscr{F}_0$, even when $f(S)$ is finite. Given $\mathscr{S}$ and f as in the example of the first paragraph of this section, suppose $u(x) = 1$ and $u(y) = 0$ so that

$$u_f(s) = 1 \quad \text{for} \quad s \in \{1, 3, 5, \ldots\}$$

$$u_f(s) = 0 \quad \text{for} \quad s \in \{2, 4, 6, \ldots\}.$$

Suppose further that every finite $A \in \mathscr{S}$ is null, so that $P(A) = 0$ for every such A. Then no extension of P from $\mathscr{S}$ to 2^S can be countably additive and, in addition, $E(u_f, P)$ is not well defined according to the definitions of the next section. The reason why $\int u(f(s)) \, dP(s)$ is not well defined is that for every λ there is an extension of P to a probability measure P^λ on an algebra that includes $\mathscr{S}$ and contains $\{1, 3, 5, \ldots\}$ such that $P^\lambda (\{1, 3, 5, \ldots\}) = \lambda$. Thus, since any value of the 'subjective probability' of $\{1, 3, 5, \ldots\}$ is consistent with P as determined for Theorem 1, the usual definition of expectation, i.e. $E(u_f, P) = P(\{1, 3, 5, \ldots\})$, makes no sense unless we are willing to allow $E(u_f, P)$ to be a set of real numbers rather than a single number (or $+\infty$ or $-\infty$), which will not be done here.

10.2. MEASURABLE AND INTEGRABLE ACTS

In addition to the assumptions on u given in the introduction, *we shall assume throughout this section and the next that* F4 *and* F5 *hold and that* P *on $\mathscr{S}$ is as specified in Theorem* 1. Our aim in the present section is to show that $u(f) = E(u_f, P)$ for certain types of acts in $\mathscr{F} \backslash \mathscr{F}_0$, provided that we assume the following dominance axiom:

> F6. *For all $f \in \mathscr{F}$ and all $x \in \mathscr{M}$, $f \succsim x$ if $f(s) \succ x$ for all $s \in S$, and $x \succsim f$ if $x \succ f(s)$ for all $s \in S$.*

As before, $\succsim$ is the union of $\succ$ and $\sim$. In addition, $f \succsim x$ means that $f \succsim g$ when $g = x$ on S, and $x \succsim f$ is defined similarly. The first part of F6 says that if you prefer y to x for every $y \in f(S)$, then you will like f as much as the constant act that yields x for every state. The second part has a dual interpretation. Thus F6, which is related to A4 and A4* in Chapter 3, is quite appealing.

Our new axiom gives a bounding result on $u(f)$ that is related to bounding aspects in the proofs of Chapter 3.

LEMMA 1. *Suppose* F6 *holds. If $A \in \mathscr{S}$ and $P(A) = 1$ then $\inf \{u_f(s): s \in A\} \le u(f) \le \sup \{u_f(s): s \in A\}$ for all $f \in \mathscr{F}$.*

Lemma 1 and later results in this section are proved in Section 5. Various terms involved in these results will now be defined. We consider several special types of acts in $\mathscr{F}$.

First, f is *measurable* if $\{s: u_f(s) \in I\} \in \mathscr{S}$ for every interval I of real numbers. Clearly, f is measurable iff $\{s: u_f(s) < a\} \in \mathscr{S}$ and $\{s: u_f(s) > a\} \in \mathscr{S}$ for every real number a. Because $u(\mathscr{M})$ is an interval, f is measurable iff $\{s: f(s) \succ x\} \in \mathscr{S}$ and $\{s: x \succ f(s)\} \in \mathscr{S}$ for every $x \in \mathscr{M}$.

Second, f is *bounded* if there is an $A \in \mathscr{S}$ and real numbers a and b such that $A \subseteq \{s: a \le u_f(s) \le b\}$ and $P(A) = 1$. For example, the f defined in the final paragraph of the preceding section is bounded since $u_f(S) = \{0, 1\}$. However, this f is not measurable since $\{1, 3, 5, \dots\}$ is not in $\mathscr{S}$. We also say that f is *bounded below* [*above*] if $A \subseteq \{s: a \le u_f(s)\}$ $[A \subseteq \{s: u_f(s) \le b\}]$ and $P(A) = 1$ for some number $a [b]$ and some $A \in \mathscr{S}$. I leave to the reader the simple proof that $f \in \mathscr{F}$ is bounded iff it is bounded below and above.

With a few obvious changes in notation, the definition of $E(u_f, P)$ – the subjective expected utility of act f – is given in Section 3.1 for measurable acts in $\mathscr{F}$. In the terms used there, u_f is $\mathscr{S}$-measurable when f is measurable (as defined above): since P is defined on $\mathscr{S}$, $E(u_f, P)$ is well defined unless $E(u_f^+, P) = \infty$ and $E(u_f^-, P) = -\infty$.

Let $\mathscr{F}^*$ denote the *set of measurable* $f \in \mathscr{F}$. As we shall see, $u(f) = E(u_f, P)$ for all $f \in \mathscr{F}^*$. However, $\mathscr{F}^*$ is not necessarily a mixture set, as shown by the following example. Let $S = \{1, 2, \ldots\}$, $\mathscr{S} = \{A \subseteq S : A \text{ or } S \backslash A \text{ is finite}\}$, and suppose that $\mathscr{M} = [0, 1]$ with $u(x) = x$ for all $x \in \mathscr{M}$. Define measurable f and g by

$$f(s) = s/(1 + s) \quad \text{for all } s,$$

$$g(s) = 1/(1 + s) \quad \text{for even } s \in S,$$

$$g(s) = (s + 2)/[(s + 1)(s + 3)] \quad \text{for odd } s \in S.$$

Here f increases in s, and g decreases in s, so both are measurable. However, $f \frac{1}{2} g$ is not measurable since

$$\{s : u_{f\frac{1}{2}g}(s) < \tfrac{1}{2}\} = \{s : u((f\tfrac{1}{2}g)(s)) < \tfrac{1}{2}\}$$

$$= \{s : u(f(s)) + u(g(s)) < 1\}$$

$$= \{1, 3, 5, \ldots\},$$

which is not in $\mathscr{S}$.

Even when $\mathscr{F}^*$ is not a mixture set, we shall see that $u(f) = E(u_f, P)$ for all f in the *mixture set* $\mathscr{M}(\mathscr{F}^*)$ *generated by* $\mathscr{F}^*$. To define $\mathscr{M}(\mathscr{F}^*)$, let

$$\mathscr{F}_1 = \{f \lambda g : f, g \in \mathscr{F}^* \text{ and } 0 \le \lambda \le 1\}$$

and, proceeding recursively, for $n > 1$ let

$$\mathscr{F}_n = \{f \lambda g : f, g \in \mathscr{F}_{n-1} \text{ and } 0 \le \lambda \le 1\}.$$

Since $f 1 g = f$, $\mathscr{F}^* \subseteq \mathscr{F}_1 \subseteq \mathscr{F}_2 \subseteq \cdots$, and we define

$$\mathscr{M}(\mathscr{F}^*) = \lim \mathscr{F}_n = \bigcup_{n=1}^{\infty} \mathscr{F}_n.$$

It is easily seen that $\mathscr{M}(\mathscr{F}^*)$ is a mixture set: it is the minimal mixture set $\mathscr{F}'$ for which $\mathscr{F}^* \subseteq \mathscr{F}' \subseteq \mathscr{F}$, i.e., $\mathscr{M}(\mathscr{F}^*)$ is the intersection of all such mixture sets $\mathscr{F}'$.

Since $f \in \mathscr{M}(\mathscr{F}^*)$ might not be measurable, it is necessary to define the meaning of $E(u_f, P)$ for this case. Given P on $\mathscr{S}$, we say that a function P' on 2^S is an *extension* of P if P' is a probability measure on 2^S such that $P'(A) = P(A)$ for all $A \in \mathscr{S}$. Obviously, u_f is 2^S-measurable, so $E(u_f, P')$ is well defined for every extension P' of P except when $E(u_f^+, P') = \infty$ and $E(u_f^-, P') = -\infty$. We shall say that $f \in \mathscr{F}$ is *integrable* if $E(u_f, P')$ is well defined and has the same value ($-\infty$ and $+\infty$ being allowed) for every extension P' of P. When f is integrable, we define $E(u_f, P)$ as the common value of the $E(u_f, P')$. Otherwise, $E(u_f, P)$ is not defined.

Our basic result for this section is that every $f \in \mathcal{M}(\mathcal{F}^*)$ is integrable with $u(f) = E(u_f, P)$ for all such f. We state this as the final conclusion of the following theorem. The other conclusions are stated in the order of proof given in Section 5.

THEOREM 2. *Suppose* F6 *holds. Then, with* $\mathcal{F}^*$ *the set of measurable acts in* $\mathcal{F}$, *and* $\mathcal{M}(\mathcal{F}^*)$ *the mixture set generated by* $\mathcal{F}^*$:

(a) $u(f) = E(u_f, P)$ *for every bounded* $f \in \mathcal{F}^*$;

(b) u *on* $\mathcal{M}$ *is bounded if* $P(A) > 0$ *for every* A *in some denumerable measurable partition of* S;

(c) *Every measurable act is bounded*;

(d) *Every* $f \in \mathcal{M}(\mathcal{F}^*)$ *is integrable, and* $u(f) = E(u_f, P)$ *for all* $f \in \mathcal{M}(\mathcal{F}^*)$.

It should be recalled that Theorem 2 presumes the representation of Theorem 1 for $\mathcal{F}_0$ and that u is a linear order-preserving function on $\mathcal{F}$ with $u(x) = u(f)$ when $f(s) = x$ for all $s \in S$, and with $u_f(s) = u(f(s))$.

10.3. COUNTABLE ADDITIVITY

Another axiom, related to B6 in Section 9.3, is needed to imply that P is countably additive when $\mathcal{S}$ is a Borel algebra of subsets of S.

F7.   *For all* $A, B, A_1, A_2, \dots \in \mathcal{S}$, *for all* $x, y \in \mathcal{M}$, *and for all* f_A, f_B, $f_1, f_2, \dots \in \mathcal{F}_0$, *if*

$$f_A = x \quad on \quad A, \qquad f_A = y \quad on \quad S \backslash A;$$

$$f_B = x \quad on \quad B, \qquad f_B = y \quad on \quad S \backslash B;$$

$$f_n = x \quad on \quad A_n, \qquad f_n = y \quad on \quad S \backslash A_n, \quad n = 1, 2, \dots,$$

and if $A_1 \subseteq A_2 \subseteq \cdots, A = \bigcup_{i=1}^{\infty} A_i$, $x \succ y$ *and* $f_A \succ f_B$, *then* $f_n \succ f_B$ *for some* n.

Given $x \succ y$, $f_A \succ f_B$ and a nondecreasing sequence $\{A_i\}$ with limit $A \in \mathcal{S}$, f_n becomes more like f_A as n increases, so one might expect that f_n will be preferred to f_B for large n. This is basically what F7 requires. Indeed, if we set $u(x) = 1$ and $u(y) = 0$, Theorem 1 and the hypotheses of F7 give

$$P(A_1) \leq P(A_2) \leq \cdots \leq P(A); P(B) < P(A); A_i \uparrow A.$$

Consequently, if P is countably additive, so that $P(A_i) \to P(A)$ then $P(B) <$

$< P(A_n)$ for large n with $f_n \succ f_B$ by Theorem 1. However, if countable additivity fails, we could have $\lim P(A_i) \leq P(B) < P(A)$, and in this case we obtain a specific violation of F7.

THEOREM 3. *Suppose $\mathcal{S}$ is a Borel algebra, P is as given in Theorem 1, and F7 holds. Then P is countably additive.*

This result makes no use of concepts defined in the preceding section. However, the mere presumption that $\mathcal{S}$ is a Borel algebra has a significant impact on that section, as seen by

THEOREM 4. $\mathcal{F}^* = \mathcal{M}(\mathcal{F}^*)$ *if $\mathcal{S}$ is a Borel algebra.*

Thus, quite apart from whether or not P is countably additive, $\mathcal{F}^*$ is a mixture set when $\mathcal{S}$ is a Borel algebra. In this case, part (d) of Theorem 2 is redundant. If F6 and F7 hold in the context of Theorem 1, and if $\mathcal{S}$ is a Borel algebra, then the set $\mathcal{F}^*$ of measurable acts is a mixture set, P is countably additive, and every $f \in \mathcal{F}^*$ is bounded with $u(f) = E(u_f, P)$.

Theorems 3 and 4 are proved in Section 6.

10.4. PROOF OF THEOREM 1

Given the hypotheses of Theorem 1, consider a measurable n-part partition $\{A_1, \ldots, A_n\}$ of S and let $\mathcal{F}_A$ be the subset of functions in $\mathcal{F}_0$ that are constant on each element of this partition. Also let $f \in \mathcal{F}_A$ be represented as the n-tuple $(f(A_1), \ldots, f(A_n)) \in \mathcal{M}^n$ with the special convention that $f(A_i)$ denotes the element in $\mathcal{M}$ assigned to s for all $s \in A_i$. It then follows directly from Theorem 9.2 that there is a linear function u_A on $\mathcal{M}$ and nonnegative numbers $P_A(A_i)$ that sum to 1 such that, for all $f, g \in \mathcal{F}_A$,

$$f \succ g \quad \text{iff} \quad \sum_{i=1}^{n} P_A(A_i) u_A(f(A_i)) > \sum_{i=1}^{n} P_A(A_i) u_A(g(A_i)),$$

where $P_A(A_i) = 0$ iff A_i is null, the $P_A(A_i)$ are uniquely determined, and u_A on $\mathcal{M}$ is unique up to a positive affine transformation.

Since u on $\mathcal{M}$, i.e. on the constant acts in $\mathcal{F}$, has the same properties as u_A on $\mathcal{M}$, Theorem 2.1 tells us that u_A is a positive affine transformation of u on $\mathcal{M}$. Therefore, with no loss in generality, we replace u_A by u: for all $f, g \in \mathcal{F}_A$,

$$f \succ g \quad \text{iff} \quad \sum_{i=1}^{n} P_A(A_i) u(f(A_i)) > \sum_{i=1}^{n} P_A(A_i) u(g(A_i)).$$

A similar form holds for every finite measurable partition of S.

We now show that the partition-specific subscript can be dropped from P. Suppose two measurable partitions $\{A_1, \ldots, A_n\}$ and $\{B_1, \ldots, B_m\}$ have some common element, say $A_1 = B_1$. Then, for all f and g that are constant on A_1 and on $S \backslash A_1$, it follows from the preceding paragraph that

$$P_A(A_1)u(f(A_1)) + [1 - P_A(A_1)]u(f(S \backslash A_1)) >$$
$$> P_A(A_1)u(g(A_1)) + [1 - P_A(A_1)]u(g(S \backslash A_1))$$

if and only if a similar inequality holds when A is replaced by B. Axiom F4 then requires $P_A(A_1) = P_B(A_1)$. Since we have the same subjective probability for a measurable event from every finite measurable partition which contains that event, we obtain the form given in the preceding paragraph with $P_A(A_i)$ replaced by $P(A_i)$. An analysis like that just completed shows that P is additive. In particular, if A and B are disjoint elements in $\mathscr{S}$, consideration of the partitions $\{A, B, S \backslash (A \cup B)\}$ and $\{A \cup B, S \backslash (A \cup B)\}$ shows that $P(A \cup B) = P(A) + P(B)$.

Finally, with $\mathscr{F}_A$ as defined in the opening paragraph of this section, u on $\mathscr{F}_A$ must be a positive affine transformation of $\sum P(A_i)u(f(A_i))$ on $\mathscr{F}_A$. Then, since $u(x) = \sum P(A_i)u(x)$ and $u(y) = \sum P(A_i)u(y)$, it follows that $u(f) = \sum P(A_i)u(f(A_i)) = E(u_f, P)$ for all $f \in \mathscr{F}_A$; hence, for all acts in $\mathscr{F}_0$, $u(f) = E(u_f, P)$.

10.5. PROOFS WITH F6

Assume throughout this section that F6 holds along with the conclusions of Theorem 1. We prove Lemma 1 first, assuming that $A \in \mathscr{S}$ and $P(A) = 1$. Given $f \in \mathscr{F}$, we are to show that $\inf u_f(A) \leq u(f) \leq \sup u_f(A)$. We shall prove only that $u(f) \leq \sup u_f(A)$ since the proof for the other bound is similar. If $\sup u_f(A) = \infty$, there is nothing to prove, so suppose henceforth that $d = \sup_f(A) < \infty$. Also let $a = \inf u_f(A)$, and define $g \in \mathscr{F}$ by $g = f$ on A and $a \leq u_g(s) \leq d$ for all $s \in S \backslash A$. Since $P(A) = 1$, $S \backslash A$ is null, and therefore $f \sim g$ and $u(f) = u(g)$. Thus it suffices to show that $u(g) \leq d$. We consider two cases as follows.

Case 1. $a < d$. Let $x_1, x_2, \ldots$ in $\mathscr{M}$ satisfy $u(x_1) \leq u(x_2) \leq \cdots$ with $u(x_n) \to d$. Fix $y \in \mathscr{M}$ with $u(y) < d$. Since $u(g(s)) \leq d$ for all $s \in S$,

$$\lambda u(g(s)) + (1 - \lambda)u(y) < u(x_n) \quad \text{for all} \quad s \in S$$

whenever $\lambda < [u(x_n) - u(y)]/[d - u(y)]$. Since there are positive λ that satisfy this when n is large, we have $g(s)\lambda y$ less preferred than x_n for such

λ according to the linearity and order-preserving properties of u. The latter part of F6 then implies that $x_n \succsim g \lambda y^*$, where $y^* \in \mathscr{F}_0$ is such that $y^*(s) = y$ for all s. Then $\lambda u(g) + (1 - \lambda)u(y) = u(g \lambda y^*) \le u(x_n) \le d$, so that $\lambda u(g) + (1 - \lambda)u(y) \le d$. Since $u(x_n) \to d$, we can get λ arbitrarily close to 1 for large n. Therefore $u(g) \le d$.

Case 2. $a = d$. If $u(y) < d$ for some $y \in \mathscr{M}$, the case 1 proof applies, so suppose that $d = \inf u(\mathscr{M})$. If $d < u(g)$ then, since $x \succ y$ for some $x, y \in \mathscr{M}$ by F4, $d < u(z) < u(g)$ for some $z \in \mathscr{M}$. But then $z \succ g(s)$ for all s, and therefore $u(z) \ge u(g)$ by F6, a contradiction. Therefore $u(g) \le d$.

This completes the proof of Lemma 1. We now turn to the proofs of the several parts of Theorem 2.

Theorem 2(a)

Let f be measurable and bounded with $A \in \mathscr{S}, P(A) = 1$, and $A \subseteq$ $\subseteq \{s: a \le u_f(s) \le b\}$, where a and b are finite. Also let $g = f$ on A and $g = y$ on $S \backslash A$ with $a \le u(y) \le b$. Act g is measurable since $\{s: u_g(s) \in I\} =$ $= [\{s: u_f(s) \in I\} \cap A] \cup B$, where $B = \emptyset$ if $u(y) \notin I$ and $B = S \backslash A$ if $u(y) \in I$. Since $S \backslash A \in \mathscr{N}, g \sim f$ and therefore $u(g) = u(f)$. Moreover, since $P(A) = 1$ with f and g measurable and bounded, $E(u_f, P) = E(u_g, P)$. We therefore show that $u(g) = E(u_g, P)$.

This follows directly from Lemma 1 if $a = b$, so assume henceforth that $a < b$ with $a = 0$ and $b = 1$ for convenience (using a positive affine transformation, if necessary). Given $n \in \{1, 2, \dots\}$, let

$$A_1 = \{s: 0 \le u_g(s) \le 1/n\}$$

$$A_i = \{s: (i - 1)/n < u_g(s) \le i/n\}, \qquad i = 2, \dots, n.$$

Since g is measurable, the nonempty A_i form a measurable partition of S. With $x_i \in \mathscr{M}$, define $f_i, g_i, h_i \in \mathscr{F}^*$ thus:

$f_i = g$ on A_i, $f_i = x_i$ on $S \backslash A_i$ $(i = 1, \dots, n)$,

$g_i = x_{i+1}$ on $\bigcup_{j=1}^{i} A_j$, $g_i = x_i$ on $\bigcup_{j=i+1}^{n} A_j$ $(i = 1, \dots, n-1)$,

$h_i = g$ on $\bigcup_{j=1}^{i+1} A_j$, $h_i = x_{i+1}$ on $\bigcup_{j=i+2}^{n} A_j$ $(i = 1, \dots, n-1)$,

where $g = h_{n-1}$. It is easily checked that $f_1 \frac{1}{2} f_2 = g_1 \frac{1}{2} h_1$ and $h_{i-1} \frac{1}{2} f_{i+1} =$ $= g_i \frac{1}{2} h_i$ for $i = 2, \dots, n - 1$. Since $u(r_1) + u(r_2) = u(r_3) + u(r_4)$ when $r_1 \frac{1}{2} r_2 =$ $= r_3 \frac{1}{2} r_4$, summation and cancellation give

$$u(g) = \sum_{i=1}^{n} u(f_i) - \sum_{i=1}^{n-1} u(g_i).$$

Since the x_i are arbitrary, choose them so that $(i-1)/n \leq u(x_i) \leq i/n$ for $i = 1, \ldots, n$. Then, by Lemma 1, $(i-1)/n \leq u(f_i) \leq i/n$. Therefore

$$(n-1)/2 \leq \sum_{i=1}^{n} u(f_i) \leq (n+1)/2.$$

Because linearity permits us to choose $u(x_i)$ arbitrarily close to $(i-1)/n$, and because Theorem 1 and $g_i \in \mathscr{F}_0$ give $u(g_i) = \sum_{j<i} P(A_j) u(x_{i+1}) + \sum_{j>i} P(A_j) u(x_i)$, it follows from a suitable choice of the x_i that $u(g_i) \leq \sum_{j \leq i} P(A_j) i/n + \sum_{j<i} P(A_j)(i-1)/n + 1/n^2$, hence that

$$\sum_{i=1}^{n-1} u(g_i) \leq (n-1)/2 - \sum_{i=1}^{n} P(A_i)(i-1)/n + 1/n.$$

This and the two preceding displayed expressions give

$$u(g) \geq (n-1)/2 - \left[(n-1)/2 - \sum_{i} P(A_i)(i-1)/n + 1/n \right]$$
$$= \sum_{i=1}^{n} P(A_i)(i-1)/n - 1/n.$$

By choosing $u(x_i)$ close to i/n, we obtain the upper bound on $u(g)$ in the following:

$$\sum_{i=1}^{n} P(A_i)(i-1)/n - 1/n \leq u(g) \leq \sum_{i=1}^{n} P(A_i) i/n + 1/n.$$

Since $\sum P(A_i)(i-1)/n \leq E(u_g, P) \leq \sum P(A_i) i/n$ according to the definition of expected value, it follows by letting $n \to \infty$ that $u(g) = E(u_g, P)$.

Theorem 2(b)

Let $\mathscr{A}$ be a denumerable partition of S with $A \in \mathscr{S}$ and $P(A) > 0$ for all $A \in \mathscr{A}$. Because the sum of the $P(A)$ cannot exceed 1, we can order the members of $\mathscr{A}$ so that $P(A_1) \geq P(A_2) \geq \cdots$ with $\mathscr{A} = \{A_1, A_2, \ldots\}$ and $A_i \cap A_j = \emptyset$ whenever $i \neq j$.

Contrary to the desired result, suppose u on $\mathscr{M}$ is unbounded, say unbounded above for definiteness. Since we have not proved that $u(f) = E(u_f, P)$ for unbounded f, a less direct procedure is needed to yield the contradiction that $u(f)$ is infinite for some f. Given u on $\mathscr{M}$ unbounded above, assume with no loss in generality that $[0, \infty) \subseteq u(\mathscr{M})$, and choose $x_i \in \mathscr{M}$, $f \in \mathscr{F}$ and $g_n \in \mathscr{F}_0$ (constant on each A_i for $i \leq n$ and on $\bigcup_{i>n} A_i$)

thus:

$$u(x_i) = P(A_i)^{-1} \qquad i = 1, 2, \ldots$$

$$f = x_i \quad \text{on} \quad A_i \quad i = 1, 2, \ldots$$

$$u(g_n(s)) = P(A_n)^{-1} - P(A_i)^{-1} \quad \text{for} \quad s \in A_i, \quad i = 1, \ldots, n$$

$$u(g_n(s)) = 0 \qquad\qquad\qquad \text{for} \quad s \in \bigcup_{i > n} A_i.$$

By Theorem 1,

$$u(g_n) = P(A_n)^{-1} \sum_{i=1}^{n} P(A_i) - n \quad (n = 1, 2, \ldots).$$

By linearity and $P(A_1) \geq P(A_2) \geq \cdots$,

$$u((f \tfrac{1}{2} g_n)(s)) = \tfrac{1}{2} P(A_i)^{-1} + \tfrac{1}{2}[P(A_n)^{-1} - P(A_i)^{-1}]$$

$$= \tfrac{1}{2} P(A_n)^{-1} \quad \text{for all} \quad s \in \bigcup_{i \leq n} A_i;$$

$$u((f \tfrac{1}{2} g_n)(s)) \geq \tfrac{1}{2} P(A_n)^{-1} \quad \text{for all} \quad s \in \bigcup_{i > n} A_i.$$

Therefore $\tfrac{1}{2} P(A_n)^{-1} = \inf\{u((f \tfrac{1}{2} g_n)(s)) : s \in S\}$. Hence, by Lemma 1, $u(f \tfrac{1}{2} g_n) \geq \tfrac{1}{2} P(A_n)^{-1}$. Then linearity and the preceding equation for $u(g_n)$ yield

$$u(f) \geq P(A_n)^{-1} - P(A_n)^{-1} \sum_{i=1}^{n} P(A_i) + n \geq n.$$

Since this forces $u(f)$ to infinity as $n \to \infty$, we obtain a contradiction to the finiteness of $u(f)$. Therefore u must be bounded above. A symmetric proof shows that u is bounded below, so u is bounded under the given hypotheses.

Theorem 2(c)

To show that every measurable act is bounded, suppose to the contrary that $f \in \mathscr{F}^*$ is unbounded. Assume for definiteness that f is unbounded above and, with no loss in generality, assume that $[0, \infty) \subseteq u(\mathscr{M})$. Modify $f \in \mathscr{F}^*$ as follows. For each member of a measurable partition which verifies that $f \in \mathscr{F}^*$ where $u_f(s) < 0$, replace $f(s)$ by y with $u(y) = 0$. Let g be f thus modified. Then $g \in \mathscr{F}^*$, g is unbounded above, and $u_g(s) \geq 0$ for all s.

Let $A_n = \{s : n - 1 \leq u_g(s) < n\}$ for $n = 1, 2, \ldots$. Then $S = \bigcup A_n$ and each $A_n \in \mathscr{S}$ since g is measurable. Let $B_n = \bigcup_{i=1}^{n} A_i$. Since g is unbounded above, $P(B_n) < 1$ for all n, and therefore $P(S \backslash B_n) = P(\{s : u_g(s) \geq n\}) > 0$ for all n. We consider two cases, according to whether $P(B_n)$ approaches 1.

Case 1. $P(S \backslash B_n) \to 0$. Then $P(A_n) > 0$ for denumerably many A_n. Let these be $A_{n_1}, A_{n_2}, \ldots$, and let $C_1 = \bigcup_1^{n_1} A_n$, $C_2 = \bigcup_{n_1+1}^{n_2} A_n, \ldots$ so that $\{C_1, C_2, \ldots\}$ is a denumerable measurable partition of S with $P(C_i) > 0$ for every i. But then Theorem 2(b) implies that u on $\mathscr{M}$ is bounded, thus contradicting our supposition that g is unbounded.

Case 2. $P(S \backslash B_n) \to \lambda > 0$. Take $u(x_n) = n$ and let

$$g_n = g \quad \text{on} \quad B_n, \qquad g_n = x_n \quad \text{on} \quad S \backslash B_n,$$

$$h_n = x_n \quad \text{on} \quad B_n, \qquad h_n = g \quad \text{on} \quad S \backslash B_n.$$

All g_n and h_n are measurable. Since g_n is bounded, Theorem 2(a) and $P(S \backslash B_n) \geq \lambda$ imply $u(g_n) \geq n\lambda$. Since $h_n(s) \succ x_{n-1}$ for all $s \in S$, F6 implies $u(h_n) \geq n - 1$. Then, since $g \frac{1}{2} x_n^* = g_n \frac{1}{2} h_n$, $u(g) + n = u(g_n) + u(h_n)$, and therefore $u(g) \geq n\lambda - 1$ for all n, which contradicts the finiteness of $u(g)$.

Theorem 2(d)

To show that all acts in $\mathscr{M}(\mathscr{F}^*)$ are integrable with $u(f) = E(u_f, P)$, consider first an $f \in \mathscr{F}_1$ with $f = g \lambda h$, where $g, h \in \mathscr{F}^*$. By Theorem 2(c), g and h are bounded, so let $A, B \in \mathscr{S}$ be such that $P(A) = P(B) = 1$, $A \subseteq \{s : a_1 \leq u_g(s) \leq b_1\}$ and $B \subseteq \{s : a_2 \leq u_h(s) \leq b_2\}$, with the a_i and b_i finite. Then $A \cap B \in \mathscr{S}$, $P(A \cap B) = 1$, and $A \cap B \subseteq \{s : \inf\{a_1, a_2\} \leq \lambda u_g(s) + (1 - \lambda)u_h(s) \leq \sup\{b_1, b_2\}\}$, so f is bounded. By linearity and Theorem 2(a),

$$u(f) = \lambda u(g) + (1 - \lambda)u(h)$$

$$= \lambda E(u_g, P) + (1 - \lambda)E(u_h, P)$$

$$= E(\lambda u_g + (1 - \lambda)u_h, P)$$

$$= E(u_{g \lambda h}, P)$$

$$= E(u_f, P).$$

The only equality here that merits further comment is $\lambda E(u_g, P) + (1 - \lambda)E(u_h, P) = E(\lambda u_g + (1 - \lambda)u_h, P)$, which uses things in Section 3.1. Since g and h are measurable and bounded, there are sequences $G_1, G_2, \ldots$ and $H_1, H_2, \ldots$ of simple $\mathscr{S}$-measurable functions on S that converge uniformly from below to u_g and u_h respectively. It follows that $\lambda G_1 +$

$+ (1 - \lambda)H_1, \lambda G_2 + (1 - \lambda)H_2, \ldots$ is a sequence of simple $\mathscr{S}$-measurable functions on S that converges uniformly below to $\lambda u_g + (1 - \lambda)u_h = u_f$. It follows that f is integrable: for any extension P' of P, $\lambda E(u_g, P) +$ $+ (1 - \lambda)E(u_h, P) = \lambda E(u_g, P') + (1 - \lambda)E(u_h, P') = E(\lambda u_g + (1 - \lambda)u_h, P') =$ $= E(u_f, P)$.

Therefore, if $f \in \mathscr{F}_1$, then f is bounded and there is a sequence of simple $\mathscr{S}$-measurable functions that coverges uniformly from below to u_f. From the proof just given, the same thing is true for every $f \in \mathscr{F}_2$. Induction then completes the proof of Theorem 2(d).

10.6. PROOFS WITH BOREL ALGEBRAS

We assume in this section that $\mathscr{S}$ is a Borel algebra, so that it is closed under countable unions.

For Theorem 3, let P be as specified in Theorem 1, and assume that F7 holds. According to the paragraph that precedes the statement of Theorem 3, if $A_n \uparrow A$ and $P(A) > P(B)$ for $A_1, A_2, \ldots, B \in \mathscr{S}$, then (by F7) $f_n \succ f_B$ for some n and therefore (by Theorem 1) $P(A_n) > P(B)$ for some n. If for every $\lambda < P(A)$ there is a $B \in \mathscr{S}$ for which $\lambda \leq P(B) < P(A)$, then $P(A_n) \to P(A)$. Therefore, if $P(A_n)$ does not approach $P(A)$, then there is an interval $[\lambda, P(A))$ with $\lambda < P(A)$ such that there is no $B \in \mathscr{S}$ with $P(B)$ in $[\lambda, P(A))$ and such that $P(A_n) < \lambda$ for all n. Suppose this to be the case.

If $P(A_{n+1} \backslash A_n) = P(A_{n+1}) - P(A_n) > 0$ for a denumerable number of n, then, since the corresponding $A_{n+1} \backslash A_n$ are disjoint and hence the sum of any finite number of their probabilities is less than λ, there must be an event $D_n = A_{n+1} \backslash A_n$ with small positive probability for which $P(A) > P(A \backslash D_n) = P(A) - P(D_n) \geq \lambda$, contrary to $P(B) \notin [\lambda, P(A))$ for all $B \in \mathscr{S}$. Hence $P(A_{n+1}) = P(A_n)$ for almost all n, and therefore there is some N such that $P(A_n) = P(A_m)$ for all $m, n \geq N$. However, with $B = A_N$, we require $P(A_n) > P(A_N)$ for some n. Hence it must be false that $[\lambda, P(A))$ contains no $P(B)$, and we conclude that

$$A_n \uparrow A \Rightarrow P(A_n) \to P(A).$$

To complete the proof of Theorem 3, suppose $\{A_1, A_2, \ldots\}$ is a denumerable partition of A with $A_n \in \mathscr{S}$ for all n. Let $B_1 = A_1$ and $B_n = \bigcup_{i=1}^{n} A_i$ for all n, so that $B_n \uparrow A$. By the preceding conclusion, $P(B_n) \to P(A)$, so that $\sum_{i=1}^{\infty} P(A_i) = \lim P(B_n) = P(A)$. Hence P is countably additive.

Theorem 4 says that $f \lambda g \in \mathscr{F}^*$ when $f, g \in \mathscr{F}^*$ and $0 < \lambda < 1$. Given any real a and $0 < \lambda < 1$, it suffices to show that $A = \{s : \lambda u_f(s) + (1 - \lambda)u_g(s) > a\}$ is in $\mathscr{S}$, assuming $f, g \in \mathscr{F}^*$. If $s \in A$ then there are rational numbers b_1 and b_2 such that $b_1 + b_2 > a$, $\lambda u_f(s) > b_1$ and $(1 - \lambda)u_g(s) > b_2$. For rationals b_1 and b_2 with $b_1 + b_2 > a$ let $B(b_1, b_2) = \{s : u_f(s) > b_1/\lambda\} \cap \{s : u_g(s) > b_2/(1 - \lambda)\}$. Clearly $B(b_1, b_2) \subseteq A$, and A is the union of all such $B(b_1, b_2)$. Since f and g are measurable, $B(b_1, b_2) \in \mathscr{S}$ and therefore $A \in \mathscr{S}$ since $\mathscr{S}$ is a Borel algebra and the number of $B(b_1, b_2)$ is countable.

CHAPTER 11

SUBJECTIVE LINEAR UTILITY FOR PARTIALLY
ORDERED PREFERENCES

Chapter 5 relaxed the assumption that $\succ$ on $\mathcal{M}$ or $\mathcal{P}$ is an asymmetric weak order, thus generalizing the two-way linear utility theory of Chapter 2. The present chapter considers a similar relaxation for $\succ$ on $\mathcal{F}$ of the preceding chapter that gives rise to a one-way subjective linear utility representation of the form

$$f \succ g \Rightarrow E(u_f, P) > E(u_g, P),$$

where u is a linear function on a convex set $\mathcal{P}$ of probability measures with $u_f(s) = u(f(s))$, and P is a probability measure on $\mathcal{S}$. We allow $\sim$ to be nontransitive, which adds a degree of realism to our model since a series of indifference comparisons $(f_1 \sim f_2, f_2 \sim f_3, \ldots, f_{n-1} \sim f_n)$ can easily accompany a strict preference judgment between end terms in the series $(f_1 \succ f_n)$. The strict preference relation need not be transitive. However, the one-way model implies that $\succ$ is acyclic.

As in the preceding chapter, $\mathcal{S}$ is a Boolean algebra of subsets of S, but instead of an arbitrary mixture set $\mathcal{M}$ we shall use a convex set $\mathcal{P}$ of probability measures $p, q, \ldots$ that are defined on an algebra $\mathcal{A}$ of subsets of a set $\mathcal{C}$ of consequences. An act is a function $f : S \to \mathcal{P}$ and, in this context,

$$\mathcal{F} = \{f: \quad f \text{ is constant on each element in some} \atop \text{measurable partition of } S\},$$

$$\mathcal{F}_0 = \{f \in \mathcal{F} : f \text{ is constant on each element in some } \textit{finite} \atop \text{measurable partition of } S\}.$$

We assume throughout the chapter that $S, \mathcal{S}, \mathcal{C}, \mathcal{A}$, and $\mathcal{P}$ are as noted with $\mathcal{P}$ closed under finite convex combinations, as in C0 of Section 5.1. Act $f \lambda g$ has $(f \lambda g)(s) = f(s) \lambda g(s)$ for all $s \in S$, where $f(s) \lambda g(s) = \lambda f(s) + (1 - \lambda)g(s)$. Since $f(s) \in \mathcal{P}$, $f(s)(D)$ for $D \in \mathcal{A}$ is the probability that measure $f(s)$ assigns to the subset D of consequences. If $f(s) = p \lambda_s q$, then f assigns the measure $\lambda_s p + (1 - \lambda_s)q$ in $\mathcal{P}$ to state s. As before, $\succsim$ is the union of $\succ$ and its symmetric complement $\sim$, and $p \succ q$ iff $f \succ g$ when $f = p$ on S and $g = q$ on S. In addition, given u on $\mathcal{P}$, we define u_f for any $f \in \mathcal{F}$ by $u_f(s) = u(f(s))$ for all $s \in S$.

The first section of the chapter discusses axioms for $\succ$ on $\mathscr{F}$ that imply the one-way representation for all $f, g \in \mathscr{F}_0$. The second section delves into the structure of the axioms and presents a comprehensive theorem for the one-way situation. We then introduce two more axioms that allow the representation to be extended to certain nonsimple acts in $\mathscr{F}$ when S has an infinite number of states. Additional remarks on the one-way representation are given in Fishburn (1975b).

11.1. AXIOMS AND SIMPLE ACTS

In addition to the usual assumption that $\succ$ on $\mathscr{F}$ is asymmetric, we shall use six basic axioms for the one-way subjective linear utility model. We denote these as G2 through G7, and state them succinctly with the understanding that they apply to all $f, g, f_1, f_2, g_1, g_2 \in \mathscr{F}$, all $p, q, r, t \in \mathscr{P}$, all $0 < \lambda < 1$, and all $\lambda_s, \mu_s, \alpha_s, \beta_s \in [0, 1]$.

G2. $\quad$ If $f_1 \succ f_2$ and $g_1 \succ g_2$ then $f_1 \lambda g_1 \succ f_2 \lambda g_2$,

G3. $\quad$ If $f_1 \succ f_2$ and $g_1 \succ g_2$ then $f_1 \alpha g_2 \succ f_2 \alpha g_1$ for some $0 < \alpha < 1$,

G4. $\quad$ There are $p', q' \in \mathscr{P}$ for which $p' \succ q'$,

G5. $\quad$ If $f_1(s) = p \lambda_s q$, $f_2(s) = p \mu_s q$, $g_1(s) = r \alpha_s t$ and $g_2(s) = r \beta_s t$ for all $s \in S$, and if $p \succ q$, $r \succ t$, $f_1 \succ f_2$ and $g_1 \succ g_2$, then there are $p', q' \in \mathscr{P}$ with $p' \succ q'$ such that $f_1' \succ f_2'$ and $g_1' \succ g_2'$ when $f_1'(s) = p' \lambda_s q'$, $f_2'(s) = p' \mu_s q'$, $g_1(s) = p' \alpha_s q'$ and $g_2(s) = p' \beta_s q'$ for all $s \in S$,

G6. $\quad$ If $f_1(s) = p \lambda_s q$ and $f_2(s) = p \mu_s q$ and $\lambda_s \geq \mu_s$ for all $s \in S$, then $f_1 \succsim f_2$ if $p \succ q$,

G7. $\quad$ If $f \succ g$ then there is a $D \in \mathscr{A}$ and $p', q' \in \mathscr{P}$ with $p' \succ q'$ such that $f' \succ g'$ when $f'(s) = p'[f(s)(D)]q'$ and $g'(s) = p'[g(s)(D)]q'$ for all $s \in S$.

Axioms G2 and G3 are similar respectively to C2 and C3 in Section 5.1, and they 'generalize' the combination of A2 and A3 applied to $\succ$ on $\mathscr{F}$. Axiom G2 is a weak independence axiom that accommodates the notion of nontransitive indifference or 'vague preferences' by requiring $\succ$ in both antecedents to obtain $\succ$ in the conclusion. Axiom G3 is a strong Archimedean axiom, but nevertheless seems plausible with α near to 1.

Since G2 and G3 apply to all constant acts in $\mathscr{F}$, it follows immediately from Theorem 3.1 that there is a linear function u on $\mathscr{P}$ for which $u(p) > u(q)$ whenever $p \succ q$. In fact, as we shall note later, our axioms imply the existence of linear u on $\mathscr{F}$ such that $u(f) > u(g)$ whenever $f \succ g$.

Axioms G4, G5, and G6 bear similarities to F4, F5, and F6 in the preceding chapter. Axiom G5 is a form of monotonicity-preservation condition which considers pairs of acts that are composed of mixtures of two probability measures in $\mathscr{P}$, such as p and q for f_1 and f_2, with the mixing coefficient (λ_s or μ_s) variable over the states. (Of course, for f_1 to be in $\mathscr{F}$ when $f_1(s) = p \lambda_s q$ for all s, if $p \neq q$ then there must be a measurable partition of S such that λ_s is constant on each member of the partition.) Given the hypotheses of G5, including $p \succ q$, $r \succ t$ $f_1 \succ f_2$ and $g_1 \succ g_2$, the axiom asserts that (p, q) and (r, t) can be replaced by a single pair (p', q') without changing the preferences between the modified f_1 and f_2, and g_1 and g_2. In many cases we would expect that either (p, q) or (r, t) could be an acceptable (p', q'), but (in the presence of G6) the axiom allows the possibility that f_1 with (r, t) in place of (p, q) is indifferent to f_2 with (r, t) in place of (p, q), and that g_1 with (p, q) in place of (r, t) is indifferent to g_2 with (p, q) in place of (r, t).

Axiom G6 is an appealing independence-dominance condition. It says that if f_1 and f_2 are composed of mixtures of p and q, if you prefer p to q, and if, regardless of which state obtains, f_1 offers as good a chance as f_2 for the preferred p, then you will like f_1 as much as f_2.

The final axiom, G7, seems different than anything encountered before. Its purpose is to ensure the existence of a 'consistent' measure P, as will be explained later. Given $f \succ g$, one generally pictures $D \in \mathscr{A}$ which satisfies the conclusion of G7 as a subset of relatively preferred consequences. Indeed, we would expect that $f \succ g$ indicates the existence of a relatively desirable D such that f is perceived by the individual to be more likely than g of yielding something in D. Given such a perception, and given p definitely preferred to q, we would expect $f' \succ g'$ when $f'(s) = p[f(s)(D)]q$ and $g'(s) = p[g(s)(D)]q$ for all $s \in S$.

In fact, if $\mathscr{C}$ contains only two consequences, say $\mathscr{C} = \{c, d\}$, and if we presume that $c \succ d$, then G7 is trivially satisfied by taking $p' = c^*$, $q' = d^*$ and $D = \{c\}$, for then $f' = f$ and $g' = g$. However, it does not appear that G7 follows from other axioms when $\mathscr{C}$ has more than two consequences.

One can look at G7 in a slightly more general light as follows. If f is not indifferent to g then, whether $f \succ g$ or $g \succ f$, the expressed preference would seem odd unless there were some $D \in \mathscr{A}$ that the individual perceives as having noticeably different chances under f and under g. If he perceives g as having a better chance than f of yielding something in D, then complementation suggests that he will perceive f as having a better chance than g of yielding something in $\mathscr{C}\backslash D$. Thus it seems most reasonable that, when $f \not\succ g$, it will be felt that f has a better chance than g of giving something in E for some $E \in \mathscr{A}$. Whether $f \succ g$ or $g \succ f$, it should follow that f' will be preferred to g' when p is definitely preferred to q, $f'(s) = p[f(s)(E)]q$ and $g'(s) = p[g(s)(E)]q$ for all $s \in S$. Even if this were false for some (p, q) with $p \succ q$, because of a bare preference for p over q that is diluted into indifference when put into the (f', g') format, it could still be true for other (p, q) pairs, and this is more than enough to satisfy G7.

The closest thing to G7 in the preceding chapter would appear to be F5 even though there are a number of differences between the two axioms. Despite these differences, both axioms serve important roles in generating a well-behaved subjective probability measure P on $\mathscr{S}$.

As shown by the following theorem, the axioms discussed above are sufficient for the one-way subjective linear utility representation for simple acts.

THEOREM 1. *Suppose G2 through G7 hold. Then there is a linear function u on $\mathscr{P}$ and a probability measure P on $\mathscr{S}$ such that, for all $f, g \in \mathscr{F}_0$, $E(u_f, P) > E(u_g, P)$ whenever $f \succ g$.*

Unlike P in the preceding chapter, P in Theorem 1 is not generally unique. Similarly, u on $\mathscr{P}$ is not generally unique up to a positive affine transformation.

We shall not prove Theorem 1 directly since it will follow as a simple corollary of a much more comprehensive theorem that is developed in the next section. The new theorem does not use any additional axioms, but it does require the definition of some new concepts.

11.2. FRACTIONAL EVENTS AND INDUCED MEASURES

The principal new concept that we shall pursue in this section is that of a fractional event. As defined earlier, an ordinary event is an $A \in \mathscr{S}$. A *fractional event* is any function from S into $[0, 1]$ that is constant on each element of some measurable partition of S. Event $A \in \mathscr{S}$ thus corresponds to the fractional event that assigns 1 to each $s \in A$ and 0 to each $s \in S \backslash A$, which is often referred to as the characteristic function of A.

In this chapter, *x and y, with or without subscripts, will be used exclusively to denote fractional events* and should not be confused with earlier uses of these symbols. The set of all fractional events is denoted $\mathscr{X}$:

$\mathscr{X} = \{x : x$ is a function from S into $[0, 1]$ that is constant on each element in some measurable partition of $S\}$.

With the usual definition that $(x \lambda y)(s) = \lambda x(s) + (1 - \lambda)y(s)$, it is easily seen that $\mathscr{X}$ is a mixture set since it is closed under finite convex combinations that produce functions that are constant on each element in some measurable partition (consider intersections of events in the partitions for x and y) of S.

In a manner of speaking, the fractional event x assigns 'probability' $x(s)$ to each $s \in S$. If $\mathscr{C} = \{c, d\}$, then an obvious bijection between $\mathscr{F}$ and $\mathscr{X}$ is obtained by corresponding f and x when $f(s)(c) = x(s)$ for all $s \in S$.

Let $\mathbf{1}$ and $\mathbf{0}$ denote respectively the universal fractional event ($\mathbf{1}(s) = 1$ for all s) and the empty fractional event ($\mathbf{0}(s) = 0$ for all s). The 'complement' of fractional event x is $\mathbf{1} - x$, which takes on the value $1 - x(s)$ for each s. We shall make use later of the fact that the set $\mathscr{X}$ of fractional events is a subset of the vector space of all real-valued functions on S that are constant on each element in some measurable partition of S. The theory developed in Section 5.4 will then give rise to a 'probability measure' P^* on $\mathscr{X}$ whose specialization to characteristic functions of ordinary events yields P on $\mathscr{S}$.

Given $x, y \in \mathscr{X}$, we consider the possibility of comparing these fractional events to see if one is 'more probable than' the other. To do this we select consequences $c, d \in \mathscr{C}$ with $c \succ d$ and form acts f and g as follows:

$$f(s)(c) = x(s) \quad \text{and} \quad f(s)(d) = 1 - x(s)$$
$$g(s)(c) = y(s) \quad \text{and} \quad g(s)(d) = 1 - y(s).$$

If the individual has a subjective probability measure P on $\mathscr{S}$, then his probability for c under f will be $\int x(s) \, dP(s)$, and his probability for c under g will be $\int y(s) \, dP(s)$. Since he prefers c to d, we would presume that he will prefer f to g if the first probability exceeds the second by a noticeable difference. Hence, if $f \succ g$, we would be inclined to say that he considers x more probable than y, while $g \succ f$ would indicate that he believes y to be more probable than x. It might happen that $f \succ g$ for one (c, d) pair but $f \sim g$ for another pair (c', d') when c' is barely preferred to d', and in this case we would still say that x is considered more probable than y.

When c and d in the preceding paragraph are replaced by measures in $\mathscr{P}$, we obtain a slightly more general definition of a comparative probability relation $\succ^*$ on $\mathscr{X}$:

$$x \succ^* y \quad \text{iff} \quad \text{there are } p, q \in \mathscr{P} \text{ with } p \succ q \text{ such that } f \succ g \text{ when}$$
$$f(s) = px(s)q \text{ and } g(s) = py(s)q \text{ for all } s \in S.$$

The relation $\succ^*$ on $\mathscr{X}$ has an important connection to axiom G5. Some readers will have noticed already that G5, G6 and G7 involve fractional events in some profusion. For G5 let $x(s) = \lambda_s$, $y(s) = \mu_s$, $x'(s) = \alpha_s$ and $y'(s) = \beta_s$. Then G5 says that if $x \succ^* y$ is established on the basis of $p \succ q$, and if $x' \succ^* y'$ is established on the basis of $r \succ t$, then there are $p' \succ q'$ that establish both $x \succ^* y$ and $x' \succ^* y'$.

We shall say that P^* is a (finitely additive) *probability measure on* $\mathscr{X}$ if it satisfies the following for all $x, y \in \mathscr{X}$:

$$P^*(1) = 1,$$
$$P^*(x) \geq 0,$$
$$P^*(x + y) = P^*(x) + P^*(y) \text{ when } x + y \leq 1.$$

Although this differs somewhat from the traditional definition, new terminology seems unnecessary. Given P^* on $\mathscr{X}$, we will define P on $\mathscr{S}$ by

$$P(A) = P^*(x) \text{ when } x(s) = 1 \text{ on } A \text{ and } x(s) = 0 \text{ on } S \backslash A.$$

Clearly, P on $\mathscr{S}$ is a probability measure (traditional) when P^* on $\mathscr{X}$ is a probability measure (nontraditional). Moreover, it follows readily from the definitions in Section 3.1 that, for all $x \in \mathscr{X}$,

$$P^*(x) = \int_S x(s) dP(s).$$

In the spirit of our one-way representation, it will be proved later that G2 through G6 imply the existence of a probability measure P^* on $\mathscr{X}$ for which $P^*(x) > P^*(y)$ whenever $x \succ^* y$. Although G7 is not involved in this proof, it plays an important role in imparting a type of consistency or regularity to P^* that will be used in connection with measures on $\mathscr{A}$ induced by P and $\mathscr{F}$.

Induced Measures

Given P^* on $\mathscr{X}$ and $f \in \mathscr{F}$, with P on $\mathscr{S}$ defined from P^* as indicated above, we define the measure P_f induced by P and f on $\mathscr{A}$ by

$$P_f(D) = \int_S [f(s)(D)] dP(s) \quad \text{for all} \quad D \in \mathscr{A}.$$

Thus, for each measurable subset of consequences, P_f gives the probability under P on $\mathscr{S}$ that some consequence in the subset will obtain when f is 'chosen'. Clearly, P_f is a probability measure on $\mathscr{A}$ when $f \in \mathscr{F}$ and P is a probability measure on $\mathscr{S}$, and it follows readily from the definitions that $P_{f\lambda g} = \lambda P_f + (1 - \lambda)P_g$. Thus, with

$$\mathscr{P}_P = \{P_f : f \in \mathscr{F}\},$$

we see that the set $\mathscr{P}_P$ of measures on $\mathscr{A}$ induced by P and $\mathscr{F}$ is closed under finite convex combinations. Moreover, since $P_f(D) = \int p(D)\, dP(s) = = p(D)$ when $f(s) = p$ for all s, $\mathscr{P} \subseteq \mathscr{P}_P$.

Given P^*, we define a preference relation $\succ_P$ on $\mathscr{P}_P$ that is induced by $\succ$ on $\mathscr{F}$ as follows:

$$P_f \succ_P P_g \quad \text{iff} \quad f \succ g.$$

If $p \succ q$ for $p, q \in \mathscr{P}$ then $p \succ_P q$ regardless of which P^* on $\mathscr{X}$ that is consistent with $\succ^*$ is adopted. The subscript on $\succ_P$ is retained to acknowledge the possibility that different P^* for which $P^*(x) > P^*(y)$ whenever $x \succ^* y$ give rise to different induced preference relations. For example, if $p, q \in \mathscr{P}_P \cap \mathscr{P}_Q$, we might have $p \succ_P q$ and $p \sim_Q q$.

The technical role of G7 can now be explained. It is used to ensure that $\succ_P$ is irreflexive which, in combination with G2 (let $f_1 = g_2 = f$, $f_2 = g_1 = g$ and $\lambda = \frac{1}{2}$), implies that $\succ_P$ is asymmetric. Without G7, we face the possibility that $P_f = P_g$ when $f \succ g$, which would give $p \succ_P p$ when $p = P_f$. With G7, this cannot happen regardless of which P^* is adopted. For suppose that $f \succ g$ and, as in G7, that $f' \succ g'$ with $p \succ q$, $D \in \mathscr{A}$, and $f'(s) = p[f(s)(D)]q$ and $g'(s) = p[g(s)(D)]q$ for all $s \in S$. Let

$$x(s) = f(s)(D)$$
$$y(s) = g(s)(D)$$

for all $s \in S$. Then $x \succ^* y$ by definition, and therefore $P^*(x) > P^*(y)$ for every P^* consistent with $\succ^*$. Since $P_f(D) = P^*(x)$ and $P_g(D) = P^*(y)$, it follows that $P_f \neq P_g$.

Theorem

The principal implications of our axioms are summarized in the following theorem.

THEOREM 2. *Suppose G2 through G7 hold. Then there is a probability measure P^* on the set $\mathscr{X}$ of fractional events such that, for all $x, y \in \mathscr{X}$,*

$$x \succ^* y \Rightarrow P^*(x) > P^*(y).$$

Given any such P^*, let $(\mathscr{P}_P, \succ_P)$ be as defined above with $\mathscr{P}_P$ the measures on $\mathscr{A}$ induced by P and $\mathscr{F}$, and $P_f \succ_P P_g$ iff $f \succ g$. Then $\mathscr{P}_P$ is closed under finite convex combinations, $\mathscr{P} \subseteq \mathscr{P}_P$, $P_f(D) = P^*(x)$ when $x(s) = f(s)(D)$ for all $s \in S$ with $D \in \mathscr{A}$, and there is a linear function u on $\mathscr{P}_P$ such that $u(p) > u(q)$ whenever $p, q \in \mathscr{P}_P$ and $p \succ_P q$.

Although we have omitted a subscript on u, it clearly depends on P^* or P. A proof of Theorem 2 is given in Section 4.

Given a particular P^* and u that satisfy the theorem, we extend u to $\mathscr{F}$ by defining $u(f) = u(P_f)$. Since $P_{f \lambda g} = \lambda P_f + (1 - \lambda)P_g$, $u(f \lambda g) = \lambda u(f) + (1 - \lambda)u(g)$ so that u is linear on $\mathscr{F}$. Moreover, by the definition of $\succ_P$,

$$f \succ g \Rightarrow u(f) > u(g).$$

Similarly, since $\mathscr{P} \subseteq \mathscr{P}_P$, u on $\mathscr{P}$ is linear with $u(p) > u(q)$ whenever $p, q \in \mathscr{P}$ and $p \succ q$.

To see that Theorem 1 follows from Theorem 2, we consider $f \in \mathscr{F}_0$. Suppose $\{A_1, \dots, A_n\}$ is an n-part measurable partition of S, with $p_i \in \mathscr{P}$ and $f = p_i$ on A_i for $i = 1, \dots, n$. Then $P_f = \sum_{i=1}^n P(A_i)p_i$ since, for each $D \in \mathscr{A}$,

$$P_f(D) = \int_S [f(s)(D)] \, dP(s) = \sum_{i=1}^n P(A_i)p_i(D).$$

Therefore $u(f) = u(P_f) = u(\sum P(A_i)p_i) = \sum u(p_i)P(A_i) = E(u_f, P)$, so that

$$E(u_f, P) = u(f) \quad \text{for all} \quad f \in \mathscr{F}_0.$$

Hence $f, g \in \mathscr{F}_0$ and $f \succ g$ imply $E(u_f, P) > E(u_g, P)$, and Theorem 1 is verified.

11.3. AN EXTENSION

We now consider an extension of the subjective expected-utility form $u(f) = E(u_f, P)$ to nonsimple measures in $\mathscr{F}$ within the context of the preceding section. To simplify integrability problems, it will be assumed that $\mathscr{S} = 2^S$, but $\mathscr{A}$ can still be any arbitrary Boolean algebra of subsets of $\mathscr{C}$.

Two more axioms are used in the extension. They are patterned after C5 and the separation axiom in Theorem 5.6. In G9, $p_i^* \in \mathscr{F}$ has $p_i^*(s) = p_i$ for all $s \in S$.

G8.   *There are $p_1 > p_2 > p_3 > p_4$ in $\mathscr{P}$ such that, for every $p \in \mathscr{P}$, either $p_2 > p$ or $p > p_3$,*

G9.   *(a) If $A \in S \setminus \{\emptyset\}$, $f \in \mathscr{F}$ with $f(s) = p$ for all $s \in S \setminus A$, $f(s) > p_3 > p_4$ for all $s \in S$ and some $p_3, p_4 \in \mathscr{P}$, and $0 < \lambda < 1$, then there are $s_*, s^* \in A$, with $g = f(s^*)$ and $h = f(s_*)$ on A and $g = h = p$ on $S \setminus A$, such that $g > f \lambda p_4^*$ and $f > h \lambda p_4^*$;*
(b) If $A \in \mathscr{S} \setminus \{\emptyset\}$, $f \in \mathscr{F}$ with $f(s) = p$ for all $s \in S \setminus A$, $p_1 > p_2 > f(s)$ for all $s \in S$ and some $p_1, p_2 \in \mathscr{P}$, and $0 < \lambda < 1$, then there are $s_*, s^* \in A$, with $g = f(s^*)$ and $h = f(s_*)$ on A and $g = h = p$ on $S \setminus A$, such that $g \lambda p_1^* > f$ and $f \lambda p_1^* > h$.

Axiom G8 is a reasonable separation condition which supercedes G4. It should hold in most situations. Although G9 is less palatable, something like it is needed to extend the subjective expected-utility form when $>$ is not presumed to be an asymmetric weak order.

Consider G9(a), where $f = g = h = p$ on the complement of a nonempty event A, and where $g = f(s^*)$ and $h = f(s_*)$ on A so that g and h are simple acts in $\mathscr{F}_0$. If A is effectively null, then the import of the conclusion of G9(a) is that $p > p \lambda p_4$. This could of course fail when λ is near to 1, owing to the diluting effect in the mixture $p \lambda p_4$, which could give $p \sim p \lambda p_4$. If A is not null, then the conclusion of G9(a) would have the best chance of holding when $f(s^*)$ is a relatively desirable measure in $f(A) = \{f(s): s \in A\}$ – to give $g > f \lambda p_4^*$, and when $f(s_*)$ is a relatively undesirable measure in $f(A)$ – to give $f > h \lambda p_4^*$.

Our extension theorem applies only to acts in $\mathscr{F}$ that are totally bounded on S. Further considerations of boundedness would follow the lines suggested in the latter part of Section 5.3.

THEOREM 3. *Suppose G2 through G9 hold with $\mathscr{S} = 2^S$, and let P and u satisfy the representation of Theorem 2. Then $E(u_f, P) = u(f)$ for every $f \in \mathscr{F}$ for which $\inf u(f(S))$ and $\sup u(f(S))$ are finite.*

A proof of this theorem appears in Section 5.

11.4. PROOF OF THEOREM 2

Our proof of Theorem 2 has two main steps. The first is to establish the existence of P^* on $\mathscr{X}$ for which $x >^* y \Rightarrow P^*(x) > P^*(y)$. This step assumes G2 through G6 and is similar to the proofs of Theorems 5.2 and 5.3, with modifications necessitated by the fact that P^* is to be a probability measure. The second step then obtains u for $(\mathscr{P}_P, \succ_P)$. This step adds G7 to our assumptions and makes direct use of Theorem 5.1.

Derivation of P*

Using the type of approach suggested by Sections 5.4 and 5.5, let $\mathscr{V}$ be the vector space of all real-valued functions on S that are constant on each element of some measurable partition of S, so $\mathscr{X} \subseteq \mathscr{V}$, and let C be the convex cone in $\mathscr{V}$ generated by $\{x - y : x, y \in \mathscr{X} \text{ and } x \succ^* y\}$. We shall note first that $\mathbf{0} \notin C$, then show that C is Archimedean, and then embed C in a maximal cone in such a way that the existence of the desired P^* will follow from the Hausner–Wendel theorem, Theorem 5.7.

Contrary to $\mathbf{0} \notin C$, suppose that there are $x_i, y_i \in \mathscr{X}$ with $x_i \succ^* y_i$ and positive numbers, say λ_i, normed so that $\sum_{i=1}^{n} \lambda_i = 1$, such that $\sum_{i=1}^{n} \lambda_i(x_i - y_i) = \mathbf{0}$. According to the definition of $\succ^*$, let $p_i, q_i \in \mathscr{P}$ with $p_i \succ q_i$ be such that $f_i \succ g_i$ when $f_i(s) = p_i x_i(s) q_i$ and $g_i(s) = p_i y_i(s) q_i$ for $s \in S$. Then, using G2 and G5, we proceed from $i = 1$ up to $i = n$ in the obvious way to arrive at the conclusion that there are $p', q' \in \mathscr{P}$ with $p' \succ q'$ along with $f, g \in \mathscr{F}$ and $f \succ g$ such that $f(s) = (\sum \lambda_i x_i(s)) p' + (1 - \sum \lambda_i x_i(s)) q'$ and $g(s) = (\sum \lambda_i y_i(s)) p' + (1 - \sum \lambda_i y_i(s)) q'$ for all $s \in S$. But then, since $\sum \lambda_i(x_i - y_i) = \mathbf{0}$, $f = g$, and this contradicts irreflexivity of $\succ$ in view of $f \succ g$. Therefore $\mathbf{0} \notin C$.

For the Archimedean property we are to show that $v, w \in C$ implies $av - w \in C$ for some $a > 0$. For definiteness let $v = \sum \lambda_i(x_i - y_i)$ and $w = \sum \mu_j(x'_j - y'_j)$ with $\lambda_i > 0, \mu_j > 0, x_i \succ^* y_i$ and $x'_j \succ^* y'_j$, with the λ_i and μ_j normalized with no real loss in generality so that $\sum \lambda_i = \sum \mu_j = 1$. Using the procedure indicated in the preceding paragraph, we obtain $f, g, f'g' \in \mathscr{F}$ with $f \succ g$ and $f' \succ g'$ along with $p \succ q$ (by one more application of G5) such that

$$f(s) = p[\sum \lambda_i x_i(s)]q$$
$$g(s) = p[\sum \lambda_i y_i(s)]q$$
$$f'(s) = p[\sum \mu_j x'_j(s)]q$$
$$g'(s) = p[\sum \mu_j y'_j(s)]q$$

for all $s \in S$. The Archimedean axiom G3 then gives $0 < \alpha < 1$ with $f \alpha g' \succ g \alpha f'$ so that, by the definition of $\succ^*$, $[\alpha \sum \lambda_i x_i + (1 - \alpha) \sum \mu_j y'_j] \succ^*$ $\succ^* [\alpha \sum \lambda_i y_i + (1 - \alpha) \sum \mu_j x'_j]$. Rearrangement and the definition of C then give $[\alpha/(1 - \alpha)][\sum \lambda_i(x_i - y_i)] - [\sum \mu_j(x'_j - y'_j)] =$ $= [\alpha/(1 - \alpha)]v - w \in C$.

It follows that C is an Archimedean convex cone in $\mathcal{V}$ with $\mathbf{0} \notin C$. To carry out the embedding step, we show first that there is a convex cone in $\mathcal{V}$ that includes $C \cup \mathcal{X} \backslash \{\mathbf{0}\}$ and does not contain $\mathbf{0}$. Let C' be the convex cone generated by $\{x - y : x \succ^* y\} \cup \mathcal{X} \backslash \{\mathbf{0}\}$, so that $C \cup \mathcal{X} \backslash \{\mathbf{0}\} \subseteq C'$. The result just stated holds if $\mathbf{0} \notin C'$. To the contrary, suppose $\mathbf{0} \in C'$, i.e. there are nonnegative a_i and b_j at least one of which is positive along with $x_i \succ^* y_i$ and $z_j \in \mathcal{X} \backslash \{\mathbf{0}\}$ such that

$$\sum a_i (x_i - y_i) + \sum b_j z_j = \mathbf{0}.$$

Either all $b_j = 0$, which contradicts $\mathbf{0} \notin C$, or all $a_i = 0$, which is impossible, or some $a_i > 0$ and some $b_j > 0$. In the last case, normalize the coefficients so that $\sum a_i = 1$ and use the procedure of the proof of $\mathbf{0} \notin C$ to get $f \succ g$ and $p \succ q$ with $f(s) = p[\sum a_i x_i(s)] q$ and $g(s) = p[\sum a_i y_i(s)] q$ for all s. Since $\sum b_j z_j(s) \geq 0$ for all s, $\sum a_i(x_i - y_i) + \sum b_j z_j = \mathbf{0}$ implies that $\sum a_i y_i(s) \geq \sum a_i x_i(s)$ for all s. Therefore, given $p \succ q$, G6 implies $g \succsim f$, thus contradicting $f \succ g$. Hence $\mathbf{0} \notin C'$.

It follows easily from Zorn's lemma in Section 5.4 that there is a maximal convex cone $\mathcal{V}^+$ in $\mathcal{V}$ which includes $C \cup \mathcal{X} \backslash \{\mathbf{0}\}$ and does not contain $\mathbf{0}$. Given $\mathcal{V}^+$, define $>_0$ on $\mathcal{V}$ by $v >_0 w$ iff $v - w \in \mathcal{V}^+$. Then $(\mathcal{V}, >_0)$ is a linearly ordered vector space: irreflexivity of $>_0$ is immediate from $\mathbf{0} \notin V^+$; transitivity is obvious since $v - w \in \mathcal{V}^+$ and $w - w' \in \mathcal{V}^+$ imply $v - w' \in \mathcal{V}^+$ by addition; completeness follows by showing that if neither $v - w$ nor $w - v$ is in $\mathcal{V}^+$ when $v \neq w$, then the convex cone generated by $\mathcal{V}^+ \cup \{v - w\}$ does not contain $\mathbf{0}$, thus contradicting maximality for $\mathcal{V}^+$; and the other properties in Section 5.4 are easily verified in the order (iii), (i), and (ii).

Given the linearly ordered vector space $(\mathcal{V}, >_0)$, we define $\gg$, $\sim^+$, $<^+$, $\mathscr{E}$, $(\mathcal{V}(\mathscr{E}), >_L)$ and f_E in the manner indicated prior to Theorem 5.7 and let $F : \mathcal{V} \to \mathcal{V}(\mathscr{E})$ be the linear function that satisfies that theorem. We let E denote the equivalence class in $\mathscr{E} = \mathcal{V}^+ / \sim^+$ that includes the Archimedean cone C and let $\mathbf{1}$ be the representative from E used in Theorem 5.7, noting that $\mathbf{1} \in C$ follows directly from G4.

Now for each $v \in \mathcal{V}$, recall that $F(v)$ is a real-valued function on $\mathscr{E}$ with value $F(v)(E)$ at $E \in \mathscr{E}$. We define P^* on $\mathcal{V}$ by

$$P^*(v) = F(v)(E),$$

where P^* is a linear functional on $\mathcal{V}$ since F is a linear function. Hence $P^*(x + y) = P^*(x) + P^*(y)$. Moreover, $P^*(\mathbf{1}) = F(\mathbf{1})(E) = f_E(E) = 1$ and, by the type of analysis used in the proof of Corollary 5.1, $P^*(v) > 0$ for all $v \in E$. In particular, if $x \succ^* y$, then $x - y \in C \subseteq E$, so $P^*(x - y) = = P^*(x) - P^*(y) > 0$. Hence $x \succ^* y \Rightarrow P^*(x) > P^*(y)$.

To finish the proof for P^*, we need to show that $P^*(x) \geq 0$ for $x \in \mathcal{X} \setminus \{\mathbf{0}\}$. If $x \in E$, $P^*(x) > 0$, so assume henceforth that $x \notin E \cup \{\mathbf{0}, \mathbf{1}\}$. Then $\mathbf{1} - x \notin \notin \{\mathbf{0}, \mathbf{1}\}$, so both x and $\mathbf{1} - x$ are in $\mathcal{V}^+$; hence $x >_0 \mathbf{0}$ and $\mathbf{1} - x >_0 \mathbf{0}$; hence, by Theorem 5.7(a), $F(x) >_L \mathbf{0}$ and $F(\mathbf{1} - x) = F(\mathbf{1}) - F(x) >_L \mathbf{0}$. Let E' be the first class in $(\mathcal{E}, <^+)$ at which $F(x)(E') \neq 0$, so that $F(x)(E') > 0$ since $F(x) >_L \mathbf{0}$. If $E' <^+ E$ then $F(\mathbf{1} - x)(E') = F(\mathbf{1})(E') - F(x)(E') = 0 - - F(x)(E') < 0$; but then E'', the first class in $(\mathcal{E}, <^+)$ at which $F(\mathbf{1} - x)(E'') \neq 0$, which requires $F(\mathbf{1} - x)(E'') > 0$, must satisfy $E'' <^+ E'$. And, with this and $F(\mathbf{1} - x)(E'') = F(\mathbf{1})(E'') - F(x)(E'') = 0 - F(x)(E'') > 0$, we get $F(x)(E'') < 0$, which contradicts the designation of E'. Therefore, it must be true that $E <^+ E'$, so that $F(x)(E) = 0$, i.e. $P^*(x) = 0$. Hence $P^*(x) \geq 0$ for all $x \in \mathcal{X}$.

Derivation of u

Given any P^* on $\mathcal{X}$ as obtained by the preceding proof, let $(\mathcal{P}_P, \succ_P)$ be as defined in Section 2 with $P_f(D) = \int [f(s)(D)] dP(s)$ for all $D \in \mathcal{A}$ and all $P_f \in \mathcal{P}_P$, and with $P_f \succ_P P_g$ iff $f \succ g$. As noted prior to the statement of Theorem 2, G7 and G2 imply that $\succ_P$ is asymmetric; $\mathcal{P} \subseteq \mathcal{P}_P$; and $\mathcal{P}_P$ is closed under finite convex combinations. In addition, G2 and G3 imply directly that C2 and C3 of Section 5.1 hold for $\succ_P$ on $\mathcal{P}_P$. Therefore, by Theorem 5.1, there is a linear function u on $\mathcal{P}_P$ for which $u(p) > u(q)$ whenever $p, q \in \mathcal{P}_P$ and $p \succ_P q$.

11.5. PROOF OF THEOREM 3

We assume throughout this section that G2 through G9 hold with $\mathcal{S} = 2^S$. In addition, P and u are presumed to satisfy the representation of Theorem 2 as derived in the preceding section. We shall use the fact that $u(f) = E(u_f, P)$ for all $f \in \mathcal{F}_0$: see the end of Section 2.

LEMMA 1. *Suppose* $f \in \mathcal{F}$ *and* $\inf u_f(S)$ *and* $\sup u_f(S)$ *are finite. Then* $\inf u_f(S) \leq u(f) \leq \sup u_f(S)$.

Proof. Assume that $\inf u(f(S))$ and $\sup u(f(S))$ are finite. Using G8, partition S into A and B (one of which might be empty) so that $p_1 \succ p_2 \succ f(s)$ for all $s \in A$ and $f(s) \succ p_3 \succ p_4$ for all $s \in B$.

Suppose first that $B = \emptyset$, so that $A = S$. Then, with $A = S$ in G9(b), for any $0 < \lambda < 1$ there are $s_*, s^* \in S$ (which can depend on λ) such that

$f(s^*)\lambda p_1^* \succ f$ and $f\lambda p_1^* \succ f(s_*)$. Then the remarks following Theorem 2 give $\lambda u(f(s^*)) + (1 - \lambda)u(p_1) > u(f)$ and $\lambda u(f) + (1 - \lambda)u(p_1) > u(f(s_*))$, so that $\inf u(f(S)) \le u(f) \le \sup u(f(S))$ on letting $\lambda \to 1$. The same conclusion is reached with G9(a) if $A = \emptyset$.

Assume henceforth in this proof that neither A and B is empty. Choose any $p \in f(A)$ and $q \in f(B)$ and define $f_1, f_2, f_3 \in \mathcal{F}$ by

$$f_1 = f \text{ on } A, \quad f_1 = p \text{ on } B,$$
$$f_2 = q \text{ on } A, \quad f_2 = f \text{ on } B,$$
$$f_3 = q \text{ on } A, \quad f_3 = p \text{ on } B.$$

Then $f_1 \tfrac{1}{2} f_3 = f_1 \tfrac{1}{2} f_2$ so that $u(f) + u(f_3) = u(f_1) + u(f_2)$. Given $0 < \lambda < 1$, G9(b) gives $s_*, s^* \in A$ such that

$$\lambda[P(A)u_f(s^*) + P(B)u(p)] + (1 - \lambda)u(p_1) > u(f_1)$$

and

$$\lambda u(f_1) + (1 - \lambda)u(p_1) > P(A)u_f(s_*) + P(B)u(p).$$

Let λ approach 1. Then

$$P(A)\inf u_f(A) + P(B)u(p) \le u(f_1) \le P(A)\sup u_f(A) + P(B)u(p).$$

Similarly, G9(a) yields

$$P(A)u(q) + P(B)\inf u_f(B) \le u(f_2) \le P(A)u(q) + P(B)\sup u_f(B).$$

Moreover, $u(f_3) = P(A)u(q) + P(B)u(p)$ since $f_3 \in \mathcal{F}_0$. Therefore, in view of $P(A) + P(B) = 1$ and $u(f_1) + u(f_2) = u(f) + u(f_3)$, addition gives

$$\inf u_f(S) + u(f_3) \le u(f) + u(f_3) \le \sup u_f(S) + u(f_3),$$

so that $\inf u_f(S) \le u(f) \le \sup u_f(S)$.

Given Lemma 1, the proof of Theorem 3 follows the approach used in Section 10.5 to prove Theorem 10.2(a). Given $a = \inf u_f(S)$ and $b = \sup u_f(S)$, Lemma 1 gives the desired result immediately if $a = b$, so, with a and b finite, assume henceforth with no loss in generality that $a = 0$ and $b = 1$. We then define $A_1 = \{s : 0 \le u_f(s) \le 1/n\}$ and $A_i = \{s : (i - 1)/n < u_f(s) \le i/n\}$ for $i = 2, \ldots, n$ and use the cited approach to obtain

$$\sum_{i=1}^{n} P(A_i)(i - 1)/n - 1/n \le u(f) \le \sum_{i=1}^{n} P(A_i)i/n + 1/n$$

along with $\Sigma\, P(A_i)(i - 1)/n \le E(u_f, P) \le \Sigma\, P(A_i)i/n$, so that $u(f) = E(u_f, P)$ results from letting $n \to \infty$.

CHAPTER 12

SUBJECTIVE LINEAR UTILITY WITH CONDITIONAL PREFERENCE COMPARISONS

We conclude Part II with an approach to subjective linear utility that differs significantly from the approach of preceding chapters. Previously, an act was viewed as a function from the set S of states into mixture sets, with $f(s)$ the entity – such as a lottery on consequences – assigned by act f to state s. The present approach views acts as primitives and not as functions on the states. Intuitively, we shall think of acts in a natural way as the courses of action an individual is to choose among in his uncertain situation.

The set of all acts will be presumed to be a mixture set $\mathcal{M}$, with members $x, y, x\lambda y$, and so forth. A natural interpretation is that $\mathcal{M}$ is the set of simple probability measures defined on a set of basic acts whose probabilities are generated by chance mechanisms as discussed in Chapter 9. Extraneous scaling probabilities have no other application in the present formulation. In a game-theoretic setting, $\mathcal{M}$ could denote the set of simple mixed strategies available to the player whose preferences are being considered.

As before, $\mathcal{S}$ is a Boolean algebra of subsets of S. Let $\mathcal{S}' = \mathcal{S} \setminus \{\emptyset\}$, the set of nonempty events. We shall apply the individual's preference relation $\succ$ to $\mathcal{M} \times \mathcal{S}'$, whose ordered pairs $(x, A), (y, B), \ldots$ will often be written more briefly as $xA, yB, \ldots$. Consequences as such play no formal role although one might view the act-state pair (x, s) as a 'consequence', i.e. as the value-relevant aspects involved with doing x and having state s obtain. However, our approach makes no assumption that all uncertainty, apart from that involved in extraneous scaling probabilities, is resolved when x and s are specified even though we would like to capture the primary sources of exogenous uncertainty in the formulation of S.

An act-event pair xA in $\mathcal{M} \times \mathcal{S}'$ is generally conceived of as "whatever might happen if x is chosen and event A obtains". If we wish to compare acts x and y without restriction, then we would compare xS and yS. More generally, in comparing xA and yB, the individual is presumed to compare x under the hypothesis that some state in A obtains against y under the hypothesis that some state in B obtains. Roughly speaking,

$xA \succ yB$ indicates that the individual would rather do x and have A obtain than do y and have B obtain.

The notation xA for (x, A) will be joined by the convention of using parentheses to enclose a combination in the first or second position of an act-event pair. Thus $x(A \cup B) = (x, A \cup B), (x \lambda y)A = (x \lambda y, A)$, and $(x \lambda y)(A \cup B) = (x \lambda y, A \cup B)$. For any event $A \in \mathscr{S}'$, we let $\mathscr{M}_A = \{xA : x \in \mathscr{M}\}$. Each $\mathscr{M}_A$ can be thought of as a copy of $\mathscr{M}$ indexed by the conditioning event A. By defining $xA \lambda yA$ as $(x \lambda y)A$, $\mathscr{M}_A$ is a mixture set. (If $A \neq B$, then $xA \lambda yB$ has no meaning in our formulation.) Thus $\mathscr{M} \times \mathscr{S}'$ can be visualized as the union of similar mixture sets since $\mathscr{M} \times \mathscr{S}' = \bigcup_{A \in \mathscr{S}'} \mathscr{M}_A$.

The most specific representation considered in the chapter is

$$xA \succ yB \quad \text{iff} \quad \int_A u(xs) \, dP_A(s) > \int_B u(ys) \, dP_B(s).$$

Here u is a utility function on act-state pairs that is linear in its first component: $u((x \lambda y)s) = \lambda u(xs) + (1 - \lambda)u(ys)$. And P_A and P_B are probability measures on the conditional algebras $\mathscr{S}_A = \{A \cap C : C \in \mathscr{S}\}$ and $\mathscr{S}_B = \{B \cap C : C \in \mathscr{S}\}$ respectively. The measure P_S for S will be denoted simply as P, and we shall note that if $P(A) > 0$ then $P_A(C) = P(C)/P(A)$ whenever $C \in \mathscr{S}_A$.

More generally, utility will be defined initially on act-event pairs with $u(x, A \cup B) = P_{A \cup B}(A)u(xA) + P_{A \cup B}(B)u(xB)$ whenever $A \cap B = \emptyset$, and with $xA \succ yB$ iff $u(xA) > u(yB)$. We shall consider this basic model in the first section, using six axioms for $\succ$ on $\mathscr{M} \times \mathscr{S}'$. The second section shows that another axiom is needed to ensure that each P_A is additive and that

$$u(xA) = \sum_{i=1}^{n} P_A(A_i)u(xA_i)$$

whenever $\{A_1, \ldots, A_n\}$ is a measurable partition of A. We then examine the extension to $u(xA) = \int_A u(xs) \, dP_A(s)$ of the preceding paragraph.

12.1. LINEAR UTILITY FOR ACT-EVENT PAIRS

This section discusses axioms for $\succ$ on $\mathscr{M} \times \mathscr{S}'$ which imply a two-way utility representation with utilities linear on each $\mathscr{M}_A$, so that $u((x \lambda y)A) = \lambda u(xA) + (1 - \lambda)u(yA)$. The representation involves a basic decomposition of $u(x, A \cup B)$ when $A \cap B = \emptyset$ that serves later as the point of departure for subjective probability measures on conditional algebras.

The six axioms used in this section are denoted as P1 through P6. We state them with the understanding that they apply to all $A, B \in \mathscr{S}'$ and all $x, y, z, w \in \mathscr{M}$. As usual, $\sim$ is the symmetric complement of $\succ$, and $\succsim = \succ \cup \sim$.

P1. $\succ$ on $\mathscr{M} \times \mathscr{S}'$ is an asymmetric weak order,

P2.   If $xA \sim zB$ and $yA \sim wB$ then $(x\frac{1}{2}y)A \sim (z\frac{1}{2}w)B$,

P3. $\{\alpha : (x\alpha y)A \succsim zB\}$ and $\{\beta : zB \succsim (x\beta y)A\}$ are closed subsets of the unit interval,

P4.   There are $x', y' \in \mathscr{M}$ such that $x'S \succ y'S$,

P5.   If $xA \succsim xB$ and $A \cap B = \emptyset$ then $xA \succsim x(A \cup B) \succsim xB$,

P6.   If $A \cap B = \emptyset$ then $x'A \succ x'B$ and $y'B \succ y'A$ for some $x', y' \in \mathscr{M}$.

The first three axioms are patterned after the Herstein–Milnor axioms of Section 2.1. Indeed, P1, P2, and P3 respectively imply that B1, B2, and B3 hold for $\succ$ on each $\mathscr{M}_A$. That is, P1 implies that $\succ$ on $\mathscr{M}_A$ is an asymmetric weak order, P2 says that if $xA \sim yA$ then $(x\frac{1}{2}z)A \sim (y\frac{1}{2}z)A$, and P3 requires $\{\alpha : (x\alpha y)A \succsim zA\}$ and $\{\beta : zA \succsim (x\beta y)A\}$ to be closed in the relative usual topology on $[0, 1]$.

These partial implications of P1 through P3 already tell us by Theorem 2.1 that for each $A \in \mathscr{S}'$ there is a linear function u_A on $\mathscr{M}$ such that $xA \succ yA$ iff $u_A(x) > u_A(y)$, with each u_A unique up to a positive affine transformation. The essential purpose of the other implications of P1 through P3 along with P4 through P6 is to allow an alignment of the u_A functions that gives $xA \succ yB$ iff $u_A(x) > u_B(y)$, plus the decomposition $u_{A \cup B}(x) = P_{A \cup B}(A)u_A(x) + P_{A \cup B}(B)u_B(x)$.

Axioms P1, P2, and P3 go beyond the Herstein–Milnor axioms for each $\mathscr{M}_A$ through their connections between events. Thus P1 postulates a consistent ordering throughout $\mathscr{M} \times \mathscr{S}'$, the independence axiom P2 admits two events – and generalizes B2 further by not requiring either $x = z$ or $y = w$, and the Archimedean axiom P3 also admits two conditioning events. In words, P2 says that if you are indifferent between (doing x and having A obtain) and (doing z and having B obtain), and indifferent between (doing y and having A obtain) and (doing w and having B obtain), then you will be indifferent between (a 50–50 gamble for x or y and having A obtain) and (a 50–50 gamble for z or w and having B obtain).

Axiom P4, which is similar to B4, F4, and G4 in preceding chapters, is unremarkable. Its main purpose is to ensure unique values for the 'probabilities' that appear in the basic theorem.

The fifth axiom generalizes an averaging condition used by Bolker (1967) in a different approach to subjective expected utility that is contrasted with other approaches in Fishburn (1981). It is worth noting that P5 uses a single act x along with disjoint events A and B. Given that you plan to do x, it says that if you would just as soon have A obtain as have B obtain, then your liking for having $A \cup B$ obtain will be intermediate to your likings for A and for B.

A specific example of P5 is illustrated by a situation in which you are considering eating a serving of mushrooms of uncertain toxicity. If you would rather eat (x) the mushrooms on the hypothesis that they are harmless (A) than eat (x) them on the hypothesis that they are poisonous (B), or $xA \succ xB$, then P5 claims that you would just as soon eat them, presuming harmless, than eat them without knowing their toxicity, and so forth. The axioms do not rule out the possibility that $xA \succ xB$ along with $xA \sim x(A \cup B) \succ xB$, which in the example would indicate that you believe with certainty that the mushrooms are harmless. Note also that $xA \sim xB$ and $A \cap B = \emptyset$ imply $xA \sim x(A \cup B) \sim xB$.

There are two existential conditions among the axioms. One is P4. The other is P6, which posits the existence of two acts for any disjoint A and B in $\mathscr{S}'$ that yield opposite preferences between A and B: $x'A \succ x'B$ and $y'B \succ y'A$. If $\mathscr{S}' = \{A, B, A \cup B\}$ with A = harmless and B = poisonous in the mushroom example, then P6 holds if (eat, A) $\succ$ (eat, B) and (throw away, B) $\succ$ (throw away, A). A breakdown of P6 occurs if there are disjoint A and B in $\mathscr{S}'$ such that, regardless of what course of action you might adopt, you would just as soon have A obtain as have B obtain. It is not difficult to imagine examples which violate P6 (e.g., you would rather see a certain flight arrive safely at its destination than to have it crash, regardless of whether you will take this flight on your trip), and in such cases the only possible way to salvage P6 is to introduce artificial acts that could yield the required preferences.

Despite its vulnerability to preferential dominance between events, P6 is somewhat less demanding than structural presumptions of several other theories, such as constant acts in Savage's model or in the approach of Chapters 10 and 11. The technical role of the axiom involves the alignment of different u_A. For example, if P6 holds, so that $u_A(x') > u_B(x')$ and $u_B(y') > u_A(y')$, or $u(x'A) > u(x'B)$ and $u(y'B) > u(y'A)$, as desired for our representation, then linearity will provide a $\lambda \in (0, 1)$ where $u(x' \lambda y', A) = u(x' \lambda y', B)$, or $u_A(x' \lambda y') = u_B(x' \lambda y')$, which provides a point of common reference for u_A and u_B. As noted later, our axioms imply a λ where $(x' \lambda y')A \sim (x' \lambda y')B$, and this type of indifference statement will be used to align u_A and u_B with $u_A(x' \lambda y') = u_B(x' \lambda y')$.

THEOREM 1. *Suppose* P1 *through* P6 *hold. Then there is a real-valued function* u *on* $\mathcal{M} \times \mathcal{S}'$ *and unique nonnegative real numbers* $P_{A \cup B}(A)$ *and* $P_{A \cup B}(B)$ *that sum to* 1 *for each pair* $A, B \in \mathcal{S}'$ *for which* $A \cap B = \emptyset$, *such that, for all* $x, y \in \mathcal{M}$ *and all* $A, B \in \mathcal{S}'$,

$$xA \succ yB \quad iff \quad u(xA) > u(yB),$$

$$u_A(\cdot) = u(\cdot, A) \text{ is linear on } \mathcal{M},$$

$$u(x, A \cup B) = P_{A \cup B}(A)u(xA) + P_{A \cup B}(B)u(xB) \text{ when } A \cap B = \emptyset.$$

Moreover, u *in this representation is unique up to a positive affine transformation.*

The proof of Theorem 1 is presented in Section 4. Following the proof we shall pause to consider what can happen when the structural axiom P6 fails but P1 through P5 hold.

12.2. AN AXIOM FOR ADDITIVITY

Despite the suggestion of Theorem 1 that $P_{A \cup B}$ might behave like a probability measure on $\mathcal{S}_{A \cup B} = \{(A \cup B) \cap C : C \in \mathcal{S}\}$, the axioms of the theorem do not permit this conclusion. We shall show this with a concrete example.

Let $\mathcal{S}' = \{A, B, C, A \cup B, A \cup C, B \cup C, S\}$ with A, B, and C mutually disjoint and $S = A \cup B \cup C$. Also let $\mathcal{M}$ be the set of all probability distributions on two basic acts and, for convenience, let $x \in \mathcal{M}$ denote the mixed act that has probability x for the first basic act and probability $1 - x$ for the second basic act. Thus $\mathcal{M}$ corresponds to $[0, 1]$. We assume that the representation of Theorem 1 holds with unique 'probabilities' given by

$$P_{A \cup B}(A) = 0.6, \qquad P_{A \cup B}(B) = 0.4,$$

$$P_{A \cup C}(A) = 0.1, \qquad P_{A \cup C}(C) = 0.9,$$

$$P_{B \cup C}(B) = 0, \qquad P_{B \cup C}(C) = 1.0,$$

and

$$P(A) = 0.1, \qquad P(B \cup C) = 0.9,$$
$$P(B) = 0, \qquad P(A \cup C) = 1.0,$$
$$P(C) = 0.5, \qquad P(A \cup B) = 0.5,$$

where $P \equiv P_S$. The basic utilities are given by

$$u(xA) = x$$
$$u(xB) = 1 - x$$
$$u(xC) = \tfrac{1}{2}$$

for all $x \in [0, 1]$, so that, according to the uP decomposition,

$$u(x, A \cup B) = 0.4 + 0.2x$$
$$u(x, A \cup C) = 0.45 + 0.1x$$
$$u(x, B \cup C) = \tfrac{1}{2}$$
$$u(x, S) = 0.45 + 0.1x.$$

For example, $u(x, A \cup B) = (0.6)x + (0.4)(1 - x) = 0.4 + 0.2x$, and the three ways of splitting S, by A and $B \cup C$, by B and $A \cup C$, and by C and $A \cup B$, all yield $u(xS) = 0.45 + 0.1x$. Note also that each u_D for $D \in \mathscr{S}'$ is linear on $\mathscr{M}$.

Define $\succ$ on $\mathscr{M} \times \mathscr{S}'$ in the example by $xD \succ yE$ iff $u(xD) > u(yE)$, for all $x, y \in [0, 1]$ and all $D, E \in \mathscr{S}'$. Then it is not hard to show that P1 through P6 hold. Hence, according to Theorem 1, the P values are unique. However, P is not additive since $P(A) + P(B) = 0.1$ and $P(A \cup B) = 0.5$.

It may also be noted that the P_D in the example do not satisfy the chain rule for probabilities which would require $P(A \cup B)P_{A \cup B}(A) = P(A)$. But $P(A \cup B)P_{A \cup B}(A) = 0.3$ and $P(A) = 0.1$.

We shall use a seventh axiom to imply that each P_A is a probability measure on $\mathscr{S}_A = \{A \cap C : C \in \mathscr{S}\}$. As will be seen, this is another structural axiom that lacks the direct intuitive appeal of most of the other axioms.

P7.   *If A, B, and C are mutually disjoint events in $\mathscr{S}'$, and if $xA \sim xB$ for some $x \in \mathscr{M}$, then there is a $y \in \mathscr{M}$ at which exactly two of yA, yB, and yC are indifferent.*

Prior to Theorem 1 we observed that if $A \cup B = \emptyset$ then P1 through P6 imply that $xA \sim xB$ for some $x \in \mathcal{M}$. Thus, what P7 requires in addition is that for any triple A, B, C of mutually disjoint events in $\mathcal{S}'$ there be a $y \in \mathcal{M}$ such that $yt(A) \sim yt(B) \succ yt(C)$ or $yt(C) \succ yt(A) \sim yt(B)$ for some permutation t on $\{A, B, C\}$. Axiom P7 fails at A, B, C if for all $x \in \mathcal{M}$ it is true that $xA \sim xB$ iff $xB \sim xC$ iff $xA \sim xC$.

Our new axiom fails in the preceding example since two of $u(xA)$, $u(xB)$, and $u(xC)$ are equal only when $x = \frac{1}{2}$, and at $x = \frac{1}{2}$ we have $u(xA) = = u(xB) = u(xC)$. In other words, every indifference class that contains two of xA, xB, and xC also contains the third. As seen by the next theorem, when this type of 'indifference coincidence' is forbidden, the P_A behave in the manner of consistent probability measures.

THEOREM 2. *Suppose P1 through P7 hold, and let u and the P_A be as specified in Theorem 1 with $P_A(\emptyset) = 0$ and $P_A(A) = 1$. Then P_A is a finitely additive probability measure on $\mathcal{S}_A$ for each $A \in \mathcal{S}'$, $P_C(A) = P_C(B)P_B(A)$ whenever $A \subseteq B \subseteq C$ and $A, B, C \in \mathcal{S}'$, and*

$$u(xA) = \sum_{i=1}^{n} P_A(A_i)u(xA_i)$$

whenever $x \in \mathcal{M}$, $A \in \mathcal{S}'$ and $\{A_1, \ldots, A_n\}$ is an n-part measurable partition of A.

With $P \equiv P_S$, the chain condition $P_C(A) = P_C(B)P_B(A)$ for $A \subseteq B \subseteq \subseteq C$ gives $P(A) = P(B)P_B(A)$ whenever $A \subseteq B$ and $A, B \in \mathcal{S}'$. Hence, if $P(B) \neq 0$, then

$$P_B(A) = P(A)/P(B),$$

so that $P_B(A)$ can be viewed as the conditional probability of the event "A given B". It follows that if $P(A) \neq 0$ for the displayed equality in Theorem 2, then we have

$$u(xA) = \frac{1}{P(A)} \sum_{i=1}^{n} P(A_i)u(xA_i),$$

which refers the matter to the unconditional measure P on $\mathcal{S}$.

It should also be noted that even when $P(A) = 0$ for $A \in \mathcal{S}'$, P_A is a uniquely defined probability measure on $\mathcal{M}_A$. When this occurs, the preceding expression for $u(xA)$ does not apply and P_A is not determined by P.

The fact that P_A is uniquely determined regardless of whether $P(A)$ is positive or zero may seem unusual. However, it is intuitively appealing. For example, the outcome of an information-producing experiment in a sequential decision process may have a smooth distribution with probability zero for each particular outcome value. Nevertheless, some outcome will be observed, and further action will be based on this observation. Despite a zero probability for each outcome of the experiment, Theorem 2 says that there is a well-defined conditional probability measure for any outcome that applies to as-yet-unresolved uncertainty in the sequential process.

A proof of Theorem 2 appears in Section 5.

12.3. MEASURABLE AND BOUNDED CONDITIONAL ACTS

If $\mathscr{S}$ is finite then Theorems 1 and 2 present a complete theory for subjective expective utility in the conditional mode adopted in this chapter. Our purpose here will be to consider the extension of the form in Theorem 2 to $u(xA) = \int_A u(xs)\,\mathrm{d}P_A(s)$, i.e. to $u(xA) = E(u_x, P_A)$ with $u_x(s) = u(xs)$ for all $s \in S$. Since $u_x(s)$ is defined in the present setting only if $\{s\}$ is in $\mathscr{S}'$, we shall assume that $\{s\} \in \mathscr{S}'$ for every $s \in S$. This does not imply that $\mathscr{S}$ is a Borel algebra unless S is finite.

By analogy to definitions in Section 10.2, xA is *measurable* if $\{s : u_x(s) \in I\} \cap A \in \mathscr{S}$ for each interval I of real numbers. It follows easily that xA is measurable iff $A \cap \{s : ys' \succ xs\}$ and $A \cap \{s : xs \succ ys'\}$ are in $\mathscr{S}$ for all $ys' \in \mathscr{M} \times \mathscr{S}$. A measurable xA is *bounded below* if $P_A(\{s \in A : u_x(s) \geq \geq a\}) = 1$ for some number a, and is *bounded above* if $P_A(\{s \in A : u_x(s) \leq \leq b\}) = 1$ for some number b. And xA is said to be *bounded* if it is bounded below and above.

The principal axiom involved in the extension is a sure-thing or dominance principle that is closely related to F6 in Chapter 10 and to G6 in Chapter 11.

P8.   *For all $x, y \in \mathscr{M}$ and all $A, B \in \mathscr{S}', xA \succsim yB$ if $xs \succ yB$ for all $s \in A$ or if $xA \succ ys$ for all $s \in B$.*

This is a very appealing assumption. It is implied by P1 through P7 when S is finite, but not otherwise.

THEOREM 3. *Suppose the hypotheses of Theorem 2 hold along with P8 and $\{s\} \in \mathscr{S}'$ for every $s \in S$. Then, for all measurable $xA \in \mathscr{M} \times \mathscr{S}'$:*

(a) $u(xA) = E(u_x, P_A)$ if xA is bounded;
(b) $u(xA) \geq E(u_x, P_A)$ if xA is bounded below;
(c) $E(u_x, P_A) \geq u(xA)$ if xA is bounded above;
(d) $E(u_x, P_A)$ is well defined and finite.

This is quite similar in form to Lemma 3.1 and Proposition 5.1, and part (a) is almost the same as Theorem 10.2(a), which said that $u(f) = E(u_f, P)$ for every measurable and bounded $f \in \mathscr{F}^*$. The similarity between the two is obvious if one corresponds $u_f(s)$ to $u_x(s)$ and replaces P by P_A.

As far as I can tell, P1 through P8 do not imply that u is bounded or that every measurable xA is bounded. Assuming this to be the case, it lies in sharp contrast to Theorem 10.2(c), where we noted that every measurable act in $\mathscr{F}^*$ is bounded. However, the two formulations are different enough that this should come as no great surprise.

We use one final condition to obtain $u(xA) = E(u_x, P_A)$ for all measurable xA without presuming that measurable acts are bounded.

P9.   For all $A, B, A_1, A_2, \ldots \in \mathscr{S}'$ and all $x, y \in \mathscr{M}$, if $A_1 \subseteq A_2 \subseteq \cdots$ and $A = \bigcup_{i=1}^{\infty} A_i$, then $xA \succ yB$ implies that there is an integer N such that $xA_n \succsim yB$ for all $n \geq N$, and $yB \succ xA$ implies that there is an N such that $yB \succsim xA_n$ for all $n \geq N$.

The previous axiom most like P9 in style is F7 in Section 10.3. Actually, P9 is somewhat stronger than what is needed for our final theorem, but it is used because of its simple statement and interpretation. If $A_n \uparrow A$ and $xA \succ yB$, we would usually expect some A_n for large n to be enough like A to give $xA_n \succsim yB$. The first part of P9 goes beyond this by requiring $xA_n \succsim yB$ for all sufficiently large n, but this still seems reasonable for most situations.

THEOREM 4. Suppose the hypotheses of Theorem 3 hold along with P9. Then $u(xA) = E(u_x, P_A)$ for all measurable $xA \in \mathscr{M} \times \mathscr{S}'$.

Proofs of Theorems 3 and 4 are sketched in Section 6.

12.4. PROOF OF THEOREM 1

The proofs of the theorems in this chapter are patterned after proofs in Fishburn (1973, 1974). As in preceding discussion, we shall subscript u in two ways, with $u_A(x) = u(xA)$ and $u_x(s) = u(xs)$. The present section proves Theorem 1. We begin with implications of P1, P2, and P3 and then work with a special condition that is shown later to follow from the axioms of Theorem 1. The section concludes with remarks on the failure of P6.

Implications of P1, P2 and P3

The following results are based on our first three axioms and use the consequences of Theorem 2.1 noted after the statement of the axioms in Section 1 for the Herstein–Milnor axioms. Here $x, y, z, w \in \mathcal{M}$ and and $A, B \in \mathcal{S}'$.

L1. $xA \gtrsim zB \gtrsim yA \Rightarrow (x \lambda y)A \sim zB$ for some λ,

L2. $xA \succ zB \succ yA \Rightarrow (x \lambda y)A \sim zB$ for a unique $0 < \lambda < 1$,

L3. $(xA \sim zB, yA \sim wB) \Rightarrow (x \lambda y)A \sim (z \lambda w)B$ for all λ,

L4. $(xA \succ zB, yA \sim wB) \Rightarrow (x \lambda y)A \succ (z \lambda w)B$ for all $0 < \lambda < 1$,

L5. $(xA \succ xB, yB \succ yA) \Rightarrow (x \lambda y)A \sim (x \lambda y)B$ for a unique $0 < \lambda < 1$.

The hypotheses of L5 tie in to P6, and L5 will be used later in connection with P6. Proofs of L1–L5 follow.

L1. The α and β sets for P3 are nonempty, closed and cover $[0, 1]$, so must have some λ in common.

L2. By L1, $zB \sim (x \lambda y)A$ for some $0 < \lambda < 1$: P1 and Theorem 2.1 imply that λ is unique.

L3. Given $xA \sim zB$ and $yA \sim wB$, successive applications of P2 and M3 give $(x \lambda y)A \sim (z \lambda w)B$ for all $\lambda \in \Lambda = \{ \sum_{i=1}^{N} \alpha_i / 2^i : \alpha_i \in \{0, 1\}$ and N is a positive integer$\}$. If $xA \sim yA$, L3 follows easily from P1 and Theorem 2.1. Assume henceforth that $xA \succ yA$. Let $T_\lambda = \{ \beta : (x \lambda y)A \gtrsim (z \beta w)B \}$ for $\lambda \notin \Lambda$, and take $\lambda_i \leq \lambda$ for $i = 1, 2, \ldots$ with $\lambda_i \in \Lambda$ and $\lambda = \sup\{\lambda_i\}$. Then $(x \lambda y)A \gtrsim (x \lambda_i y)A \sim (z \lambda_i w)B$ by Theorem 2.1 for A or $\mathcal{M}_A$ and by the first sentence of the present proof. Thus $\lambda_i \in T_\lambda$ for all i, so $\lambda \in T_\lambda$ by P3. Hence $(x \lambda y)A \gtrsim (z \lambda w)B$. A similar proof $(zB \succ wB)$ gives $(z \lambda w)B \gtrsim (x \lambda y)A$.

L4. Let $xA \succ zB$, $yA \sim wB$ and $0 < \lambda < 1$ be given. Assume throughout this paragraph that $xA \gtrsim yA \sim wB \gtrsim zB$. It follows easily from $xA \succ zB$, $yA \gtrsim zB$ and Theorem 2.1 that $(x \lambda y)A \succ zB$. Also, by $yA \sim wB$, $xA \gtrsim wB$ and either Theorem 2.1 $(xA \succ wB)$ or L3 $(xA \sim wB)$, we have $(x \lambda y)A \gtrsim wB$. Now if $wB \sim zB$ then $zB \sim (z \lambda w)B$ and therefore $(x \lambda y)A \succ (z \lambda w)B$. On the other hand, if $wB \succ zB$ then $wB \succ (z \lambda w)B$ by Theorem 2.1, and therefore $(x \lambda y)A \succ (z \lambda w)B$.

Suppose next that $xA \succ zB \succ yA \sim wB$. By L2, $zB \sim (x \mu y)A$ for a unique $0 < \mu < 1$. If $\lambda \geq \mu$ then $(x \lambda y)A \gtrsim zB \succ (z \lambda w)B$ by Theorem 2.1, and hence $(x \lambda y)A \succ (z \lambda w)B$. Alternatively, if $\lambda < \mu$, then $zB \sim (x \mu y)A \succ yA \sim wB$ implies $(z \rho w)B \sim (x(\rho \mu)y)A$ for all ρ by L3 and the mixture-set axioms. Let $\rho = \lambda/\mu$. Then $(x \lambda y)A \sim (z(\lambda/\mu)w)B \succ (z \lambda w)B$, where $\succ$ results from $\lambda/\mu > \lambda$ and Theorem 2.1.

The final case for L4 is $yA \sim wB \succ xA \succ zB$. Its proof is similar to the proof in the preceding paragraph.

L5. Let $xA \succ xB$ and $yB \succ yA$ be given. Suppose first that $xA \sim \sim yA$. Then $yB \succ xA \succ xB$ so, by L2, $xA \sim (x \lambda y)B$ for a unique $0 < \lambda < 1$. By Theorem 2.1, $(x \lambda y)A \sim xA$, so $(x \lambda y)A \sim (x \lambda y)B$. Since $(x \beta y)A \sim xA$ for all β, the uniqueness of λ follows. A similar proof applies if $xB \sim yB$.

We assume henceforth in the proof of L5 that $xA \nsim yA$ and $xB \nsim yB$, and consider cases as follows.

Case 1. $yA \succ xA$. Then $yB \succ yA \succ xA \succ xB$, so, by L2, $yA \sim (x \alpha y)B$ and $xA \sim (x \beta y)B$ for unique $\alpha, \beta \in (0, 1)$. By Theorem 2.1, $0 < \alpha < \beta < 1$. By L3, $(x \rho y)A \sim (x(\rho \beta + (1 - \rho)\alpha)y)B$ for all ρ. Solve $\rho = \rho \beta + (1 - \rho)\alpha$ for ρ to get $0 < \rho^* = \alpha/(1 + \alpha - \beta) < 1$. The only ρ where $(x \rho y)A \sim (x \rho y)B$ is ρ^*. For suppose $\mu \neq \rho^*$. Then $(x \mu y)A \sim (x(\mu \beta + (1 - \mu)\alpha)y)B$. If $\mu > \rho^*$ then $\mu > \mu \beta + (1 - \mu)\alpha$, and Theorem 2.1 $(yB \succ xB)$ gives $(x(\mu \beta + (1 - \mu)\alpha)y)B \succ (x \mu y)B$. If $\rho^* > \mu$, then the converse holds. The conclusion of L5 holds with $\lambda = \rho^*$.

Case 2. $xA \succ yA$. If $xB \succ yB$ also, then case 1 applies symmetrically, so assume that $yB \succ xB$. Thus

each of xA and yB is $\succ$ to each of yA and xB.

Case 2a. $xA \gtrsim yB \succ xB \gtrsim yA$. Then L2 and Theorem 2.1 imply $yB \sim \sim (x \alpha y)A$ and $xB \sim (x \beta y)A$ for unique α, β with $0 \leq \beta < \alpha \leq 1$. By L3, $(x \rho y)B \sim (x(\rho \beta + (1 - \rho)\alpha)y)A$, and the proof proceeds as in case 1.

Case 2b. $yB \succ xA \succ yA \succ xB$. This is similar to case 2a.

Case 2c. $yB \succ xA \succ xB \gtrsim yA$. L2 implies $xB \sim (x \alpha y)A$ and $xA \sim \sim (x \beta y)B$ for unique $\alpha \in [0, 1)$ and $\beta \in (0, 1)$. Then L3 implies $(x(\rho + (1 - \rho)\beta)y)B \sim (x(\rho \alpha + (1 - \rho))y)A$ for all ρ. Solve $\rho + (1 - \rho)\beta = \rho \alpha + (1 - \rho)$ for ρ to get $0 < \rho^* = (1 - \beta)/(2 - \alpha - \beta) < 1$. Uniqueness of ρ^* follows from Theorem 2.1.

Case 2d. $xA \gtrsim yB \succ yA \succ xB$. This is similar to Case 2c.

Aligning Linear Utility Functions

Given u_A on $\mathcal{M}$ for each $A \in \mathscr{S}'$, we use the following axiom to linearly transform these linear functions to obtain the results in Lemma 1. The next subsection shows that P1 through P6 imply P6*.

P6*.   *For each $A \in \mathcal{S}'$ either* (i) *$xA \sim yS$ for all $x \in \mathcal{M}$ and some $y \in \mathcal{M}$, or* (ii) *there are $x, y, z, w \in \mathcal{M}$ such that $xA \sim zS$, $yA \sim wS$ and $zS \succ wS$.*

LEMMA 1. *Suppose* P1, P2, P3, *and* P6* *hold. Then there is a real-valued function u on $\mathcal{M} \times \mathcal{S}'$ such that, for all $x, y \in \mathcal{M}$ and all $A, B \in \mathcal{S}'$,*

$$xA \succ yB \quad iff \quad u(xA) > u(yB), \qquad u(\cdot A) \text{ is linear on } \mathcal{M}.$$

Moreover, u is unique up to a positive affine transformation.

Proof. For each $A \in \mathcal{S}'$ let u_A be a linear function on $\mathcal{M}$ that gives $xA \succ yA$ iff $u_A(x) > u_A(y)$. We define u on $\mathcal{M} \times \mathcal{S}'$ as follows.

First, $u(xS) = u_S(x)$ for all $x \in \mathcal{M}$. Second, if P6*(i) holds for A, then u_A is constant and we set $u(xA) = u(yS)$ for all $x \in \mathcal{M}$, where $xA \sim yS$. Finally, if P6*(ii) holds for A with x, y, z, and w as noted therein, transform u_A linearly so that $u_A(x) = u(zS)$ and $u_A(y) = u(wS)$, and define u on $\mathcal{M}_A$ by $u(tA) = u_A(t)$ for all $t \in \mathcal{M}$.

By construction, $u(\cdot A)$ is linear for each $A \in \mathcal{S}'$. Moreover, if $xA \succ yB$ iff $u(xA) > u(yB)$, for all $xA, yB \in \mathcal{M} \times \mathcal{S}'$, it is clear from the restrictions in the construction process that v on $\mathcal{M} \times \mathcal{S}'$ satisfies the requirements of Lemma 1 if and only if v is a positive affine transformation of u.

It remains to verify that u preserves $\succ$. We show first that $u(xA) = u(yS)$ iff $xA \sim yS$. If A obeys P6*(i) then this is obvious, so suppose that A comes under P6*(ii) with alignment as follows:

$$zA \sim z'S, \qquad u(zA) = u_A(z) = u(z'S)$$

$$wA \sim w'S, \qquad u(wA) = u_A(w) = u(w'S)$$

$$z'S \succ w'S, \qquad u(z'S) > u(w'S).$$

Suppose first that $xA \sim yS$. There are three cases depending on whether $xA \succ zA$, $zA \succsim xA \succsim wA$, or $wA \succ xA$. The proofs of the latter two cases are similar to the first case, so we detail only the first case:

$$xA \sim yS \succ zA \sim z'S \succ wA \sim w'S.$$

By Theorem 2.1, $zA \sim (x\lambda w)A$ for a unique $0 < \lambda < 1$; and, by L3, $(y\lambda w')S \sim (x\lambda w)A$. Therefore $zA \sim (y\lambda w')S$. By linearity, $u(zA) = \lambda u(xA) + (1-\lambda)u(wA)$ and $u(z'S) = \lambda u(yS) + (1-\lambda)u(w'S)$. Since $u(zA) = u(z'S)$ and $u(wA) = u(w'S)$ by alignment, $u(xA) = u(yS)$.

Conversely, suppose that $u(xA) = u(yS)$. There are three cases depending on whether $u(xA) > u(zA)$, $u(zA) \geq u(xA) \geq u(wA)$, or $u(wA) > u(xA)$. We detail only the first of these where

$$u(xA) = u(yS) > u(zA) = u(z'S) > u(wA) = u(w'S).$$

For a unique $\lambda \in (0, 1)$, $u(zA) = \lambda u(xA) + (1 - \lambda)u(wA)$ and $u(z'S) = \lambda u(yS) + (1 - \lambda)u(w'S)$. By linearity, $zA \sim (x\lambda w)A$ and $z'S \sim (y\lambda w')S$. Therefore $(x\lambda w)A \sim (y\lambda w')S$, and, by $u(wA) = u(w'S)$, $wA \sim w'S$. If either $xA \succ yS$ or $yS \succ xA$ then L4 contradicts $(x\lambda w)A \sim (y\lambda w')S$. Therefore $xA \sim yS$.

We have just proved that $u(xA) = u(yS)$ iff $xA \sim yS$. Since u_A and u_S are intervals, it follows easily that $u(xA) > u(yS)$ iff $xA \succ yS$, and that $u(yS) > u(xA)$ iff $yS \succ xA$.

Henceforth in the proof of Lemma 1 let

$$I = \{u(xS) : x \in \mathcal{M}\} = u_S(\mathcal{M}).$$

Suppose first that $u(xA) \in I$ and $u(yB) \in I$, with $u(xA) = u(zS)$ and $u(yB) = u(wS)$ for definiteness. Then $xA \sim zS$ and $yB \sim wS$ by the preceding paragraph. If $xA \succ yB$ then $zS \succ wS$, and therefore $u(zS) > u(wS)$ and $u(xA) > u(yB)$. Conversely, if $u(xA) > u(yB)$, then $u(zS) > u(wS)$, and hence $zS \succ wS$ and $xA \succ yB$. Similar results hold if $yB \succ xA$ or if $xA \sim yB$.

Suppose next that $u(xA) \in I$ with $xA \sim zS$, and that $u(yB) \notin I$. If $u(xA) > u(yB)$, then $u(zS) > u(yB)$ and $zS \succ yB$, so $xA \succ yB$. If $xA \succ yB$ then $zS \succ yB$, and therefore $u(zS) > u(yB)$ and $u(xA) > u(yB)$. The situation for $u(yB) > u(xA)$ is similar.

Finally, suppose neither $u(xA)$ nor $u(yB)$ is in I. Then the desired order-preserving result is obvious if one of $u(xA)$ and $u(yB)$ exceeds the interval I and the other is less than I. Thus, the only remaining case arises for both $u(xA)$ and $u(yB)$ exceeding I (or both less than I), which is equivalent to $xA \succ zS$ and $yB \succ zS$ for all $z \in \mathcal{M}$. In this exceeding case we have $x', x^*, y', y^* \in \mathcal{M}$ with $u(x'A) \in I$ and $u(x^*A) \in I$ such that

$$x'A \sim y'B \quad \text{and} \quad u(x'A) = u(y'B)$$

$$x^*A \sim y^*B \quad \text{and} \quad u(x^*A) = u(y^*B)$$

$$x'A \succ x^*A \quad \text{and} \quad u(x'A) > u(x^*A),$$

with $u(xA) > u(x'A) > u(x^*A)$ and $u(yB) > u(y'B) > u(y^*B)$. Let α, β be the unique numbers in $(0, 1)$ where

$$u(x'A) = \alpha u(xA) + (1 - \alpha)u(x^*A) \quad \text{and} \quad x'A \sim (x\alpha x^*)A,$$

$$u(y'B) = \beta u(yB) + (1 - \beta)u(y^*B) \quad \text{and} \quad y'B \sim (y\beta y^*)B.$$

Since $x'A \sim y'B$, $(x\alpha x^*)A \sim (y\beta y^*)B$.

Given these things, suppose first that $u(xA) = u(yB)$. Then $\alpha = \beta$ since $u(x'A) = u(y'B)$ and $u(x^*A) = u(y^*B)$. Hence $(x\alpha x^*)A \sim (y\alpha y^*)B$. Since $x^*A \sim y^*B$, L4 gives $xA \sim yB$. Conversely, if $xA \sim yB$, then L3 gives $(x\alpha x^*)A \sim (y\alpha y^*)B$. Then $\alpha = \beta$ follows from Theorem 2.1, and therefore $u(xA) = u(yB)$.

Suppose next in our final case that $u(xA) > u(yB)$. Then $\alpha < \beta$. Since $yB \succ y^*B$, Theorem 2.1 implies $(y\beta y^*)B \succ (y\alpha y^*)A$. Hence $(x\alpha x^*)A \succ \succ (y\alpha y^*)B$. Since $x^*A \sim y^*B$, L3 forbids $xA \sim yB$, and L4 forbids $yB \succ xA$. Therefore $xA \succ yB$. Conversely, if $xA \succ yB$, then L4 gives $(x\alpha x^*)A \succ \succ (y\alpha y^*)B$. It follows that $\beta > \alpha$, which requires $u(xA) > u(yB)$. A similar proof applies if $u(yB) > u(xA)$ or if $yB \succ xA$. ∎

Completion of the Proof

We complete the proof of Theorem 1 by establishing P6* and then breaking up $u(x, A \cup B)$ according to the decomposition in the theorem.

LEMMA 2. P1 *through* P6 *imply* P6*.

Proof. If $\mathscr{S} = \{\emptyset, S\}$, there is nothing to prove, so suppose that $A \in \mathscr{S}'$ with $A \subset S$, and let $B = S \backslash A$. Then P6 implies $xA \succ xB$ and $yB \succ yA$ for some $x, y \in \mathscr{M}$. By L5, $(x \lambda y)A \sim (x \lambda y)B$ for a unique $0 < \lambda < 1$. Then P1 and P5 imply $(x \lambda y)A \sim (x \lambda y)S$.

If $xA \not\sim yA$, then $(x \lambda y)A$ is between (by $\succ$) xA and yA by Theorem 2.1. Hence $(x \lambda y)S$ is also between xA and yA. Then P4 and L2 show that P6* (ii) holds for A.

Suppose next that $xA \sim yA$. If u_A is constant, then P6*(i) holds for A. If u_A is not constant and $xS \not\sim yS$ then $(x \lambda y)A$ is between xS and yS, and P6*(ii) holds with the use of L2. Finally, suppose $xA \sim yA \sim xS \sim \sim yS$ with u_A not constant and $zA \succ xA$ for definiteness. We consider three cases for zA versus zB.

Case 1. $zB \succ zA$. Since $xA \succ xB$, L5 gives $(z \lambda x)A \sim (z \lambda x)B$ for a unique $0 < \lambda < 1$. Then P1 and P5 imply $(z \lambda x)S \sim (z \lambda x)A$. By Theorem 2.1, $(z \lambda x)A \succ xA$. Thus $(z \lambda x)S \sim (z \lambda x)A \succ xA \sim x$, so P6*(ii) holds.

Case 2. $zB \sim zA$. Then $zS \sim zA$ by P5. Hence $zS \succ xS$, and P6*(ii) holds.

Case 3. $zA \succ zB$. This is similar to case 1. ∎

LEMMA 3. *Suppose* P1 *through* P6 *hold along with the representation of Lemma* 1. *Then, for all* $A, B \in \mathscr{S}'$ *for which* $A \cap B = \emptyset$, *there are unique nonnegative numbers* $P_{A\cup B}(A)$ *and* $P_{A\cup B}(B)$ *that sum to* 1 *and satisfy*

$$u(x, A\cup B) = P_{A\cup B}(A)u(xA) + P_{A\cup B}(B)u(xB)$$

for all $x\in\mathcal{M}$.

Proof. Let u be any function on $\mathcal{M}\times\mathcal{S}'$ that satisfies Lemma 1, and let A, B be any pair of disjoint events in $\mathcal{S}'$. Take $xA\succ xB$ and $yB\succ yA$ by P6, with $(x\lambda y)A\sim (x\lambda y)B$ by L5. Then $\lambda u(xA) + (1-\lambda)u(yA) = = \lambda u(xB) + (1-\lambda)u(yB)$, so

$$\lambda[u(xA) - u(xB)] = (1-\lambda)[u(yB) - u(yA)] > 0.$$

By P5, $(x\lambda y)(A\cup B)\sim (x\lambda y)B$ so that, by Lemma 1,

$$\lambda[u(x, A\cup B) - u(xB)] = (1-\lambda)[u(yB) - u(y, A\cup B)].$$

Divide this by the preceding equality to get

$$\frac{u(x, A\cup B) - u(xB)}{u(xA) - u(xB)} = \frac{u(y, A\cup B) - u(yB)}{u(yA) - u(yB)}.$$

If $zA\succ zB$, the preceding analysis yields $[u(z, A\cup B) - u(zB)]/[u(zA) - u(zB)] = [u(y, A\cup B) - u(yB)]/[u(yA) - u(yB)]$, and if $zB\succ zA$, then $[u(z, A\cup B) - u(zB)]/[u(zA) - u(zB)] = [u(x, A\cup B) - u(xB)]/[u(xA) - u(xB)]$. It follows that there is a unique number ρ such that, for all $x\in\mathcal{M}$ for which $xA\not\sim xB$, $\rho = [u(x, A\cup B) - u(xB)]/[u(xA) - u(xB)]$, or

$$u(x, A\cup B) = \rho u(xA) + (1-\rho)u(xB).$$

If $xA\sim xB$, then $x(A\cup B)\sim xA$ by P5, so the equation just written holds also when $xA\sim xB$. Hence it holds for all $x\in\mathcal{M}$, and the unique ρ is clearly invariant under positive affine transformations of u. Any $xA\succ xB$ shows with the use of P5 that $0\le\rho\le 1$. The conclusion of Lemma 3 follows with $P_{A\cup B}(A) = \rho$ and $P_{A\cup B}(B) = 1-\rho$. ∎

On the Failure of P6

Because P6 has limitations described in Section 1, it seems worthwhile to note what can happen when P1 through P5 hold, but P6 fails. Two examples will illustrate the possibilities. The first has nonoverlapping preferences; the second has overlapping preferences.

EXAMPLE 1. Let $\mathcal{S} = \{\emptyset, A, B, S\}$ with $A\cap B = \emptyset$ and $S = A\cup B$. Suppose P6* fails with

$$xA\succ yS\succ zB \quad\text{for all}\quad x, y, z\in\mathcal{M}.$$

L1 through L5 have no bearing here, P1 through P5 can be presumed to hold, but P6 clearly fails.

If u_S is unbounded above or below, if u_A is unbounded below, or if u_B is unbounded above, then it is clearly impossible to align these functions to yield a u on $\mathcal{M} \times \mathcal{S}'$ that satisfies the representation of Lemma 1. We suppose henceforth that u_S, u_A and u_B are bounded. Then suitable affine transformations of u_A and u_B provide a u with $u(xD) = u_D(x)$ that satisfies Lemma 1, except for uniqueness of u up to a positive affine transformation.

Let us assume further that the following sure-thing axiom holds along with P1 through P5:

P10.   If $xA \succsim yA$ and $xB \succsim yB$ then $xS \succsim yS$; if $xA \succ yA$ and $xB \succ yB$ then $xS \succ yS$.

This axiom is implied by P1 through P6 as can be seen from Theorem 1. Given P1 through P5, and P10, a theorem in Harsanyi (1955) implies that for any choice of linear u_A, u_B, and u_S, there are $a \geq 0, b \geq 0$ and k such that

$$u_S(x) = au_A(x) + bu_B(x) + k \quad \text{for all} \quad x \in \mathcal{M}.$$

Axiom P4 requires $a + b > 0$. Suppose in fact that $a > 0$ and $b > 0$. Then for *any* chosen $\lambda \in (0, 1)$ we can obtain u on $\mathcal{M} \times \mathcal{S}'$ that satisfies the representation of Lemma 1 along with

$$u(x, A \cup B) = \lambda u(xA) + (1 - \lambda)u(xB) \quad \text{for all} \quad x \in \mathcal{M}.$$

Since $A \cup B = S$, this has the decomposition form needed for Theorem 1 or Lemma 3. Indeed, all aspects of Theorem 1 except for uniqueness hold if we take $P(A) = \lambda$ and $P(B) = 1 - \lambda$. But since λ could be any number in $(0, 1)$, it has no meaning in terms of the individual's subjective probability for event A.

EXAMPLE 2. Again let $\mathcal{S} = \{\emptyset, A, B, S\}$, but now let $\mathcal{M} = \{(\alpha, \beta, \gamma): \alpha \geq 0, \beta \geq 0, \gamma \geq 0, \alpha + \beta + \gamma = 1\}$ with α, β, and γ respectively the probabilities assigned by a mixed act to basic acts f, g, and h. Define u on $\{f, g, h\} \times \mathcal{S}'$ by $(u(fA), u(fS), u(fB)) = (3, 1, 0), (u(gA), u(gS), u(gB)) = (1, 0, -1)$ and $(u(hA), u(hS), u(hB)) = (0, -1, -4)$. Extend u linearly for $x = (\alpha, \beta, \gamma)$ and $C \in \mathcal{S}'$:

$$u((\alpha, \beta, \gamma)C) = \alpha u(fC) + \beta u(gC) + \gamma u(hC),$$

and define $\succ$ by $xC \succ yD$ iff $u(xC) > u(yD)$. Then it is easily checked that P1 through P5, P6*, and the obvious generalization of P10 hold, so that Lemma 1 (including uniqueness) applies completely. But P6 fails since $xA \succ xB$ for all $x \in \mathcal{M}$.

According to the given u values, we have

$$u(x, A \cup B) = \tfrac{2}{5}u(xA) + \tfrac{1}{5}u(xB) - \tfrac{1}{5} \quad \text{for all} \quad x \in \mathcal{M},$$

and the coefficients here are uniquely determined. By Lemma 1, we can transform u linearly to get rid of $k = -\tfrac{1}{5}$, and when this is done we obtain

$$u(x, A \cup B) = \tfrac{2}{5}u(xA) + \tfrac{1}{5}u(xB).$$

Although this resembles the decomposition form in Lemma 3, we would hesitate to think of the coefficients as the subjective probabilities of A and B since they do not sum to 1. Because $\tfrac{2}{5} + \tfrac{1}{5} < 1$, a positive affine transformation of u can introduce an extra term (k) into the additive form, as just illustrated, but this does not happen when P6 holds.

12.5. PROOF OF THEOREM 2

We presume P1 through P7 along with u and the P_A as specified in Theorem 1. As indicated in the hypotheses of Theorem 2, P_A is extended to all of $\mathcal{S}_A$ by taking $P_A(\emptyset) = 0$ and $P_A(A) = 1$.

To verify additivity and the chain rule, take $A, B \in \mathcal{S}'$ with $A \cap B = \emptyset$. Let $D \in \mathcal{S}'$ be such that $A \cup B \subseteq D$. If $A \cup B = D$ then $P_D(A) + P_D(B) = P_D(A \cup B) = 1$ by Theorem 1 and $P_D(D) = 1$. Suppose henceforth that $A \cup B \subset D$, and let $C = D \backslash (A \cup B)$ so that $\{A, B, C\}$ is a partition of D. Let α through ν be the unique ρ values (see end of proof of Lemma 3) for the following six cases, for all $x \in \mathcal{M}$:

$$u(xD) = \alpha u(x, A \cup B) + (1 - \alpha)u(xC)$$

$$u(x, A \cup B) = \beta u(xA) + (1 - \beta)u(xB)$$

$$u(xD) = \gamma u(xA) + (1 - \gamma)u(x, B \cup C)$$

$$u(x, B \cup C) = \delta u(xB) + (1 - \delta)u(xC)$$

$$u(xD) = \mu u(xB) + (1 - \mu)u(x, A \cup C)$$

$$u(x, A \cup C) = \nu u(xA) + (1 - \nu)u(xC).$$

For additivity we need to show that $P_D(A \cup B) = P_D(A) + P_D(B)$, which is the same as $\alpha = \gamma + \mu$. The chain rule will be shown later to follow from $\alpha\beta = \gamma$.

Combine successive pairs of the preceding equalities to get

$$u(xD) = \alpha\beta u(xA) + \alpha(1 - \beta)u(xB) + (1 - \alpha)u(xC),$$

$$u(xD) = \gamma u(xA) + \delta(1 - \gamma)u(xB) + (1 - \gamma)(1 - \delta)u(xC),$$

$$u(xD) = v(1 - \mu)u(xA) + \mu u(xB) + (1 - \mu)(1 - v)u(xC).$$

The first two of these imply that

$$k_1 u(xA) + k_2 u(xB) + k_3 u(xC) = 0 \quad \text{for all} \quad x \in \mathcal{M},$$

where $k_1 = \alpha\beta - \gamma, k_2 = \alpha(1 - \beta) - \delta(1 - \gamma),$ and $k_3 = (1 - \alpha) - (1 - \gamma)(1 - \delta)$, and $k_1 + k_2 + k_3 = 0$.

We show that $k_1 = k_2 = k_3 = 0$ using P7. Since we know from P6 and L5 that the hypotheses of P7 hold, there is a $y \in \mathcal{M}$ at which exactly two of yA, yB, and yC are indifferent. Assume for definiteness that $yA \sim yB$ and $yA \nsim yC$. Since $u(yA) = u(yB), (k_1 + k_2)u(yA) + k_3 u(yC) = 0$, or $k_3[u(yC) - u(yA)] = 0$. Hence $k_3 = 0$ since $u(yA) \neq u(yC)$. Then $k_1 + k_2 = 0$ and $k_1[u(xA) - u(xB)] = 0$ for all $x \in \mathcal{M}$, so it follows from P6 that $k_1 = 0$. Hence $k_1 = k_2 = k_3 = 0$, so that

$$\alpha\beta = \gamma \quad \text{and} \quad \alpha(1 - \beta) = \delta(1 - \gamma).$$

In similar fashion, the first and third $u(xD)$ expressions in the preceding paragraph yield $\alpha\beta = v(1 - \mu)$ and $\alpha(1 - \beta) = \mu$. Since $\alpha\beta = \gamma$ and $\alpha(1 - \beta) = \mu$ imply that $\alpha = \gamma + \mu$, additivity is verified.

The chain rule of Theorem 2 says that $P_K(G) = P_K(H)P_H(G)$ whenever $G \subseteq H \subseteq K$ with $G, H, K \in \mathcal{S}'$. If either $\subseteq$ is $=$, then the desired conclusion is obvious. Henceforth suppose that $G \subset H \subset K$. Let $A = G$, $B = H \backslash G, C = K \backslash H$, and $D = K$. Then $\alpha\beta = \gamma$ in the preceding paragraph gives $P_D(A \cup B)P_{A \cup B}(A) = P_D(A)$, or $P_K(H)P_H(G) = P_K(G)$.

The final part of Theorem 2, for $u(xA) = \sum_i P_A(A_i)u(xA_i)$ follows easily from the basic uP decomposition and the properties just established for the P_A.

12.6. PROOF OF THEOREMS 3 AND 4

We assume throughout this section that P1 through P8 hold, that $\{s\} \in \mathcal{S}'$ for all $s \in \mathcal{S}$, and that u and the P_A are as specified in Theorem 2. With $u_x(s) = u(xs) = u(x, \{s\}), u_x(A)$ is defined as $\{u_x(s) : s \in A\}$. We begin with a typical bounding lemma.

LEMMA 4. *If* $xA \in \mathcal{M} \times \mathcal{S}'$ *and* inf $u_x(A)$ *and* sup $u_x(A)$ *are finite, then* inf $u_x(A) \leq u(xA) \leq$ sup $u_x(A)$.

Proof. With $a = \inf u_x(A)$ and $b = \sup u_x(A)$, both finite, suppose to the contrary of $a \leq u(xA) \leq b$ that $b < u(xA)$. By linearity and the overlap caused by P6, $u(\mathcal{M} \times \mathcal{S}')$ is an interval. Hence $b < u(yB) < u(xA)$ for some $yB \in \mathcal{M} \times \mathcal{S}'$. Then $yB \succ xs$ for all $s \in A$, so $yB \succsim xA$ by P8. But this contradicts $xA \succ yB$, as implied by $u(xA) > u(yB)$. A similar contradiction follows from $u(xA) < a$. ∎

Theorem 3

To prove Theorem 3(a) assume that $xA \in \mathcal{M} \times \mathcal{S}'$ is measurable and bounded with $P_A(\{s \in A : a \leq u_x(s) \leq b\}) = 1$. Let $B = \{s \in A : a \leq u_x(s) \leq b\}$. Then, since $P_A(B) = 1$, $u(xA) = u(xB)$ by Theorem 2 (or even Theorem 1), and $E(u_x, P_A) = E(u_x, P_B)$ using the chain rule. If $a = b$, then the desired result is immediate. Suppose henceforth that $a < b$ and for convenience take $a = 0$ and $b = 1$. Let

$$A_1 = \{s : 0 \leq u_x(s) \leq 1/n\} \cap B$$

$$A_i = \{s : (i-1)/n < u_x(s) \leq i/n\} \cap B, \qquad i = 2, \dots, n.$$

With $J = \{i : A_i \neq 0\}$, Theorem 2 implies that $u(xB) = \sum_J P_B(A_i)u(xA_i)$. By Lemma 4,

$$\sum_{i=1}^{n} P_B(A_i)(i-1)/n \leq u(xB) \leq \sum_{i=1}^{n} P_B(A_i)i/n.$$

By definition, $E(u_x, P_B) = \lim_{n \to \infty} \sum_{i=1}^{n} P_B(A_i)(i-1)/n$. Since the difference between the two sides of the preceding inequality on $u(xB)$ goes to zero, we get $u(xB) = E(u_x, P_B)$, hence $u(xA) = E(u_x, P_A)$.

The other parts of Theorem 3 follow easily from part (a). Since $u(xA) = P_A(A^+)u(xA^+) + P_A(A^-)u(xA^-)$ for an arbitrary measurable xA when A^+ and A^- as defined by $A \cap \{s : u_x(s) \geq 0\}$ and $A \cap \{s : u_x(s) < 0\}$ respectively are nonempty, it will suffice to consider an $A \in \mathcal{S}'$ for which $u_x(s) \geq 0$ for all $s \in A$.

Thus, suppose xA is measurable with inf $u_x(A) \geq 0$ and with xA unbounded above. Let

$$A_n = A \cap \{s : u_x(s) < n\}$$

$$B_n = A \cap \{s : u_x(s) \geq n\}$$

for $n = 1, 2, \dots$. Then $A = A_n \cup B_n$, $A_1 \subseteq A_2 \subseteq \cdots$, $\bigcup_{n=1}^{\infty} A_n = A$, and

$u(xA) = P_A(A_n)u(xA_n) + P_A(B_n)u(xB_n)$ provided that $A_n, B_n \in \mathcal{S}'$, which is true by measurability and unboundedness above for all large n.

By Lemma 4 and its proof, $u(xA_n) \geq 0$ and $u(xB_n) \geq n$ for all large n, so $u(xA) \geq nP_A(B_n)$ for large n. Since $u(xA)$ is finite, this forces $P_A(B_n)$ to zero as $n \to \infty$, so that $P_A(A_n) \to 1$. By definition,

$$E(u_x, P_A) = \sup\left\{ \int_{A_n} u_x(s)\, dP_A(s) + nP_A(B_n) : n = 1, 2, \ldots \right\}$$

$$= \sup \{P_A(A_n)u(xA_n) + nP_A(B_n) : \quad n = 1, 2, \ldots \},$$

where Theorem 3(a) is used in the second line. Since the term in braces does not decrease as n increases, $E(u_x, P_A)$ equals the limit of $P_A(A_n)u(xA_n) + nP_A(B_n)$, and since

$$u(xA) = P_A(A_n)u(xA_n) + P_A(B_n)u(xB_n) \geq P_A(A_n)u(xA_n) + nP_A(B_n),$$

it follows that $u(xA) \geq E(u_x, P_A)$.

This effectively verifies part (b) of the theorem. Part (c) is proved in a symmetric manner (or in precisely the same way be taking negatives), and (d) follows from these as indicated above by the A^+, A^- comments.

Theorem 4

Now assume that P9 holds. Consider the latter part of the preceding proof with $A_n \uparrow A$. Because $u(\mathcal{M} \times \mathcal{S}')$ is a nondegenerate interval, P9 and order preservation imply in a straightforward way that $u(xA_n) \to u(xA)$ as $n \to \infty$. Since $P_A(A_n) \to 1$ also, it follows that $P_A(A_n)u(xA_n) \to u(xA)$. Moreover, since $nP_A(B_n) > 0$ for all n, we conclude that $\sup \{P_A(A_n)u(xA_n) + nP_A(B_n)\} \geq u(xA)$, i.e. that $E(u_x, P_A) \geq u(xA)$.

Thus, according to Theorem 3 and this result, $u(xA) = E(u_x, P_A)$ for all measurable xA that are bounded below, hence also for all measurable xA that are bounded above. And, if xA is unbounded both below and above, then $u(xA) = P_A(A^+)u(xA^+) + P_A(A^-)u(xA^-) = P_A(A^+)E(u_x, P_{A^+}) + P_A(A^-)E(u_x, P_{A^-}) = E(u_x, P_A)$.

REFERENCES

Allais, M.: 1953, 'Le comportement de l'homme rationnel devant le risque: critique des postulats et axiomes de l'École Americaine', *Econometrica* **21**, 503–546.

Anscombe, F. J. and Aumann, R. J.: 1963, 'A Definition of Subjective Probability', *Annals of Mathematical Statistics* **34**, 199–205.

Aumann, R. J.: 1962, 'Utility Theory Without the Completeness Axiom', *Econometrica* **30**, 445–462 (also **32**, 210–212).

Bernoulli, D.: 1738, 'Specimen theoriae novae de mensura sortis', *Commentarii Academiae Scientiarum Imperialis Petropolitanae* **5**, 175–192. Translated by L. Sommer, *Econometrica* **22** (1954), 23–36.

Blackwell, D. and Girshick, M. A.: 1954, *Theory of Games and Statistical Decisions*, Wiley, New York.

Bolker, E. D.: 1967, 'A Simultaneous Axiomatization of Utility and Subjective Probability', *Philosophy of Science* **34**, 333–340.

Chipman, J. S.: 1971, 'Non-Archimedean Behavior Under Risk: An Elementary Analysis-with Application to the Theory of Assests', in J. S. Chipman, L. Hurwicz, M. K. Richter, and H. F. Sonnenschein (eds.), *Preferences, Utility, and Demand*, Harcourt Brace Jovanovich, New York, pp. 289–318.

de Finetti: 1937, 'La prévision ses lois logiques, ses sources subjectives', *Annals de l'Institut Henri Poincaré* **7**, 1–68. Translated by H. E. Kyburg in H. E. Kyburg and H. E. Smokler (eds.), *Studies in Subjective Probability*, Wiley, New York, 1964, pp. 97–158.

DeGroot, M. H.: 1970, *Optimal Statistical Decisions*. McGraw-Hill, New York.

Farquhar, P. H.: 1977, 'A Survey of Multiattribute Utility Theory and Applications', *TIMS Studies in the Management Sciences* **6**, 59–89. Errata, *Management Science* **24** (1978), 785.

Fishburn, P. C.: 1964, *Decision and Value Theory*, Wiley, New York.

Fishburn, P. C.: 1967, 'Bounded Expected Utility', *Annals of Mathematical Statistics* **38**, 1054–1060.

Fishburn, P. C.: 1970, *Utility Theory for Decision Marking*, Wiley, New York.

Fishburn, P. C.: 1971a, 'A Study of Lexicographic Expected Utility', *Management Science* **17**, 672–678.

Fishburn, P. C.: 1971b, 'One-Way Expected Utility with Finite Consequence Spaces', *Annals of Mathematical Statistics* **42**, 572–577.

Fishburn, P. C.: 1973, 'A Mixture-Set Axiomatization of Conditional Subjective Expected Utility', *Econometrica* **41**, 1–25.

Fishburn, P. C.: 1974, 'On the Foundations of Decision Making Under Uncertainty', in M. Balch, D. McFadden, and S. Wu (eds.), *Essays on Economic Behavior Under Uncertainty*, North-Holland, Amsterdam, pp. 25–44.

Fishburn, P. C.: 1975a, 'Unbounded Expected Utility', *Annals of Statistics* **3**, 884–896.

Fishburn, P. C.: 1975b, 'A Theory of Subjective Expected Utility with Vague Preferences', *Theory and Decision* **6**, 287–310.

Fishburn, P. C.: 1976, 'Axioms for Expected Utility in n-Person Games', *International Journal of Game Theory* **5**, 137–149.

Fishburn, P. C.: 1980, 'Multilinear Expected Utility', *Mathematics of Operations Research* **5**, 502–509.

Fishburn, P. C.: 1981, 'Subjective Expected Utility: A Review of Normative Theories', *Theory and Decision* **13**, 139–199.

Fishburn, P. C. and Farquhar, P. H.: 1979, 'Finite-Degree Utility Independence', forthcoming in *Mathematics of Operations Research*.

Fishburn, P. C. and Roberts, F. S.: 1978, 'Mixture Axioms in Linear and Multilinear Utility Theories', *Theory and Decision* **9**, 161–171.

Harsanyi, J. C.: 1955, 'Cardinal Welfare, Individualistic Ethics, and Interpersonal Comparisons of Utility', *Journal of Political Economy* **63**, 309–321.

Hausner, M.: 1954, 'Multidimensional Utilities', in R. M. Thrall, C. H. Coombs, and R. L. Davis (eds.), *Decision Processes*, Wiley, New York, pp. 167–186.

Hausner, M. and Wendel, J. G.: 1952, 'Ordered Vector Spaces', *Proceedings of the American Mathematical Society* **3**, 977–982.

Herstein, I. N. and Milnor, J.: 1953, 'An Axiomatic Approach to Measurable Utility', *Econometrica* **21**, 291–297.

Jensen, N. E.: 1967, 'An Introduction to Bernoullian Utility Theory. I: Utility Functions', *Swedish Journal of Economics* **69**, 163–183.

Keeney, R. L.: 1968, 'Quasi-Separable Utility Functions', *Naval Research Logistics Quarterly* **15**, 551–565.

Keeney, R. L. and Raiffa, H.: 1976, *Decisions with Multiple Objectives*, Wiley, New York.

Kelley, J. L.: 1955, *General Topology*, American Book Company, New York.

Kelley, J. L., Namioka, I., *et al.*: 1963, *Linear Topological Spaces*, Van Nostrand, Princeton, New Jersey.

Ledyard, J. O.: 1971, 'A Pseudo-Metric Space of Probability Measures and the Existence of Measurable Utility', *Annals of Mathematical Statistics* **42**, 794–798.

Luce, R. D. and Krantz, D. H.: 1971, 'Conditional Expected Utility', *Econometrica* **39**, 253–271.

Luce, R. D. and Suppes, P.: 1965, 'Preference, Utility and Subjective Probability', in R. D. Luce, R. R. Bush, and E. Galanter (eds.), *Handbook of Mathematical Psychology III*, Wiley, New York, pp. 250–410.

MacCrimmon, K. R.: 1968, 'Descriptive and Normative Implications of the Decision-Theory Postulates', in K. Borch and J. Mossin (eds.), *Risk and Uncertainty*, Macmillan, New York, pp. 3–32.

Pfanzagl, J.: 1968, *Theory of Measurement*, Wiley, New York.

Pollak, R. A.: 1967, 'Additive von Neumann–Morgenstern Utility Functions', *Econometrica* **35**, 485–494.

Pratt, J. W., Raiffa, H., and Schlaifer, R.: 1964, 'The Foundations of Decision under Uncertainty: An Elementary Exposition', *Journal of the American Statistical Association* **59**, 353–375.

Pratt, J. W., Raiffa, H., and Schlaifer, R.: 1965, *Introduction to Statistical Decision Theory*, McGraw-Hill, New York.

Ramsey, F. P.: 1931, 'Truth and Probability', in F. P. Ramsey (ed.), *The Foundations of Mathematics and Other Logical Essays*, Harcourt, Brace and Co., New York. Reprinted in H. E. Kyburg and H. E. Smokler (eds.), *Studies in Subjective Probability*, Wiley, New York, 1964, pp. 61–92.

Savage, L. J. : 1954, *The Foundations of Statistics*, Wiley, New York. Second revised edition, Dover Publications, New York, 1972.

Slovic, P. and Tversky, A. : 1974, 'Who Accepts Savage's Axioms?', *Behavioral Science* **19**, 368–373.

Suppes, P. : 1956, 'The Role of Subjective Probability and Utility in Decision Making', *Proceedings of the Third Berkeley Symposium on Mathematical Statistics and Probability, 1954–1955* **5**, 61–73.

von Neumann, J. and Morgenstern, O. : 1944, *Theory of Games and Economic Behavior*, Princeton University Press, Princeton, New Jersey. Second edition, 1947; third edition, 1953.

INDEX

THEORY AND DECISION LIBRARY

An International Series in the Philosophy and Methodology
of the Social and Behavioral Sciences

Editors:

Gerald Eberlein, *University of Technology, Munich*
Werner Leinfellner, *University of Nebraska*